only the lonely

the roy orbison story

10TH ANNIVERSARY SPECIAL EDITION

Design: David Houghton
Printed by: MPG Books, Bodmin

Published by: Sanctuary Publishing Limited, 82 Bishops Bridge Road, London W2 6BB

Photographs: courtesy of Pictorial Press Limited (including cover), London Features International, Rex Features Limited, UPI/Bettmann Newsphotos, Central Press Photos Limited and Brian Poole

ISBN: 1-86074-241-6

only the lonely

the roy orbison story

10TH ANNIVERSARY SPECIAL EDITION

ALAN CLAYSON

To the families of Karen, Sam and Miriam

Also by Alan Clayson from Sanctuary

The Quiet One: A Life Of George Harrison

Ringo Starr: Straight Man Or Joker?

Death Discs: An Account Of Fatality In The Popular Song

Jacques Brel: The Biography

Hamburg: The Cradle Of British Rock

View From The Exterior: Serge Gainsbourg

Reviews for Only The Lonely

"A very readable account of one of pop's most remarkable vocalists, *Only The Lonely* gives you a clear sense of the man and the times in which he lived. A detailed yet affectionate analysis of Orbison's music."
Record Collector

"An impressive, well-informed book with a lively anecdotal style."
Sounds

"Unravels the fascinating story of Roy Orbison's tragic but triumphant life."
Cincinnati Enquirer

"Alan Clayson's fascinating, well-researched biography paints a vivid picture of the life and times of the pop music icon."
Flint (MI) Journal

About The Author

Born in Dover, England in 1951, the author lives near Henley-on-Thames with his wife Inese and sons, Jack and Harry. Described by the *Western Morning News* as the "AJP Taylor of the pop world", Alan Clayson has written many books on music – including the best-selling *Backbeat*, subject of a major film – as well as for journals as disparate as *The Independent*, *Record Collector*, *Medieval World*, *Folk Roots*, *The Times*, *Discoveries*, *The Beat Goes On* and, as a teenager, the notorious *Schoolkids Oz*. He has been engaged to broadcast on national TV and radio, and lecture on both sides of the Atlantic.

Before he become better known as a pop historian, he led the legendary Clayson And The Argonauts in the late 1970s, and was thrust to "a premier position on rock's Lunatic Fringe" (*Melody Maker*). The 1985 album, *What A Difference A Decade Made*, is the most representative example of the group's recorded work.

As shown by the formation of a US fan club in 1992, Alan Clayson's following has continued to grow, along with demand for his production talents in the studio, and the number of his compositions performed by such diverse acts as Dave Berry – in whose Cruisers he played keyboards in the mid-1980s – and (via a collaboration with ex-Yardbird Jim McCarty) New Age outfit, Stairway. He has worked with the Portsmouth Sinfonia, Wreckless Eric, Twinkle and Screaming Lord Sutch among others.

Alan Clayson is presently spearheading a trend towards an English form of *chanson*, and feedback from both Britain and North America suggests that he is becoming more than a cult celebrity. Moreover, *Soirée*, a new album released in autumn 1997, may stand as Alan Clayson's artistic apotheosis if it were not for the promise of surprises yet to come.

Acknowledgments

I owe a particular debt to the following for their metaphorical yells of encouragement and for trusting me with archive material: David Cox, Roger Dopson, Martin Hawkins, Stuart Hobday, Allan Jones, Spencer Leigh, Steve Maggs, Steve Rowley, Charles Salt, John Tobler and Michael Towers.

I have also drawn from conversations with Chet Atkins, Cliff Bennett, Bill Dees, Fred Foster, Paul Munday, Joe Melson, Gordon Stoker and Kay Vasquez – and thank them for their candour. In this respect, I am even more in the debt of Barry Booth, Brian Poole and, of course, Steve and Michelle Howe.

Thanks is also due in varying degrees to Evie Baldwin, B and T Typewriters, Roger Barnes, Dave Berry, Stuart and Kathryn Booth, Rob Bradford, Trevor Burrows, Terry Clarke, Gordon and Rosemary Clayson, Ron Cooper, Pete Cox, Greg and Debi Daniels, Kevin Delaney, Peter Doggett, Tim Fagan, Pete Frame, Anne Freer, Bernard Futter, Eric Goulden, Paul Hearne, David Horn, Graham Larkbey, Graham and Yvonne Lambourne, Brian Leafe, Fraser Massey, Jim McCarty, Cohn Miles, David Nicolle (Reading Evening Post), Peter O'Brian, Darrell Paddick, Sarah Parish, Ray Phillips, Tony Peters (Acuff-Rose), Athenia Pierce (Wink Chamber of Commerce), Denis Reed, Patsy Riches, Andy Taylor, Geoff Taggart, Paul Tucker, Marion Vause and Chris Warman – plus Inese who shielded me as far as possible from the real world as well as Jack and Harry who like to be included.

"By Hercules! The man was greater than Caesar or Cromwell – nay, nearly equal to Odin or Thor! The Texans ought to build him an altar!"

Thomas Carlyle speaking of Jim Bowie

Contents

Preface To The 1998 Edition

Through the adventurous grace of Sanctuary, *Only The Lonely* has finally reached the public the way that nature intended. Hopefully, it will utilise your time in more interesting a fashion than the first edition – written in the year following Roy Orbison's death in 1988 (and subjected, in my view, to hamfisted editing) – and that it will pass at last the litmus test of any biography of this nature in that the reader is drawn to the music, and finds the text as entertaining as the person who inspired it.

Alan Clayson, August 1998

PROLOGUE

Dream Baby

Most London Teddy Boys had heard of Sunglasses Ron. A menacing hybrid of Edwardian rake and Mississippi gambler, Ron, so it was rumoured, had worn his shades day and night since Buddy Holly died. What Ted didn't know of a deed poll Presley or someone who planned his life and bank balance around every Jerry Lee Lewis tour of Britain? How many are the forearms tattooed with the image of Chuck Berry or pairs of family pets named Gene and Vincent?

By day a Kentish landscape gardener, seventeen-year-old Stephen Howe had also been bitten by the rock 'n' roll bug. Through the influence of his elder brother Mick, this sandy-haired youth's favourite singing star came to be Roy Orbison – whose first hit records antedated Steve's birth.

Though his albums were filed in the "Rock 'N' Roll" section in Virgin's Oxford Street megastore, Orbison's was not a name that sprang immediately to mind when discussing the behemoths of classic rock. Had he not overcome an essentially retiring disposition and snapped into the idiosyncratic style that, from 1959, would sell over thirty million units, his good-in-parts rockabilly inventory might have been a body of work desired for its very obscurity rather than any intrinsic worth. Without needing to hear 'Ooby Dooby', 'Rockhouse' *et al*, rock 'n' roll connoisseurs might have mentioned him in passing alongside Warren Smith, Johnny "Peanuts" Wilson, Charlie Feathers, Malcolm Yelvington(!) and Sonny Fisher – the list is endless of those who flowered momentarily in the wake of Elvis Presley. Instead, Roy

Orbison's later achievements infused his earlier outpourings with a considerably greater historical interest.

Accompanying himself on guitar, one of the first Orbison songs mastered by Steve Howe was 'The Clown', a 1957 demonstration recording never intended for release. From the elementary fretboard chords he'd taught himself, Steve began to compose songs after the manner of his idol. His faith in his not inconsiderable vocal talent would be justified when his facsimile of Roy's 'Danny Boy' received high commendation in a talent contest organised by the *Evening Post*.

This newspaper was local to Reading, home of Steve's girlfriend, Michelle Booth. In her final year at Highdown Comprehensive, Michelle's musical tastes had run to Elvis Presley and, a long way behind, Bryan Ferry. Unlike other girls of her age, she'd been quite unmoved by the outrages of The Sex Pistols, Generation X and other punk rockers who, by 1978, had become rather passé anyway. After pairing off with Steve during a fortnight in a Bognor holiday camp, her previous preferences were tested and found wanting by the magic of Roy Orbison, whose old records Steve had been systematically buying up from his brother.

Early one Friday evening in March 1983, Michelle left Reading by train to spend the weekend with Steve and his family in Gravesend – a destination too appropriately named. After waiting in vain to greet her at the station, Steve informed the police before driving home to spend a sleepless night. At five am on that chilly morning, a squad car pulled up to whisk Steve to the Middlesex where Michelle was on a life support system. She'd sustained near-fatal injuries when flung from the speeding Inter-City train just past Brentford. Her broken body had been spotted beside the track by a railwayman on an early shift.

In the intensive care cubicle, Steve could only identify her by a mole on her left shoulder. In the thick of the inserted tubes and drips, her wounds were so numerous and serious that you wouldn't have known she was a human being. From the first, there was almost no hope of her recovery. However, though that pitiful, helpless life could have been taken without effort, the Grim Reaper decided to spare Michelle Booth.

Foul play was suspected but confirmation of this would have to hang fire until the patient stirred – if she ever would – from a deep coma. To improve the chances of arousal, she was spoon-fed familiar sounds. Her twin sister, Sharon, chattered about school; Steve whispered sweet nothings, and, from a cassette player for hours on end, Roy Orbison sang.

Hearing of the schoolgirl's plight, certain showbusiness celebrities made thoughtful gestures. Comedian Spike Milligan sent flowers. From rock 'n' roll revivalists, Darts, came a signed photograph. A letter even arrived from high society gadfly-turned-pop singer, Roddy Llewellyn. Michelle's eyes opened but there was no flicker of understanding yet. A shot in the dark was someone's idea to contact Roy Orbison. Perhaps a personal message from him might lift her closer to the brink of consciousness.

There are not untrue stories of stars employing secretaries whose job it is to rip open fan mail, extract any cheques, cash or the more useful gifts and throw the unread letters away. Roy Orbison, however, was of a different stamp. In his Tennessee fastness, the: Big O acted immediately on Michelle's behalf. Seated before a tape recorder microphone, "I was recovering from heart surgery myself and I was hoping that if I could say something on a tape without referring to hospitals or accidents or anything that she might not relate to, then it might help." For what it was worth, he wished her all the best for the future and invited her to be his guest of honour when next his concert itinerary reached a convenient venue in southern England. "I was hoping that she would have that in her mind and just sort of be wanting to come to that concert but I think that her own strong willpower brought her through."

Though she couldn't recall hearing Roy during her oblivion, Michelle was convinced that his pre-recorded presence was of subliminal benefit "because when I came home from the hospital and the tapes were played again, I could remember a lot of the words to songs I'd never heard of before." She also recalled being first offered a cigarette in the train corridor by her ill-favoured assailant who she described to the police as resembling a penguin. His gorge rising at her spirited resistance to his sudden and thuggish embrace, this sex maniac threw her from him for the sake of himself.

Technically, the case remained unsolved. After a reconstruction of the crime – with Sharon standing in for her sister – several witnesses came forward and an Alan George Westlake was charged. As he waddled to the dock at the Old Bailey, you could appreciate the penguin allusion, enhanced further by a domed forehead and pear shape. Through the oratory skills of his barrister, Westlake was acquitted but only painful months of therapy and further operations would enable Michelle Booth to re-enter the world outside: "I don't think I'll ever recover completely but physically I'm getting on quite well. My walking's not half as good as I'd like it to be but I'm coming along." Scotched, nonetheless, was her ambition to become a nurse. No stranger to life's hard knocks himself, Roy Orbison would advise Michelle that, "It's not getting over it. It's getting used to it," when, on 20 March, 1979, he more than kept his promise.

Straight from a television appearance in Los Angeles, he'd flown to Heathrow where he touched down around lunch time that Thursday. The British tour was scheduled to start in Manchester in two days. Despite a lost night's repose, he instructed his chauffeur to drive not to the usual West End hotel but to bear left down the M4 motorway towards Reading. Turning off at the A329, the limousine nosed through the lugubrious suburbs of a university town reckoned by makers of television documentaries to be the most "average" in the United Kingdom.

The route that Roy's driver chose to the Booths' red-brick semi-detached in Southcote did Reading little justice by avoiding the central junction separating its looming Victorian biscuit factory from the prison that had held Oscar Wilde. Probably of more interest to a historian of Orbison's persuasion was the adjacent abbey ruins where Henry Beauclerc was laid to rest and the well-known English folk song, 'Summer Is Acumen In', was said to have originated.

On any other occasion, this might have been a pleasant diversion. Nothing, however, would deflect him from his iron purpose. Off the roaring A4 to Bath stood Fawley Road, a forlorn cul-de-sac where vehicles like his were seen only on formal occasions. When the car braked outside Number Six, Roy Orbison – an American legend for nearly thirty years – took a giant leap for Michelle Booth.

CHAPTER ONE

Born To Lose

A cross between a boardroom industrialist and punch-drunk cowpoke, Glenn McCarthy, so it was said, "made John Wayne look a cissy". A former labourer, this self-made oil tycoon's preoccupation with winning was common to even those fellow Texans who did not share his combative flamboyance. "I always wanted to be a millionaire," reckoned Roy Orbison too, "even when I was thirteen. I'd made up my mind to be one by the time I reached thirty."[1]

This dream would come true well before that age but Orbison never forgot the struggle. For one noted for his onstage reticence, one complete sentence was his equivalent of the Gettysburg Address. It wasn't empty words, therefore, when he told the capacity crowd at the last performance he'd ever give, that they made him feel young again. His latest single, 'You Got It', had been received as ecstatically as any of the old songs that Sunday. As an old trouper, he had gauged that the intangible buzz that had been in the air for months would slam 'You Got It' up the charts – possibly all the way. Once more, Roy Orbison was back in favour – but for how long this time?

On the nostalgia ticket, his bread and butter had been typified by the municipal two-thousand seater where he'd been booked for that final evening – 4 December, 1988 – in Akron near Lake Erie. Yet when the breaks had come, Roy had never deserted the network of one-horse-town halls, glum high school gyms and army camp messes that had sustained him during leaner years. As well as strengthening a vocational safety net, he was keeping another promise made in his teens when "no shows came to where I was. I said, well, if I get to be a star, I'm going to play smaller places – anywhere that wants to hear me."[2]

You couldn't get much closer to the centre of North America's southern region as the western end of Texas where Roy Orbison grew up. It was, indeed, very much beyond the pale of the showbusiness mainstream – apart from its intermittent use by Hollywood for "western" locations. In 1948, for example, director Howard Hawks shot a John Wayne cattle drive drama on the east side of the Panhandle. Only two miles from the actual "Red River" of the film's title, the Chisholm Trail to Missouri had passed along the main street of Vernon, the Wilbarger county town where Roy Kelton Orbison was born on 23 April, 1936.

Howling the state's independence from Mexico since 1836, the Texas Centennial Exposition was in full swing as Roy in his cradle caught and held the rich drawl that would forever betray his upbringing. The cowboy accent might be ineradicable but, for Texans born in the twentieth century, more likely career options than gunslinging and bronco busting would be found in oil. Though this "black gold" had been discovered near Nacodoches in 1866, it would take nearly fifty years for full scale production to be feasible. Meanwhile, other deposits had been uncovered all over Texas – often spurting wildly for days as entrepreneurs overcame legal, mechanical and personnel hurdles.

Dallas remains oil capital of Texas but further west were other targets of exploitation. Though agriculture was still the area's most vital occupation, many farming families became attracted to more lucrative opportunities in the urban sprawls growing round the oil fields to the west. The change was symbolised by the many local newspapers – such as *The Wink Bulletin* – who came to use an oil derrick as a heading emblem.

For many raised in pastoral quiet, adjustment to the petrol fume brashness of Fort Worth or El Paso was initially an affront to the strait-laced small town individualism and moral attitude more prevalent in certain areas of Texas than anywhere else in North America. In the hamlet of Bee Cave in 1912, the justice of the peace sentenced a sheep rustler to hang. Insulted when the Supreme Court overruled this decision, Bee Cave refused to ever elect another JP. Eventually, it was lost in one of the encroaching conurbations that absorbed four-fifths of the state's population.

That such a community should have been so swallowed would have been unthinkable for a mid-Victorian studying a map of the American West on which the few forts and settlements amid wide white spaces only emphasised its emptiness. Until 1836, Texas didn't even belong to the United States but was part of Mexico. However, increasing US immigrant infiltration of the northern marches of its empire worried the Mexican government. Worry became alarm when the newcomers revolted against the military dictatorship of President Santa Anna who had seized power in 1823. For ten years after the US army under General Houston routed the Mexicans at San Jacinto, Texas enjoyed the best of both worlds as a unified republic that could still claim affinity to the greater world in the north. Even when annexed to the United States in 1846, the Lone Star State retained a quasi-imperial insularity in its common unconscious. Today, *The Wink Bulletin*, again, "subscribes to the belief that freedom is a gift of God and not a grant from any government".

For years, travellers in Texas were more likely to encounter the depressed forbearance and olive faces of the Mexican poor than the wide-awake optimism and fast mouths of the conquerors. Among chief objections to Santa Anna's rule was that schools taught only in Spanish. But it wasn't until 1854 that it was possible to establish an English-speaking system for the entire state. No English newspapers were published in Texas until the 1860s. As long as Spanish remains a second language in its schools, Mexican decor decorates its homes, and *fajitas* and Jalepena peppers are on its restaurants' menus, Texas in part will be forever Mexico.

Furthermore, even after the first "iron horse" crossed to West Texas in 1835, pipe dreams of raising cattle amid its seas of mesquite grass were disturbed by visions of intense and unwelcome attention from the bloodthirsty Apache and Comanche. With scalp bounty still being paid by the government, the Indians were not subdued conclusively and herded onto reservations until 1880. As terrifying in their way were white bandits such as the notorious Sam Bass whose activities triggered the founding of the "Texas" Rangers.

While it is too sweeping to imply that a few decades transformed Texas from trackless wastes to settled countryside, it isn't easy to appreciate how suddenly modern Texas smouldered into form – and how much of the Old West lingers there still. A retired computer operator can jet miles above the very ruts a wagon containing his father in infancy made *en route* to Santa Rita during the gold rush. Moreover, the abandoning of the Pony Express for the telegraph – "whispering wires" – is not too distant a memory for families like the Orbisons who'd been resident in Texas for more than two generations.

Theirs was a close-knit family who, from peasant stock, had embraced the innately decent "sir" and "ma'am" virtues of small town America, smelling haughtiness and affectation a mile off. Marrying in 1932 when both were nineteen, Orbie Lee and Nadine Orbison would produce, by the onset of the Second World War, three sons – Grady, the remarkable Roy and Sammy. A former nurse, Nadine was well-equipped to cope with her youngsters' maladies – such as Roy's bi-annual attacks of flu – and to shield the household from potentially indelible and unhygienic spin-offs of her husband's job as a car mechanic. In time, the greasy overalls to be washed and any oil-black fingernails at dinner weren't necessarily Orbie Lee's.

Years later, Roy would cite his parents as his "biggest influence"[3] when annotating his life history. Certainly, through spending all day under his Dad's feet as brake linings were fitted and tyres changed, so began Roy's life-long love affair with automobiles; how they worked, the differences between them and the sheer magic of their whizzing springs and pistons. From earliest youth, he could take a small engine to bits and put it back together. Mr Orbison would also allow his sons to shunt vehicles around in first gear when they came in for repair. Long before they were officially entitled to take a car on the public highway, the hand and foot co-ordination needed to drive was second nature to the Orbison children.

Less laudable a legacy from the workshop was that, like their father, Roy and Sammy would be unable to stop smoking – though Roy "had a big drink of whiskey once. I asked my father what it was and he told me. I said, 'Can I have some?' and he said, 'Sure.' So I slugged back a big shot of whiskey, and I think I was sick for about six days. So that turned me off drink forever. I still don't drink."[4] Neither did any of the Orbisons use bad language beyond the mildest expletives.

All the males on Orbie Lee's side were inclined to suffer from poor eyesight, requiring the wearing of spectacles – in Roy's case, from the age of four. By most standards, they weren't an outstandingly comely brood either. With a preponderance of receding chins, jug-handle ears and pouchy jowls, a family grouping made you think of a cageful of ruminating hamsters. From their father, Grady and Sammy had inherited greater height and more robust constitutions than the middle son whose slighter build and washed-out complexion – from an infantine bout of jaundice – were in keeping with an unimposing presence: "I was totally anonymous – I mean, I was unknown even at my home."[5]

True to his upbringing, Roy was unswervingly polite with a fathomless sense of moderation but, if the others guffawed and slapped thighs, he'd only smile placidly. At the breakfast table, he'd listen quietly, his deliberated replies to questions unfailingly to the point. Yet he was a likable if self-contained little boy and, when not "hiding somewhere", eager to please. Playing "cowboys and indians", Roy would never object if persistently chosen to be the bad guy – although he'd never look anywhere near the part until well after he'd outgrown the game. When he started school at six, he tried hard at football though he "just never was big enough".[6]

For all the incalculable ordeals and jubilations that lay ahead, Roy would have a juvenile look about him all his life. Always, his soft blue-grey eyes would be as guileless as a new schoolboy's: "I am very much the same person I was when I was six years of age. It's hard to say and almost impossible to explain. I knew then about religion; I knew then about history – and I could play the guitar."[7]

In the rural south before the television became an indispensable domestic fixture, "musical evenings" were a frequent occurrence in many homesteads. Stately colonial mansions with granite gables might have tinkled to the strains of Debussy and. Handel but at the Orbisons' bungalow with its pot-bellied stove, the backbone of the entertainment issued from the guitars of Dad and Nadine's brother, Uncle Kenneth. Of these most common folk instruments of the South, models with Gene Autry on a rearing horse etched on the table had been readily available on the Sears-Roebuck mail-order catalogue since the early thirties.

Home-made southern folk music lay at the bedrock of the "western" in "country-and-western". Before the commercial translation of "country" into a late twentieth century commentary on the aspirations of middle America, today's Garth Brooks compact disc consumer might once have proffered the excuse, "I just had the radio on. I wasn't listening to it." "Listening to it" used to suggest association with uneducated, bigoted southern whites – "redneck" descendants of the pioneers, caricatured as clannish, unsophisticated and anti-intellectual. At its worse, country-and-western was a breeding ground for blue collar right wing sloganising, encouraging suspicion of labour unions, minority groups and foreigners: the yellow rose of Texas is the only girl for me.

This was laced with alternate pious fear and matey camaraderie towards not so much God as "the man in the sky" or "The Lord" who was entreated-as the need arose – as either a militant enforcer of redneck prejudices, homespun prairie Plato or as a sort of divine pimp. Above all, The Lord was a Man. He had a crewcut, a Charles Atlas physique and – though blessed with enough self-discipline to seldom indulge himself – an amused tolerance of boozing and womanising. He admired such diverse go-getting Texans as Glenn McCarthy and country-and-western star, Buck Owens – who cashed in with 'Cryin' Time', 'Act Naturally' and more of that simple, unaffected kinda music folks like a-tappin' their boot leather to. With the Man In The Sky's approval, Buck ploughed back some of his dough into right wing politics. Too tough to get weepy when he heard 'Cryin' Time', The Lord could still be a maudlin old bastard, flicking the odd dime at an *Indios manza* or Chicano beggar. Nonetheless, like any right-thinkin' Man, he sure hated queers, commies and niggers.

As one San Antonio guitarist, Doug Sahm, discovered on mercifully few occasions, disapproval of long hair on men was expressed by actions beyond merely bawling "get yer 'air cut" from a passing car. Echoing both Jerry Lee Lewis and I Corinthians xi 14, even Roy Orbison as late as 1966 would say, "As a male, I personally don't like feminine hair on men. And I imagine women don't like it either." He added, however, "If fellows are wearing their hair, not just to be different, but because they like it, then I say that's great. The important thing is to be yourself."[8]

In 1970, a Houston radio station was twice firebombed by some good ol' boys who begged to differ over its radical anti-Vietnam policy. Of more abiding sensitivity, airplay problems for what once was classified as "sepia" or "race" music was – and still is – but one aspect of ingrained racial tension in the Deep South. Negroes as slaves had been cattle. Free and human, they were a nuisance, undesirable and embarrassing. Especially so were the more uppity ones like singer Nat "King" Cole who had to be worked over by anti-black extremists midway through his act before a mixed southern audience in a packed auditorium.

Though nowhere as malignantly colour prejudiced as other states, even those Texan whites who bought Cole's records – similar in style to those of Caucasian crooners like Crosby or Perry Como – might well have been appalled when compulsory segregation in schools was declared unconstitutional in 1958. Thirty years afterwards, when explaining why nearly all the children in the classes for the severely retarded were black, a southern headmistress said, "Well, it's often very hard to tell if a child is mentally handicapped or just black."[9]

Any admixture of negro blood was deemed sufficient to restrict its owner to "coloured" public conveniences and launderettes not displaying the sign "Whites Only Or Maids In Uniform". It was alleged that, quite legally, C&W entertainer, Marty Robbins as "Johnny Freedom" cut several blatantly racist singles during what must have been the lowest point of his career. This episode remains vehemently denied by his fans – and it has to be said that it was when outlines between C&W and black music dissolved that Robbins/Freedom and many other white Texan performers were able to venture beyond regional popularity. Unlike his younger brother-in-law, Orbie Lee Orbison hadn't been directly acquainted with black music though, from fretboard symbols on sheet music, he had taught himself to get by on a few chords in a plain strumming fashion, reminiscent of folk-blues exponent, Huddie Ledbetter – "Leadbelly". Furthermore, Orbie Lee liked Jimmie Rodgers, a country singer whose songs were couched in rural black phrasing and imagery, with yodelled refrains. Little made Orbie Lee happier than copying 'T For Texas', 'Muleskinner Blues' and other of his seventy-eight rpm records by the ol' Blue Yodeller as the late Jimmie was known. It was fortunate for his family that Orbie Lee's singing matched his enthusiasm; strong yet soothing, age would never deepen his voice below a youthful-sounding baritone.

Sensibly, neither father nor uncle goaded the boys to learn the guitar too. Of the three, it was the unobtrusive Roy who seemed the most musical. At first, it was hard to believe that a voice so like his dad's could come from such a pale slip of a child but, "Once I started singing, it was sort of a wonder, and it didn't hurt anybody, and it made me feel good, and some people even said, 'Roy, that's nice.'"[6] When questioned, Roy would answer that he wanted to be a singer when he grew up although, "I didn't know then that you could actually make a living out of it."[10]

A fascinated listener while Orbie Lee practised, Roy as usual waited until he was asked: "It all started with me walking down a dusty road with my father, and him asking what I wanted for my [sixth] birthday, and me saying, 'I want a mouth-organ.' He asked me if I wouldn't rather have a guitar, and, well, I jumped at the guitar." In the highest oral tradition, the knowledge was handed on like an Olympic torch: "He taught me the basic chords on the guitar – nothing intricate." His left hand not yet big enough to fully-shape the chords, the first song he could manage was 'You Are My Sunshine', a Great War whimsy which walked a tightrope between joy and obsessional despair: "From the very first moment, it was me *and* the guitar, playing and singing."[4]

Roy's new combined skill would become his passport for staying up late when, at the outbreak of hostilities, his family moved from Vernon to an apartment above a chemist's in Fort Worth. The US War Office, concerned about the stalemate its forces supporting the Allies had reached against the Axis powers and Japan, had sent for Orbie Lee Orbison. At the defence plant where giant chimneys were trained on the sky like anti-aircraft guns, he – and, later, Nadine too – became an infinitesimal cog in provisioning the bloodshed afar with B-24 bombers.

His daily patriotic chore of cranking and riveting done, Mr Orbison would walk from the familiar oily odour to his evening meal through the tangles of lugubrious streets with modern buildings already caked in grime and soot from the plant, the oil refineries and the army chemical corps. In the fever of mobilisation, long black trains bumped the brand-new flying weapons he had made towards the constant drone of Dyers air-base in Abilene.

Amid clusters of passing soldiers, he might recognise a face or two for many would be billeted on the Orbisons throughout these dangerous years. Most welcome among them were Uncle Kenneth and various cousins on leave from the Pacific or European theatres of war: "They didn't know whether they were coming back or not so the level of intensity and the singing and partying just for right now was very high."[10] With his father and – when around – uncle, Roy would vamp his handful of chords to the *omnes fortissimo* sing-songs in a nicotine haze that would bring to a head an evening of boozing war-hysteria. Cognisant with events were numbers like Harold Adamson's 'Comin' In On A Wing And A Prayer' and, from The Andrews Sisters, 'You're In The Army Now'.

During a lull in the "yee-hah" exuberance, little Roy might be led forth for a turn before being packed off to bed – where his brothers were already. The heart-and-soul exhilaration of those nights left their mark on the young performer too: "And still, today, that's how I do it – with everything I have. That spirit...the easy camaraderie of musicians, that lifestyle is ingrained in me." There would be periodic and almost overwhelming vocational vacillations but, "By the time I was seven, I was finished, you know, for anything else."[5]

Preferences in Roy's now extended repertoire included 'Born To Lose' and the topical 'No Letter Today', both on the same seventy-eight by the versatile "western swing" band, Ted Daffan and his Texans, whose stamping ground then was the Dallas-Fort Worth-Houston triangle. Another favourite was the Charlie Chaplin-penned ballad, 'Eternally'. Others likewise figured in the record sales charts, first published in North America in *Billboard* magazine in 1940. Best sellers would be assigned to one of three tabulations – popular, country-and-western and "sepia" – or "rhythm-and-blues" as it became. This meant that you could top, say, the sepia chart without figuring at all in the parallel dimension of pop, unless your disc picked up enough spins on pop-orientated radio and consequent sales in matching chart return shops. As Roy Orbison would observe later, "A huge country hit can sell sixty thousand, whereas you have to sell three to four hundred thousand to get in the pop-charts."[11] Only on rare occasions could you score in all three.

Like sepia music, although there were many shades of country-and-western, you knew it when you heard it – whether at its purest in the rootin'-tootin' narrative and abrupt instrumental *accelerandos* of bluegrass or melancholy schmaltz epitomised by such as Red Foley's 'Thank You For Calling', composed by Cindy Walker. This slow waltz sounds unintentionally funny today via the enhancing of Foley's doleful melodrama with depressively creaky fiddle and a ringing telephone. Other samples of country kitsch like 'Tragic Romance' by Cowboy Copas – a very early "death disc" – walked the line with many listeners because, as the genre's greatest figure, Hank Williams, pontificated, "The tunes are simple and easy to remember, and the singers – they're *sincere* about them."[12]

The "sincerity" of vocalists of the Johnny Freedom persuasion, plus its overall lowbrow stylistic determination, ensured that a C&W show hitting town – though aimed at an adult audience – would be disregarded by liberal local media. Besides, country-and-western had not been thought a significant market when record companies began investigating specialist regional music in the twenties. Until Lubbock in West Texas spawned the nation's first full-time C&W station in 1953, "You didn't have stations that played just country or just anything else," recalled Roy Orbison. "There weren't so many records then so they played everything."[10]

However, through the machinations of an insurance company that owned a Nashville station, there was relayed in 1925 *Barn Dance*, an "in person" C&W presentation from which sprang the renowned *Grand Ole Opry* broadcast from the city's Ryman theatre. Twiddling the dial, you might also chance on *Louisiana Hayride*, *Ozark Jubilee* or disc jockeys like KDAV's "Longhorn Joe", the first to air Hank Williams.

More of a trace element in America's musical melting pot was that fusion of blues accordion and Frenchified patois (Creole) with added washboard and fiddle. Called "Cajun" in Louisiana, "Zydeco" in Texas, its influence was felt by, amongst others, the, celebrated Jimmie Rodgers and his protégé, Ernest Tubb, as well as "King Of The Hillbilly Piano Players", Moon Mullican who – anglicising it as necessary – carried it into the C&W mainstream. In 1947, Mullican's first million-seller was inspired by Harry Choates' 'Jole Blon' ("pretty blonde"), the Cajun "national anthem" and one that "was, is still" one of Roy Orbison's favourite songs: "But I could only learn it by slowing down the record. I would put my finger on the record and slow it down, and even then just word for word...the words that were so painfully put together have fallen by the wayside and I don't remember it. I remember the melody and some of the expressions in it, but it made no sense."[4]

Those distracted times at Fort Worth also nurtured in him an abiding passion for history which grew to an encyclopaedic understanding of people and places, interactions and outcomes: "That's how I correlate things," he admitted. "I get one thing that makes me think of another."[4] Principal among connected pastimes were the collection of war memorabilia and the building of miniature military aeroplanes. As he functioned only awkwardly in group activities, other of Roy's solitary diversions included swimming, fishing and sketching. Still much a creature of habit when grown to man's estate, "I never get interested in any new thing all of a sudden. I've had many long term interests and I'm happy with those."[8]

These pursuits had little bearing on his sojourn at elementary (primary) school where his teachers had to struggle to write on termly reports anything out of the ordinary about Roy's academic progress. He was solid enough in most subjects. As well as a sound conceptual grasp of mathematics, there were hints of a flair for creative writing and art but there was always the feeling that he was afraid to take literary risks for fear of getting into trouble. That might also account for why, unless pushed, he rarely participated in formal discussion either. All that made him remotely extraordinary was that, unlike most other children, he did not need much coaxing to sing solo for class assemblies. "Even if I didn't want to, I'd be the single source of attention. It grew on me, I guess."[2] The discovery that, execrable though he may be, the whole school is listening to him can create false impressions of talent in the immature mind but Roy seemed to take it in his stride, never conceited about applause that was often more than cursory. Back in class, he'd be nondescript once more – like Superman reverting to his Clark Kent persona.

In 1944, the education of the two younger Orbisons was disrupted when a polio epidemic in the Fort Worth area made it prudent for them to decamp to their grandmother's in Vernon. There they'd stay until peace was declared and the whole family could go home. It was during this hiatus that Roy Orbison's slow transition to pop stardom began. Rather than an oscillating series of close shaves, chances-in-a-million and lucky breaks, it was a gradual development of a natural aptitude in tandem with unconscious forces within his background.

Fort Worth in wartime hadn't been Al Capone's Chicago exactly but living in its crowded, rip-roaring ferment had brought to Roy an abstracted worldliness. Much of his old shy self remained but it was with a new inner confidence that the eight-year-old singing guitarist made himself conspicuous on a Saturday morning *Amateur Hour* on Vernon's KVWC radio station. So often did he bicycle to its studio to defy all comers with selections born of those hot-eyed carousings in the city, that he was granted a regular non-competitive spot as "featured popular vocalist". By the time his kin came back – with, incidentally, not a single war fatality – Roy was the show's host.

On regional commercial radio – and, later, television – throughout the United States, slots would be block booked for a certain period each week. During this time, plugs for a sponsor's product would riddle more obvious entertainment, be it records, talent contest, drama or 'live' music. Roy Orbison "listened to the radio all the time and that was the big thing when I was growing up. We didn't have the telly and things like that for relaxing. Even if I wasn't, someone else in our house was playing the radio. I learned all the songs." With C&W, pop and western swing, plus subliminal shots of R&B, Zydeco, Spanish-Mexican sounds and "classical music" clogging the ether for sometimes every waking hour in the family home. "All of those influences probably settled into one thing and I'm the result of whatever it was."[14]

More than this, in the footsteps of older performers such as Jim Reeves and Webb Pierce, other musical Texans as well as Roy first reached a wider public via local radio. The career of the incredible PJ Proby, for instance, started on a Houston station in 1949 while Waylon Jennings, "youngest DJ in the USA" appeared on KDAV which also hosted a thirty-minute showcase on Sundays by a trio of Lubbock schoolboys, "Buddy, Bob and Larry". Neither "Buddy" nor KTRM Beaumont's portly programme director, JP Richardson, knew then to what extent their lives – and deaths – would interweave.

As an occupation *per se*, Roy's stint on KVWC beat paper rounds and car washing – except that, in keeping with the show's title, no-one ever received payment for their gladly-given services. Roy's first cash-in-hand engagement took place one weekend in spring 1946. Who could ever forget the day a medicine show came to town? Straight from the pages of a Buffalo Bill annual, the horse-drawn covered wagon came to its groaning halt in the dusty main street.

Such a sight was not, however, a twitch in the death throes of the

Wild West. Indeed, as the oil business skidded more rapidly into its later recession, medicine shows and similar accoutrements of tourism would become more common. Dude ranches, restored frontier forts, rattlesnake round-ups and establishments like Abilene's Old Betsy Muzzle Loading Shop added to the mythologising of the recent cowboys-and-injuns past by feature film, musical and TV series. Beyond simply sporting a stetson as part of everyday dress, some organisations such as the Texas Cowboy Reunion Association would seek to preserve True West culture, irrespective of financial gain.

This was not, however, the case with the pageant that trundled into Vernon that day. Behind its facade of antiquity chugged a pantechnicon transporting the electricity generator for its coloured lights and public address system. Some wooden benches were set out on the dirt in front of the makeshift stage. Directly after lunch, the huckster in his card-sharp finery yapped his spiel for the snake-bite tonics and cure-all elixirs for sale. As the planting of a "feed" or stooge among onlookers was too crass a ploy in such a smallish community, attention was held between the many inducements to buy with random skits, comedy routines – and a talent competition with a first prize of fifteen dollars.

Carried away with the impromptu carnival atmosphere of the visitation, radio star Roy Orbison agreed to mount the platform. With the frozen faces of his own parents among the mob staring up at him, he stood motionless before the lowered microphone, bar a knee trembling with nerves. This wasn't the privacy of his own home. Neither was it confined to the unseen protective bubble of KVWC, or the lower expectations of an elementary school assembly. Those closest to him knew that for Roy to be a slouch, after all the *Amateur Hour* fuss, might reduce him to the reclusive mediocrity of old.

For the first of his ordained two numbers, he played it safe with 'Morning Dew', a semi-comic hillbilly excursion that always went down well whenever its composer, Grandpa Louis Jones, did it on the *Grand Ole Opry*. Furthermore, Roy had already tried it out both on the radio and at a school concert. Led by the classmate who'd badgered him to go up there, the clapping that burst forth after he'd finished so emboldened Roy that he speculated next with something a bit racy. From Grandpa Jones levity, the smart-alec gabble of 'Jole Blon' removed Vernon in bright sunshine to the witching hour in a Creole dance hall: "That was the song that did it for me."[4]

Nonetheless, in spite of his KVWC reputation and the protracted cheering after 'Jole Blon' there was a split decision, and Roy had to share the princely purse, with a fifteen-year-old who'd played last. Even then, he ended up with only three dollars and a quarter because "my buddy went with me and carried my guitar and rooted for me, so he figured he ought to have half. That was my first taste of a manager."[6]

Though his smile afterwards might have been slightly forced, this win was the limit of the young Roy Orbison's impact on Vernon. A few months later, the family crossed three hundred miles west to Winkler County where Orbie Lee had obtained better-paid employment as general mechanical factotum – a "roustabout" – on an oil field. As Wilbarger had been the setting for *Red River*, so Winkler would be in 1956 for *Giant*, the James Dean film that captured the entrenchment of the oil barons on the Llano Estacado ("staked plain") farming enclosures there. Thirty miles from the Mexican border, and equidistant from Odessa and El Paso, the dreary oil town of Wink would be Roy's home for the period of his adolescence when "the intensity of your emotions...is something awe-inspiring, no matter how painful it might sometimes seem. I believe that none of us ever really grows out of that."[5]

As if in prophecy, the newly-arrived Roy Orbison on the threshold of manhood watched a tiny black cloud on a boundless horizon crescendo to a heaven-darkening thunderstorm of Wagnerian intensity. Such weather, however, was rare in a semi-tropical climate so dry that few had settled on the Staked Plain before 1800. During the worst droughts, the clayey soil was borne away by gales strong enough for a character in Marty Robbins' 'El Paso' to be "as wild as the West Texas wind". Irrigation from the mud-brown Pecos flowing between banks of cottonwood would transform the scrubby grassland to its west to yield pumpkins, chile and the excellent wine of El Paso. To the east where the Orbisons were, "There's nothing. No trees, no lakes, no creeks, a few bushes."[6]

A few saplings would sprout round the Orbisons' freshly-built bungalow at 100 Langley Drive – and even in residential areas in No Treeson, the road to Odessa. For those who viewed it in travelogues, West Texas seemed truly abundant with the "spacious skies for amber waves of grain" in 'America The Beautiful' – and some who actually lived there were elated too by the unbroken terrain "so flat you can see today going and tomorrow coming by merely looking in the other direction".

Roy Orbison, on the other hand, "got out of there as quick as I could, and I resented being there but it was a great education. It was as tough as could be but no illusions, you know? No mysteries in Wink."[6] It would be a mistake to envisage the thousand-odd souls who populated what was then not much more than a village, as brutish yokels dwelling in broken-down shacks beside a rutted track. Once they might have been but, by the early fifties, the forties would touch Wink. In the year of the Orbisons' coming, Wink's stature had become such that a branch of the County State Bank opened on Hendricks Boulevard. Soon afterwards, the wooden Wink Wildcats stadium would be torn down to make way for a modern steel-based structure in readiness for the 1949 football season. Feelers to the world of *haut couture* could be put out via the town's Sears-Roebuck office.

Although he'd got to be quite handy with a cue in Vernon, Roy found Wink's pool hall intimidating straightaway. In this stronghold of cool, "macho guys from the oil field" glared with gormless menace at weedy, four-eyed interlopers. At least there was a cinema – albeit one of the theatre type rather than a new-fangled drive-in like you'd get in Odessa. Rather than vegetate at home in the weeks prior to his and Grady's enrolment at Wink High School, Roy became addicted to films. With quiet pride, he'd mention how he'd "give up a good meal even when I'm hungry to see a movie I've looked forward to. I like the kind of picture that entertains without necessarily showing life at its realest and rawest."[8]

This was the apotheosis of Hollywood's cynical, neurotic "film noir": all platinum blondes in sleazy dives; rain-sodden night lit by neon advertisements, and lonesome anti-heroes, narcissistic and defeatist like James Cagney – or, in a different medium, Hank Williams. Though espionage thrillers like *Pick Up On South Street* would reveal preoccupations with anti-Communism, the film industry was yet to alienate sections of its public with any real criticisms of the aggressive redneck populism of the fifties.

In a lighter vein, there was much to please Roy in this escapist post-war era of outer space "things" – and the Saturday morning western epics which often strayed into the realms of musical comedy as did Paramount's *Son Of Paleface* in 1952. While identifying with Roy Rogers the "Singing Cowboy", and slobbering over Jane Russell, the teenage moviegoer was so taken when Bob Hope "looked into the mirror and went 'grrr'"[5] that for weeks after, he sickened his family with his efforts to mimic what was more a throaty gurgle than leonine growl.

Roy now had his own bedroom from whence also emanated, according to his mother, "many hours of mad twanging and singing and howling"[15] – much of it before the mirror no doubt. From the confidential record cards from Vernon, the junior High School already had some inkling that Orbison Minor was musical if nothing else. Briefly, he had a go at the baritone saxophone but was put off by its unpredictable harmonics and, compared to guitar, illogical learning process. Culturally window-shopping further, he looked in at the school's *a cappella* choir which, under the baton of some musical archivist, would delve into archaic traditions derived largely from Anglo-Celtic oral sources. Such stirring songs of the old frontier as 'The Old Chisholm Trail', 'Sam Bass' and 'Bill Was A Texas Lad' had been forged in cow camps, wagon trains and shotgun shacks to be ranted to available violin or banjo accompaniment. However, after the West was won, and the likes of Geronimo had spent their last days as tourist attractions, these items came to be little heard formally outside school concerts, folk festivals and Lions Club functions; their value lying in the less premeditated (and more authentic) insight into the myriad undercurrents that polarise what we know as "historical events", "famous people" and "current affairs" – definitely more so than the Texas portrayed in *The Lone Ranger*.

The choir blended Roy's historical and musical concerns but he wearied of its hearty clubbism: "To be with someone else is a bit inhibiting. It's foreign to me."[2] Not entailing so much active participation was an after-school class for "musical appreciation". Some hopeful teachers would try to arouse spotty adolescent interest in classical music via the tedium of Brahms' *German Requiem* but less highbrow were Brooklyn composer Aaron Copland's ballets, *Billy The Kid* and *Rodeo*, each incorporating folk themes, dance rhythms and harmonies invoking the Old West. However, to the post-war Average Joe, "classical music" meant an earful of all that stuff Liberace,

Mantovani and Leroy Anderson go in for sometimes – you know, pruned-down muzak arrangements of Handel's *Largo*, Ravel's *Bolero*, the *Warsaw Concerto*, *Tales Of Hoffman*, the *Lone Ranger* theme and all that. Roy was especially fond of the string-laden Mantovani, then perhaps the most popular light orchestra conductor in the world, a James Last of his day, Annunzio Mantovani was to Roy "my kind of artist. He seems to want to satisfy something in everyone. He's quite the same each time you hear him, dependable you might say. I've never liked too many severe changes. He fits in well with me."[8]

Wink High knew what to expect from Roy too. Becoming as well-known for his guitar playing and "good" voice as the volleyball captain and school bully were in their chosen spheres, he was a reliable stand-in for intervals between acts at the school play. All the same, the ilk of 'Jole Blon' and 'Tennessee Waltz' were frowned upon by the Church of Christ in Texas where the Orbisons worshipped. Though he would always be a Christian by instinct, Roy would drift from this church's hellfire fundamentalism that forbade dancing and secular music.

If it lacked other facilities, there was no shortage of religious denominations in Wink. As well as the Church of Christ, there were four non-conformist ministries whose service schedules were published each Thursday in *The Wink Bulletin* – "the only newspaper in the world that cares about Wink". While also reflecting conservative Democratic political leanings on its editorial page, this chronicle focused heavily on goings-on at the "Wink-loving" High School – predominantly sport and the Lions Club which met every Monday at the community centre.

An amalgam of local worthies propagating good causes, the Lions Club maintains a considerably higher profile in the States than do their Transatlantic cousins. Whereas a Briton would be hardly aware that the Lions Club was behind the embattled jumble sale in the church hall, in brasher North America, the organisation made damn sure everyone knew of its existence with blaring public processions, paramilitary parades and "rah-rah-rah" political rallies.

Social secretary of the Wink wing was Mr RA Lipscomb who also happened to be the High School principal. Not ignored, therefore, were the cost-cutting resources available there – such as use of its auditorium for dancing. As no professional bands of import would travel as far out as Wink for less than a king's ransom, why not check if there was any cheaper – better still, free – talent locally. That Orbison boy played in the popular style, didn't he? He could lead some sort of combo that could go the distance at the next dinner-and-dance.

With such a brainwave, Mr Lipscomb would not be opening a floodgate to an evening of interminable teenage row. In the late forties, the young had to put up with much the same sort of music as their parents liked. The petrification of the entertainment industry following the War ensured that popular musicians in all fields were generally well into their thirties before achieving worthwhile recognition. Hank Williams and Johnnie Ray were exceptions but usually there was either humble servitude in the ranks of an established band or else you'd only get work by doing the good old good ones. You jumped from nursery rhymes to Bing Crosby as if the connecting years were spent in a coma.

Unless you'd been born into showbusiness, you were not encouraged to think of it as a viable career. Country-and-western, even jazz was harmless enough as long as it wasn't taken seriously enough to interfere with school. Most easily accessible to the lower cultural echelons of Wink was the "western swing" that Roy had encountered in Fort Worth. Arising from the Texas of the mid-twenties, "western swing" was as curious a hybrid as Zydeco. Merging musical virtuosity and a swinging dance beat to jovial, infectious effect, this "hillbilly jazz" bubbled in a lurid pot-pourri of bluegrass breakdowns, Tin Pan Alley standards, jump blues and adapted urban jazz, spiced with the occasional heel-clattering Mexican fandango. Much more common than front line horns were pedal steel guitar and at least two fiddles plus novelties like jew's harp or mouth-organ for a Spike Jones touch. In the course of a set, an outfit might veer fitfully from Duke Ellington's 'Satin Doll' to 'Steel Guitar Rag' to Louis Jordan's 'Choo Choo Ch'Boogie' to 'When You're Smilin'' to originals like Bob Wills and his Texas Playboys' 'My Window Faces The South' with "honky-tonk" vocal refrain. Its popularity peaking in World War Two, western swing, nevertheless, lives on in the sounds of such as Asleep At The Wheel – high on the bill at Wembley's 1989 Country Festival – and Britain's Drew's Brew and Jive Alive.

However, in the hick towns of Texas in the forties the form was often adulterated as parochial bands made do. While bull fiddle, Sears drum kit and yellow-keyed piano took a bashing, Bob Wills' horn section or Ted Daffan's slick phalanx of fiddlers might be re-arranged for piano-accordion and crudely-amplified guitar: "We would undo the strings," Roy Orbison recalled, "and put the microphone inside then put the strings back on...and we had an amplifier."[10]

Such ingenuity was not new to the blues which hovered only as distant thunder in white West Texas. Born in 1933 in Happy less than a day's drive from Wink, Buddy Knox couldn't recall hearing a single record by a black artist until he visited New York.[16] Measuring his own artistic development against that of a Tennessean youth of about the same age, Roy Orbison felt that, "The basic difference was that Elvis was surrounded by black music almost exclusively; black music and country music was just beamed every day in his area. But in my area, no, that wasn't the case."[4]

Unlike Elvis Aron Presley in the blues city of Memphis, only the most free-spirited white teenager was likely to gravitate to juke joints in run-down districts of Odessa, Midland or Fort Worth to fraternise with the state's most shunned sub-culture. Through the static, a Wink listener might tune in by accident to muffled bursts of what segregationalists heard as "the screaming idiotic words and savage music" of faraway Shreveport's rhythm-and-blues station KWKH where "Stan The Man And His No-Name Record Jive" punctuated the likes of The Midnighters' 'Sexy Ways', 'Sixty Minute Man' by The Dominoes and 'Too Many Drivers' from Smiley Lewis – all about sex, and all banned by white radio. "If you don't want to serve negroes in your place of business," ran one racist handbill, "then do not have negro records on your juke box."

Instead, why not have some *nice* music? We've got some fine records here by Doris Day, Eddie Fisher, Horace Heidt and his Musical Knights, 'Xmas Singalong With Mitch Murray'... You like "real" singing? Here's 'The Loveliest Night Of The Year' from *The Great Caruso* movie the one that Mario Lanza put in the pop charts in 1950. A bit "square"? How about Johnnie Ray, "Prince of Wails"? My dad says he's horrible but Hank Williams thinks "he's sincere and shows he's sincere. That's the reason he's popular."[12]

Through his hammy cry-guy act, Ray introduced an exhibitionism long prevalent in rhythm-and-blues. A big onstage moment was when he piled into his hit cover of The Drifters' 'Such A Night'. Such a whitewashing of an R&B smash for the pop charts was always anticipated – even welcomed – by black recording artists of the early fifties as it brought their music, if not their performances, to another world with money to waste. Some like The Platters and their role model, The Ink Spots, were even smooth enough to cross over completely.

Likewise making it from C&W to pop were Slim Whitman and Jim Reeves – but both favoured a light "sweetcorn" approach as opposed to the "hard country" of Hank Williams. As with R&B, pop stars plundered the C&W motherlode, exemplified when Patti Page ("The Singing Rage") and electric guitarist Les Paul each recorded Cowboy Copas' 'Tennessee Waltz' in 1948. Furthermore, jobbing Tin Pan Alley tunesmiths were more at home with C&W than R&B, as witnessed by the clippety-clop offerings of Frankie Laine, Tennessee Ernie Ford and Vaughan 'Riders In The Sky' Monroe – all sounding like they'd cut their teeth on a branding iron. Not so much a redneck's meat were silver screen gems like Bill Hayes' 'Ballad Of Davy Crockett' and Doris Day's whip-crack-away highlights from *Calamity Jane*.

Falling meekly into line, Roy Orbison at thirteen did not resent having to conform to adult taste. Not knowing any better and at the stage where he could "step out in front of an audience and not be scared to death",[10] he was excited by any opportunity to extend himself beyond assemblies, intermissions and parents' evenings. Without his musical prowess, Roy – who wasn't much of a scrapper – might have had to resign himself to miserable years as the Fat Owl of Wink High. Instead, he'd been adopted as a sort of mascot by those broad-shouldered shower-room studs who liked his singing but saw him as no rival for female favours.

Roy, however, with hormones raging, thought that his prime position in the school band might give him licence to talk to girls, a sex that had been untouchable thus far. Even so, if they did appreciate how sensitive and vulnerable he was, certain callous, giggling little madams couldn't care less about humiliating him. Raw physical beauty their only assets, they'd torment him with indifference or, with coquettish malice, attempt to lead him into some blushing *faux pas*. Others less spiritually ugly would confide in Roy as they would a brother about their romantic trials and tribulations, thereby dashing any hopes Roy himself might treasure in that direction, "Because every relationship I'd ever been in, the girl already had one going when we first met – even as far back as kindergarten."[5]

How many are there among the great whose will to succeed was rooted in the indignities and frustrations of schooldays? Similarly motivated, perhaps, were Roy's first less-than-immortal band recruits. With Charles Evans, a short but plump Wink High pupil who plucked the double bass, was the lanky James Morrow, a mandolin player. Both Morrow and Orbison now possessed solid-body electric instruments. With a matching amplifier, Roy's was a red Gibson Les Paul, "cutaway" to give easier access to the higher frets. These days, you see, he no longer confined himself to just stroking chords: "Like at fifteen, I tried to be a lead guitar player, playing intricate melody lines and such. I didn't get very far, so by sixteen, I'd set my mind to playing just rhythm guitar to accompany my voice."[5]

From a mutable pool of other musicians, Orbison never failed to marshal some kind of backing band for Lions Club knees-ups in the school hall. However, when the ambitious Mr Lipscomb was up for election to the Club's district presidency, Roy's boys were required to cast their net at his campaign gatherings throughout West Texas. Finding the rapid turnover of personnel prohibitive for this itinerary, Roy whittled down the group to a mobile nucleus of five. With Morrow and Evans as his Rosencrantz and Guildenstern, the line-up was completed by pianist Richard West and drummer Billy Parr Ellis who thwacked his snare drum with brush sticks so as not to drown the others.

To further suit his empire-building, Mr Lipscomb christened the new quintet "The Wink Westerners": "We had to have the name 'Wink' in there, and 'Westerners' were meant to represent West Texas which he was running for," Orbison recalled. "So it was 'West Texas' as opposed to 'western' music because we played all kinds."[17]

Loosely categorising themselves as "western swing", among the dozen or so numbers at the Wink Westerners' command were smooth approximations of 'Jersey Bounce', 'Moonlight In Vermont' and other big band sobrieties. These interspersed with current C&W and pop favourites which ranged from Webb Pierce to Hoagy Carmichael – who was reputed to have "discovered" Frankie Laine, another repertory source. As well as customary requests for 'Georgia On My Mind' and 'Jezabel' there was always some clever dick who wanted to hear 'Cry' or some other Johnnie Ray number, abhorrent to those no longer young. Roy never minded singing them – or any by Frank Sinatra, admired as "a go-getter all the way".[8]

At the drop of a hat, he'd also pitch into 'Long Black Veil', a murder ballad recorded in 1949 by fellow Texan, Lefty Frizzell – "The first singer I heard on the radio that really blew me away." Though not as generally influential as Hank Williams, Frizzell – born in 1928 – left more of a mark on Roy Orbison for "this technique which involved sliding the syllables together that just about used to slay me".[5]

In the beginning, almost all The Wink Westerners' bookings came about through either the Lions Club or school. As an amateur group formed by schoolboys, they were content then merely to have somewhere to perform. The next step – if there was to be a next step – would be to play to an audience for money.

Collaborating with club owners and impresarios, radio stations would also promote C&W jamborees, square dances and other Saturday night entertainments featuring local heroes only a rung higher than The Wink Westerners. Many of them would give living credence to the assertion, "I never did hear a cowboy with a real good voice. If he had one to start with, he always lost it bawling at cattle"[18] – or at oil field navvies. Sometimes, these hopefuls were lucky enough to support a big star at prestigious venues like Fort Worth's Panther Hall. Drawing the crowds would be names as homely as a hitching post: Ernest Tubb, The Carter Family, Hank Snow, Eddy Arnold. Their backing combos – called The Texas Troubadours, perhaps, or The Tennessee Playboys – would bolster a fierce sense of regional identity less precisely than local acts such as the Fannin County Boys who featured a lead guitarist called Joe Melson. Mixing foot-stompin hoedown, quaking sentiment and singalong evergreens, the unvarnished "sincerity" of a lot of these artists, professional or otherwise, was as contrived in image as that of Liberace. In place of that exquisite's candelabra and sequins were cartoon cowboy outfits; ten gallon hats, furry chaparajos, rhinestones and loud embroidery.

Hank Williams' sole superfluous adornment was a plain white fedora. Yet, in the early fifties, this gangling, besuited Alabaman's popularity guaranteed standing room only for virtually all his two hundred one-nighters He seemed to make a virtue of his whining downhome intonation, untutored phrasing and eccentric breath control. However, without milking an audience as much as Tubb *et al* he was committed more inescapably to the essence of his songs than previous country performers. Although his accompanying Drifting Cowboys utilised the expected steel guitar and mournful violin, Williams' plaintive vocal resolution was underpinned by unusual absorption with rhythm, hinged on his own guitar chopping.

At the time, Roy Orbison "didn't reckon him as the genius I now perceive him to be",[5] but, from the "big fun" of 'Jambalaya' to the wounded 'Your Cheatin' Heart', Hank created more C&W "standards" than anyone else. He saw himself, however, as more a folk singer like Leadbelly who, defined as a blues shouter for convenience, actually covered all waterfronts from 'The Old Chisholm Trail' via children's play rhymes to, yes, blues. Williams' work also spanned other idioms. The incorporation of blues into his stylistic arsenal is best exemplified in titles like 'Moanin' The Blues' and 'Howlin' At The Moon'. As his fame spread beyond the south, his compositions were covered for the pop market by the likes of Tony Bennett, Jo Stafford and Rosemary Clooney. In backhanded corroboration, Orbison "found his stuff too 'Tin Pan Alley-ish' for my tastes back then".[5] But for his early death in 1953, Williams might have crossed over to the pop Hot 100 in his own right.

For all his eclecticism, that Hank Williams was bracketed as simply a country-and-western singer belied the efforts of his mentors, Fred Rose and Roy Acuff. Before combining as a management-publishing-production concern – Acuff-Rose – both had been known country-and-western personalities; Rose mainly as a songwriter, Acuff as *Grand Ole Opry* compere and guiding light of The Smoky Mountain Boys from whom Williams had derived aspects of his style. Though their plans for their boy were thwarted by the Grim Reaper, other Acuff-Rose clients such as Cindy Walker and Bordleaux and Felice Bryant were steered from country to more generalised pop.

As well as business ministrations, the partners also had – to a diminishing extent – a creative say in output. Rose, for instance, co-wrote with Williams songs such as the comic-sad 'Kaw-liga', complete with throbbing tom-toms. This blueprint would provoke later Red Indian pastiches published by Acuff-Rose such as John D Loudermilk's 'Indian Reservation' in 1969 – and, five years earlier, 'Indian Wedding' by one who had flown to the highest pinnacle of pop as Hank Williams should have done.

In the year before Williams' passing, the singer with The Wink Westerners had been rewarded for services rendered when chosen as West Texas's musical representative at the International Lions Conclave in Chicago – his first trip up north. Moreover, the group itself had moved up a bit, appearing regularly on local radio. Nevertheless, to pay for equipment, Roy for one was still obliged to seek onerous holiday jobs; some obtained through Orbie Lee who was no longer a common roustabout but a drilling superintendent. However, after a bash in Kermit, a village a few miles north-east of Wink, the five were approached by a dance promoter who offered them four hundred dollars to perform at one of his revels the following week. Courageously stretching out their limited repertoire for an entire evening, the band's first endeavour as semi-professionals netted each member the same as that pocketed by Roy for a fortnight shovelling tar the previous vacation. "So then I really and truly knew I wanted to go into showbusiness because I loved singing and you could make money at it too,"[14] he realised.

CHAPTER TWO

The Cause Of It All

"To lead a Western Band is his after school wish/and of course to marry a beautiful dish"[1] was the valediction printed beneath Roy Orbison's photograph in Wink High's yearbook when he graduated in 1954. This doggerel had come from the hand of a compiler who'd latched onto the twin artistic and fleshly forces that were still kindling Roy during an adolescence "which was at times pretty frustrating".[2]

He'd never found school work arduous or been in terror over exams. However, who could pretend that a Euclid theorum or even the battle of Saratoga Springs could keep him from fantasising about girls? Sucking at a Coke in the Wildcat Den cafe on Hendricks Boulevard, he'd languish round the juke box, trying not to notice Jack and Jill cooing over each other in the corner. Later, Jack'd whisper to her and, entwined, they'd slip out to Lover's Lane to get up to Roy knew not what. So full of themselves they were, all those condescending hard-faced jerks – "oil and grease and sand and being a stud and being cool"[3] – with their tittering girlfriends on their arms.

Into the bargain, the so-called "Western Band" had almost touched the ceiling of its fortunes, and the inevitable cracks were visible. To the marriage bed had gone Richard West, lucky boy. It had been farewell also to Charlie Evans who, casting aside childish follies like The Wink Westerners, now had to work to keep alive. With his own earnings from music hardly adequate, Roy too had reached a vocational crossroad. If you went by his High School attainments, he turned out to be the brainiest Orbison, if no Einstein. While his musical ability was apparent, an inwrought commitment to honest labour led him to seek proper qualifications – "something to fall back on".[6] A good all-rounder academically, he listened to the sound advice of Orbie Lee who, from first hand, "knew there'd be a demand for geologists".[4]

With every intention of majoring in this subject, Roy was accepted on a degree course at North Texas State University in Denton near Fort Worth of blessed memory. At last, he'd be shot of Wink and its "what's the best beer you've ever drunk" twittering. He'd had quite enough of the oil fields, thank you. His spirit had nearly broken during a long hot summer job as a labourer for the Natural Gas Company in El Paso, "cutting up steel and loading it onto trucks and chopping weeds and painting water towers. Our straw boss was Mr Rose, and he wouldn't cut me any slack. I worked in the blazing heat, hard, hard labour, and then I'd play at night, come home and, some nights be too tired to eat or even to undress. I'd lay down, and I wouldn't even turn over. I'd wake up in the same spot and hit the oil patch again."[3]

If he had to return to the family trade, his degree would put him a cut above the likes of Mr Rose. He wouldn't have to work his way up to a responsible position as his father had done. Waiting at the end of his four years at college would be a respectable profession, a mortgage – maybe wedding bells: "I guess it was an attempt at being legitimate and not a free spirit."[3]

From this conventional objective, however, he'd be corrupted from a distance. Freeze-framed over his text books as he then was, Roy Orbison was poised on the verge of something he'd desire – had always desired – more than any tin-pot university grade. He hadn't known what it was but he knew he'd be disappointed if he didn't find it. He'd want it more than Jesus cried for Calvary.

Already Roy had noticed that, "If you had a guitar and walked into a place, they'd say, 'Hello, Elvis.'"[5] With Presley as carrier, the bacillus of rock 'n' roll had started to distress the Land of the Free. Nevertheless, for a year before the nationally-broadcast Ed Sullivan television show would only dare televise him from the waist up, the lewd stage antics and hillbilly-blues shout-singing of Elvis Presley had been both adored and hated throughout the South – even in far-flung Wink. During his penultimate term at school, Roy had been rivetted when the "Hillbilly Cat" careened from the radio with his first single, the seventy-eight rpm 'That's All Right', on a Memphis record label with a chicken logo. Because it was a jumped-up treatment of a negro blues, some disc jockeys hadn't been keen on scheduling such a racially-integrated disc. By August 1954, however, it had muscled in at Number Three in the country-and-western chart.

As their British compeers' would over The Sex Pistols a quarter of a century on, so adult redneck blood had run cold at Presley's noise, gibberish and loutish excesses. It was just like nigger music. If you want a more objective opinion, ask that Limey bandleader who was there the night Nat "King" Cole got what he deserved. "I don't think 'rock and roll' will come to Britain," confirmed Ted Heath. "You see, it is primarily for the coloured population."[6]

Many teenagers were just as aghast as their parents yet in a nonplus of repellent fascination. Before he'd even heard 'That's All Right', Roy Orbison had borrowed his father's car and set out on 16 April, 1954 for Dallas Sportatorium – just over 200 miles away – to catch this "unspeakably untalented, vulgar young entertainer" as a television guide would describe him. Everyone was talking about Elvis.

At the venue – a C&W jamboree – Roy "couldn't over-emphasise how shocking he looked and seemed to me that night".[7] It was like nothing the bespectacled Wink Westerner had ever experienced before. Presley, sneering gently, didn't care how terribly he behaved up there – breaking guitar strings, spitting out his chewing gum, swivelling his hips in a rude way, doing the splits, knee-dropping and crawling to the edge of the stage. He told off-colour jokes "which weren't funny, and his diction was real course like a truck driver's". With conflicting emotions, Roy noted "pandemonium in the audience because the girls took a shine to him and the guys were getting a little jealous".[4] Nonetheless, while pulling out all the stops and unfettered by sickness, the lurid Presley's instinctive control kept the mob just short of open riot – though females continued to shriek and faint in repudiation of their beaux's sporadic heckling. By the close, every potentially ugly juncture had been bypassed as all tuned into the situation's epic vulgarity. More than anyone, Elvis himself conveyed the impression that "what comes out is not show. There are a lot of people who are good actors at singing so that they make you think they sound good but, with Elvis, he lives it altogether."[8]

Even those who barracked were tacitly sick of the corny monotony they still had to endure at graduation balls, village hops and other parched occasions arranged and supervised by grown-ups to keep teenagers off the street. With Elvis, "It was everybody wanting to hear the feel of music; people really wanted to be involved with music but at the time that generation had no music to be involved in."[9] Beyond specific songs, all that counted was the rhythmic kick. Let's dance – not hoe down or strict tempo – let's rock 'n' roll. In fact, let's get real, real gone for a change.

From the uproaring go-man-go abandon, shell-shocked Roy Orbison turned a thoughtful steering wheel. There was the contradiction of Presley carrying on like a pool hall hood while garbed in the flash duds Roy associated with blacks and homosexuals: pink socks, hip-hugging slacks, black shirt, white tie, green jacket with upturned collar. However, against these and his brilliantined but girly cockade and ducktail, the sideburns down to his earlobes had showed he was a Man. Rearing up on that Dallas platform had been all that Orbison's upbringing and character had taught him to both despise and fear.

Yet the quiet, cautious Roy had been entranced by the glorious trash he'd just heard. It wasn't that far removed from the more up-tempo C&W the Westerners played. Other bands, so he understood, were already inserting Elvis numbers into their sets – among them Bonham's Fannin County Boys and a Nacodoches combo led by a Bob Luman. Moreover, some R&B records had found their way onto Wink nickelodeons, and were spun often enough to escape purging. Nowadays, Frankie Laine and Tennessee Ernie slid in and out alongside the ambulatory shuffle of Fats Domino and the sly lyricism of Chuck Berry. When all was said and done, Berry's first hit, 'Maybellene' – which Elvis had sung in Dallas – owed almost as much to C&W for all its springing from a blues environment. Of this new craze, Roy "really loved hearing it and couldn't wait for the next records to come out, but, at the same time, I was kind of ready to go myself."[10] To this end, The Wink Westerners would be slipping in a couple of sanitised rock 'n' roll items before their leader departed for Denton in October.

Settling into campus life, the impressionable Winkler county freshman was delighted that pop was encouraged there as much as "serious" music – sometimes in preference to it. Every Saturday, there was a free concert in the Main Hall. Shortly before college went down that autumn, one evening's diet of orchestral favourites and western folk song was interrupted when onto the rostrum strutted two fellows from the year above Roy. One was holding a guitar. With the merest preamble, Dick Penner and Wade Moore lurched into a number they'd made up themselves one lazy afternoon on a hostel roof. As a song, it was as nonsensical as its title, 'Ooby Dooby', but they brazened it out deadpan to warm response. As for Roy, "It knocked me flat. I was astounded because they made more music than the whole orchestra."[4]

Though it had been conceived as a western swing novelty, 'Ooby Dooby' had also reminded Roy of the Elvis Presley show – minus, of course, the unruly climate. Talking to Wade and Dick afterwards, Roy learned that 'Ooby Dooby' was "rockabilly". Its precedents were, apparently, traceable to particular records such as Hank Williams' 'Move It On Over', 'Wild Side Of Life' by Hank Thompson and Tennessee Ernie's 'Shotgun Boogie'. Nevertheless, drawing from all points on a spectrum from western swing to blues, rockabilly was the blanket term used to cover a strand of rock 'n' roll based on sparse instrumentation and primaeval rowdiness.

Anyone who'd mastered basic techniques could have a go. The core of its contagious backbeat was a slapped double bass and slashing acoustic guitar; drums not entering the fray till later. Over this rudimentary impetus, you could holler more or less any old how as long as you got "gone" enough to lend unhinged sorcery to the simplistic hep-cat couplets about clothes, lust, violence and doin' the Ooby Dooby with all o' your might. Two verses of this, and an electric guitarist would take off from simple fills to full-blooded clangorous solo amid yells of encouragement – "yep!", "woo-hoo!", "play that thing!" – until the levelling vocal surged back in.

This archetype was a launch pad for liberal non-conformity within its prescribed constraints. Sometimes, both or either guitar would be supplemented or replaced, however incongruously, with piano, violin, saxophone, harmonica, banjo or mandolin. Though singers were usually male, Wanda Jackson and Janis Martin – the "female Elvis" – were conspicuous among the exceptions. The idea was to find an individual vocal style even with well-known material. You could embroider it with yelps, hiccups, low grumbling, high pitched whining, insane falsettos – anything went.

Nevertheless, though you often had to be sharp to spot differences, there were vague regional shades of rockabilly. West Virginia, for example, leaned towards an acoustic bias whereas East Texas – as epitomised by the earthy 'Rockin' Daddy' by Houston floor-layer, Sonny Fisher – gave credence to one critic's summary of the form as "the blues with acne".

In West Texas, rockabilly was tackled with a lighter touch as an extension of western swing with few overt rhythm-and-blues overtones. Following the shock of Elvis, though Roy Orbison had listened hard to black music throughout his first college term, it wasn't always with much pleasure: "I had heard groups like The Clovers and their hits like 'One Mint Julep', all based on seventh chords, and I didn't really like them."[5] While commuting from Denton to the Westerners' growing orbit of engagements, he had also volunteered to put the icing on Moore and Penner's endeavours by hacking his limited but proficient lead guitar. Unavoidably, their 'Ooby Dooby' *pièce de résistance* with its standard blues chord changes, was seized upon by the Westerners. Mutating into a semi-instrumental, it was a much-requested highlight.

Response to another request, made at a New Year's Eve party in 1954, facilitated the group's complete switch over to rockabilly. Someone wanted 'Shake Rattle And Roll', a rousing opus first recorded by blues belter, Joe Turner. It had just been diluted for the white market by Bill Haley And The Comets, a northern dance band formerly known as Bill Haley's Saddlemen and, before that, The Four Aces Of Western Swing. Younger victims of the same passion, The Wink Westerners obligingly struck up 'Shake Rattle And Roll' that festive night – "but we had nearly ten minutes to go to the [midnight] hour so we kept playing the same song." This rave-up was strung out with call-and-response sequences to work up audience participation, taking it down easy and then building up the tension to 1955: "By the time we were finished, I was fully converted,"[11] Roy recalled.

By "going rockabilly", the Westerners would effectively outlaw themselves from the stuffy if lucrative adult functions on which they'd depended for virtually all their bookings.

Doing their bit to cast out the pestilence, many town committees had banned rock 'n' roll, often extra-legally, as obscene and subversive: "It was strange because we played in movie theatres; we played on a barge, a boat, we played anywhere that we could draw a crowd," Roy said. "But there were places, certain auditoriums, that we couldn't play because it was rock 'n' roll. At certain times in the day, we couldn't play. Sometimes we had to play in the afternoon and not play at night. It wasn't really, really bad but there were restrictions."[10]

Out with all the 'Moonlight In Vermont' corn went the old name. Not only was "Wink Westerners" reminiscent of school and the Lions Club but it was also rather too Ernest Tubb. What was needed was a punchier, more teen-orientated image. Thanks in part to Elvis, the word "teenager" had been coined by the media to donate all those 'twixt twelve and twenty who were deciding whether or not they wanted to grow up. Because of fuller employment and increases in wages since the War, teenagers had become a separate target for advertising. Rockabilly, for instance, had caught on as teen music. Furthermore, no adult would be seen dead in its outrageously-coloured "cat" clothes. Enlarging on the Presley ideal, in came check box jackets with padded shoulders; loud cowboy or Hawaiian shirts and tapered peg trousers – plus the narcissistic greasy coiffeur.

As this look would not yet enchant the more bigoted heterosexual chauvinists in redneck counties like Winkler, Roy's band weren't to squeeze into cat clothes immediately but, after deep thought, somebody came up with a suitable name. On the radio, there's this new girl group in Chicago called "The Teen Queens", right? Let's be "The Teen *Kings*", yeah?

When The Teen Kings began hawking their musical goods in spring 1955, joining Ellis, Morrow and Orbison on stage was the burly Jack Kennelly who clutched the belly of his "TK"-embossed bull fiddle between his thighs as he plucked that dissolute rockabilly throb. On a Spanish guitar with attached electronic pick-up was a short but effervescent youth, Johnny "Peanuts" Wilson, who – for now – didn't mind thrashing a finger-lacerating rhythm while the older Roy hogged the lead guitar and vocal departments. Sharing the front man's instrumental solos, the gifted James Morrow would henceforth alternate between mandolin, tenor saxophone and – if handy – piano.

This motley crew of oil field apprentices, pen-pushers and a geology student rapidly attracted steady grassroots support. After winning a "Battle of the Bands" tournament judged on the volume of applause, The Teen Kings made their television debut on a light entertainment programme transmitted from Odessa to each of the local Texan networks. Though he was now dying his hair jet black as Elvis had done, The Teen Kings' singer was no figure of such offensive magnetism. Indeed, because the quintet toed a subdued, amiable line before the cameras, they were re-booked for a whole series of fortnightly half-hour showcases sponsored by Pioneer, a Midland furniture conglomerate.

With this exposure, the next milestone loomed ahead: "Television was new; we were new, and we were quite big in the area, so we decided to make a record."[9] Already, they had an audible yardstick whereby they could measure their own worth alongside that of rivals. Under the supervision of a Major Bill Smith, they had a stab at recording a few numbers in his studio, situated where Fort Worth dissolves into Dallas. In what can now be seen as the mediaeval period of recorded sound, both demonstration and master tapes went down in single takes on heavy-duty equipment. There was no avenue for superimposition – "overdubbing" – or contrived atmospherics beyond reverberation and "bathroom" echo.

The most logical choice for an A-side was the show-stopping 'Ooby Dooby', the only repertory selection peculiar to The Teen Kings alone. As well as being either too well-known or too recent to revive, nothing else bore a stamp distinctive enough to set the group apart from any other up-and-coming rockabilly outfit. Individually, Roy and – to a lesser extent – James and Johnny had yet to find their feet as composers. The group's principal asset, if it had one, was the assured if over-eloquent lead vocal. Although it was short on the endearing imperfections of a Sonny Fisher or Gene Vincent, Roy's own reaction to that first tape was "that if I heard that voice again, I would know that I'd heard it before. I wasn't thinking, 'Boy, that's great; that's beautiful,' or that I sing wonderfully well...it was just that I said, 'There might be something there.'"[12]

There might well have been but what had all this extra-mural messing about to do with geology? He'd applied himself diligently enough to his studies to start with but gradually Roy's double life gave his tutors concern. The cash flow from music had become such that even Orbie Lee was convinced that, if Roy kept at it, he might just make a reasonable living as a musician. However, owing to the prior claims of The Teen Kings, the singing scholar began cutting lectures and handing in skimped essays. Finally, the candle burnt to the middle when a run of late nights spent either performing or catching up with course work caused him to oversleep and thereby miss an important exam. There were, nevertheless, no hard feelings when, after discussing Orbison's academic future with his parents, the university authorities upheld his transfer closer to home. At the state teachers college in Odessa, he'd try for an inferior qualification – an "associate's degree" – in English and history with a view to becoming a secondary schoolmaster.

If he had not been so fully occupied with music, Orbison's studious nature, excellent memory and methodical tenacity might well have earned him geology honours. However, to other trainee teachers in Odessa, he couldn't be imagined swishing a cane or oppressing children with gerundives. His television reputation as a rockabilly rebel had preceded him but, belying any "wellawellawella" bumpkin expectations, Roy of The Teen Kings was a well-read, impassive sophomore. When you got to know him, he revealed a dry wit and deferential rural charm. Nevertheless, rumours about him had spread, magnified and become truth. Do you know that, on stage, he's demented like someone having a fit? He and his band are making a record. He knows Elvis.

To be strictly accurate, Orbison *had* met Presley by then. When Elvis appeared at Panther Hall in 1955, Roy as a star of local TV wormed his way backstage to invite him to guest on a Pioneer furniture broadcast. During the fleeting conversation in the bustling dressing room, Orbison was flattered when the very approachable idol readily agreed to a two-song intermission spot before the studio audience. On the day, however, The Teen Kings comprehended the folly of going on after the King of Western Bop: "The crowd weren't too pleased when we came back for the second half. All of Elvis's contemporaries, even the household names, were in awe of his talent."[13]

One such "household name" who'd also made the mistake of

following Elvis onto the boards – "though it wasn't totally anti-climactic"[14] – was another Odessa student, Pat Boone, who Roy had seen acting in a Greek tragedy. Boone was more adept than Orbison at reconciling college cloisters with the stage: "At the same time, he had a TV show in Dallas, a radio show, he was touring and he still got straight As."[15] Only two years older than Roy, Pat had led an eventful life. By the age of thirteen, he'd become something of a singing *wunderkind* on Nashville radio and bigwig dinner-dances. During what he'd later write off as "an age of confusion and doubt",[16] he eloped to Texas with his high school sweetheart, Shirley – daughter of C&W sweetcorn merchant, Red Foley. After the nuptials, Pat paid his own way through teachers training college by performing with a country band. Brushing aside all opposition in a television talent competition in Gallantin, he was snapped up by Dot Records.

To his bemusement, Dot had him covering black R&B rather than the hayseed material with which both he and his father-in-law were most at ease. Nonetheless, this strategy paid dividends when, in 1955, the undergraduate metamorphosed into a pop star with a polite and embarrassed version of Fats Domino's 'Ain't That A Shame'. For the old and square, Pat Boone was a clean, well-mannered compromise to that ghastly Presley. Through the medium of teen magazine articles, this more palatable personification of rock 'n' roll provided copy deeper than his conception of a "dream girl" and whether he ever dated fans. Revelling in his married state, Pat preached that your parents' word was law; get your hair cut; don't talk dirty. These worthy ideals were incorporated later into *Twixt Twelve And Twenty*, the Boone manual for wholesome boys and girls: "We all have bad habits. Personally I'm not too good at getting up in the morning, and I happen to enjoy scrambled eggs for breakfast."[16] When he – like Elvis – moved into films, he'd further parade his dearth of private vices by baulking at kissing his leading ladies. Well, you never know what these things lead to...

Caught between the truculent in-concert sensuality of Presley – that he could never hope to emulate – and his own stolid compliance to middle-aged values, Roy found the Boone stance reassuring, a relief almost. Already, there were vinyl indications that the saintly Pat aimed to drop that raucous R&B that had been forced on him, and get on with the lush "quality" stuff *à la* Como or Sinatra. This was on the premise that rock 'n' roll was just another fad that chanced to be going a bit stronger than the Jitterbug or the Creep. As late as 1959, Sinatra would still be voted "Favourite Male Star" in a *Billboard* disc jockey poll.

As Boone was in his final Odessa year before embarking on a post-graduate course at Columbia, he and Orbison had only a passing acquaintance, "But he was already into his career, and that's what impressed me – that he was going to school *and* singing."[10]

Pat may have provided distant answers to Roy's artistic and moral dilemmas but a less eminent collegian had made a more personal impression as the aphrodisiacal promise of the 1956 spring gave way to a wondrous summer. At long last, requited love had come to Roy Orbison in the form of an attractive, vivacious brunette from Houston. Well-built for her sixteen years, Claudette Frady had never lacked would-be swains back home. Self-confident, intelligent and with an easy smile that showed off her fine teeth and mischievous eyes, she was just the sort of dolly little darlin' that a Wink High football *palooka* would be proud to be seen with at the Wildcat Den.

When Claudette and Roy began "walking out" together, common room gossips assumed that it was the attraction of opposites. Jubilant as he was, Roy's courtship of his "steady" was conducted as if Pat Boone was chaperoning them. In days before the birth pill and the Swinging Sixties, pre-marital sex was a much bigger issue. To sceptical cronies, a changing room lothario would brag of carnal capers that everyone knew were either exaggerations or downright lies. He may hare got to "third base" but only a "cheap" girl didn't "save herself" for her future husband. Her whole being might be screaming for sex as much as the pimpled fumbler of her bra strap but a true daughter of the fifties would have none of it while yet unwed.

Roy and Claudette, however, were above undignified groupings. Within weeks of their first date, she had accepted his proposal. Before the wedding in Wink later that year, Claudette even consented to spending a few days with her fiancé in the sprawling industrial city of Memphis, Tennessee. Nonetheless, according to Sam Phillips at whose house they stayed, the lovebirds "slept in separate rooms. I just found him to be an almost grown kid, you know? He had so much damn innocence about him – and he never really changed from that."

This Mr Phillips hadn't always been so accommodating. His colleagues had opined that the wild-eyed radio announcer had finally flipped his lid when, lumbered with a wife and two sons, he dropped everything in 1950 to rent a minuscule recording studio next to a used car lot on the junction of Union and Marshall Avenues. This institution, he'd calculated, would become a Mecca for local musicians. The untidy river port of Memphis was, after all, the "home of the blues".

For the first three years, the visionary Sam kept the wolf from the door with R&B masters. Many became hits when leased to Chess in Chicago and other northern record companies. However, in 1952, he declared his independence with the formation of his own label – "Sun". Two years on, he hit the jackpot when Elvis Presley came by. Here was the money-making "white man who could sing the blues" that he'd despaired of ever finding.

When Presley took the South by storm, there were howls of disbelief when Sun auctioned his contract to the mighty RCA in November 1955. What on earth was Sam playing at now? He reckoned that he could spawn another Elvis anytime he liked. There were now plenty to choose from. Not a day would go by without demo tapes thudding onto Sun's doormat, trembling string-callused fingers pressing the bell, and tongue-tied telephone callers begging auditions by the great Sam Phillips. From all across the nation they came – even from Alaska and Canada. In the South itself, they were like wasps round a jam-jar. Quite a few of these were worth a listen too. With Elvis gone, Phillips had put his money on Carl Perkins whose immediate Hot 100 smash, 'Blue Suede Shoes', caused RCA to wonder if they'd signed the wrong man.

To give Perkins a clearer run in the rockabilly stakes, Sam promoted another likely lad, Johnny Cash, as the label's C&W specialist. While an air force radio operator in Germany during the Cold War, the Arkansas-born Cash had taught himself to pick country-style guitar, and developed a liking for alcohol. Discharged in 1954, he was drawn to Memphis where, whilst working as a door-to-door salesman, he met a pair of garage mechanics who, between them, twanged electric guitar and upright bass. With these newfound friends, Johnny landed a weekly show on local radio, singing not rockabilly but mainly straight C&W of a religious bent. These anthems he delivered in a heavily masculine growl. After two months of this, "Johnny Cash And The Tennessee Two" approached Sun for a try-out. Disregarding their devotional tariff, Sam Phillips asked if they'd anything teenagers might like. Cash responded with a string of secular songs he'd composed in the Fatherland.

With his lowdown bass and facial scar, Johnny was too butch to be one more Elvis but, after his first crop of Sun singles were all country hits, he became a virtual fixture on *Louisiana Hayride*. Moreover, his manager, Bob Neal, was able to negotiate a strenuous round of engagements for Cash and the Two that would see them into next year and, beyond. After the initial leg of poorly-paid bookings – some hundreds of miles apart – it dawned on them what a joyless grind now blighted their lives. This irreversible imposition caused the itinerary to degenerate into a subsidised booze-up. Giggling drunk or on another planet, on more than one night, you'd think they'd never totter on stage. As a result, the moody, introspective Johnny became an erratic performer, walking a line between rubbish and dazed inspiration.

He was on form, however, for a regional television appearance in autumn 1955 – on which The Teen Kings had procured a guest spot. Watching Cash off- camera, Roy was struck by Cash's vocal singularity: "Very distinctive, yeah...if you hear John once, you hear him again, you know it's the same singer. So that works in your favour. It won't get you a hit record but it will help build if you have the rest of the goods."[4] Cash felt much the same about Orbison. In a genial mood afterwards, he complimented Roy on 'Ooby Dooby'. Why not give Sam Phillips a call? You can say Johnny Cash recommends you. Thus began an unlikely but lifelong amity between hard-drinkin' Johnny and virtuous Roy.

Cash hadn't been the only one to suggest Sun to The Teen Kings. For any aspiring rockabilly outfit, it made sense to start at the top. With Cash as the final incentive, the group's leader had screwed-up enough courage by December to dial Mister Starmaker Phillips. It might not have been the best time to ring as it wasn't all smiles then between the neurotic Sam and his antipathetic C&W protégé. When the nervous Orbison mentioned his referee, the Sun mogul erupted with rage. "Johnny Cash doesn't own my record company!" he thundered before clanging down the telephone.

"Well?" demanded the others that evening. Unconvincingly, Roy exonerated himself from blame. What now? As the heated inquest impinged upon the graveyard hours, someone propounded that The Teen Kings fund their own record. What? Let's put it out ourselves. People are already inquiring where they can buy 'Ooby Dooby'. We can sell it at bookings, and send it to major companies as a demo. Maybe Mercury, RCA, Columbia, one of them might accept it as a master. Roy was among the uneasy minority but the motion was carried so everybody could go to bed.

Charged by the hour, the harshly regulated session at Major Smith's had had a dollar sign over every fretful quaver. More inviting to outfits of The Teen Kings' calibre was the rates policy and closer proximity of a newly-completed studio in Clovis, a town on the New Mexico border. No regimental clock-watcher, its proprietor, Norman Petty was amenable to working at a paper loss in exchange for first refusal on publishing rights for items recorded – and, if not rushed, a group would make a more marketable job of these. For a lump sum, Mr Petty would record your song for however long it took. According to one client, Bob Montgomery the "Bob" in Buddy, Bob And Larry – "Everything in Petty's studio was cut as a demo just about. People were coming in, recording there and then submitting their stuff to a label. If Norman liked them, he would go all out to interest a label in the demos."[17]

Petty was well-placed to do this as his own instrumental trio had recorded for Columbia and ABC; the proceeds from 'Mood Indigo', a moderate hit of 1954, enabling the building of the studio. It had been intended for the exclusive use of The Norman Petty Trio but came the day when organist Petty realised that he had been the unknowing owner of the only such facility in the area. Confident in his own technical know-how as an engineer and producer, he went public in late 1955.

Among the first paying customers were The Teen Kings who coughed up for an afternoon taping 'Ooby Dooby' and a workmanlike if ponderous 'Tryin' To Get To You', featuring the versatile Morrow on clarinet. The latter had been released originally by an act called The Eagles on Mercury but, more pertinently, Elvis was doing it in concert but hadn't yet put it out himself.

If Sun wouldn't have them, there were enough more parochial independent labels too glad to issue The Teen Kings' first two sides. Before they acted hastily, Mr Petty mailed a copy of 'Ooby Dooby' to his Columbia recording manager, Mitch Miller in New York. Not letting his personal loathing of rock 'n' roll stop him, Miller had bid for Presley in November. He didn't like The Teen Kings much either but, with Norman's foot in the door with 'Mood Indigo', he thought it tactful to pass the song itself to Sid King and his Five Strings, one of the C&W acts on Columbia's roster that he'd allowed to attempt rockabilly.

After some less fruitful letters of rejection, The Teen Kings surrendered their 'Ooby Dooby' to a small West Texas company, Je-Wel, who ministered to its pressing and, from a car boot, its sale-or-return circulation to whatever record shops would take a few.

From the two versions of their song going the rounds, Wade Moore and Dick Penner sat back and waited for their royalties. That they'd probably make more out of 'Ooby Dooby' than The Teen Kings was not lost on Roy who had lately come up with two or three numbers that he felt were at least equal to some of the group's non-originals. He was too shy to sing them the one about his "brand new wife" but an earlier Orbison composition, the rocking 'Go Go Go' was a bit like Bill Haley's 'Hot Dog Buddy Buddy', and was absorbed into The Teen Kings' increasingly wilder stage presentation. No longer merely rattling off a fixed programme without fuss, Roy especially was now "anything but timid in my performances. I was very much an extrovert, sensation-seeking fellow. I moved around more than Elvis or anyone."[7] An eye-witness, Kay Vasquez, confirmed Orbison's "leaping all over the place in some sort of leopard-skin get-up" on one occasion. Gyrating, snarling and rolling about as if he had a hornet in his pants was, however, not a pleasure but a duty as it was for Bill Haley And The Comets. Paunchy and kiss-curled, Haley would apologise to the press for his band's stage frolics, but, having got lucky with 'Rock Around The Clock', they'd have been daft not to have played up to it, wouldn't they? Anyway, one of The Comets had served under Benny Goodman.

Though Roy Orbison "felt that for my style, it was a bit shallow", there had become such a keen differentiation between vocalist and backing group that these days, while The Teen Kings toiled behind him, Roy had to carry the visuals almost single-handed. His prominence was affirmed in the billing – "Roy Orbison And The Teen Kings" – and his wearing of stage gear that contrasted with the group uniform of checked shirt and buff suit. The others might have been happy to go along with this new status quo but Johnny Wilson – temperamentally, a better qualified wildman – was casting covetous glances at Orbison's monopoly of the spotlight. Dishing out the same old chords while Roy put on the agony, "Peanuts" harboured thoughts of chucking in The Teen Kings one day. He'd form another group with himself as Elvis. Besides, unless they pulled another stroke soon, The Teen Kings might fizzle out anyway, having taken local impact to its limit.

Foreseeing this eventuality himself, Roy sought advice from the fatherly manager of an Odessa record store, a Mr Hollerfield. Though sympathetic, this gentleman bemoaned the consigning of 'Ooby Dooby' to the fly-by-night Je-Wel who, he said, had an abysmal distribution set-up. However, as Roy was still a minor, he could wriggle out of whatever written pledges he'd made to them. When Sam Phillips was logging thousands of car miles peddling records in the early days of Sun, Hollerfield had befriended him as he was now befriending Roy. He'd talk to Sam on The Teen Kings' behalf. He'd call right now and play Sam 'Ooby Dooby' over the wire.

Sure enough, Sam remembered "Poppa" Hollerfield and trusted that he was in good health. Yes, the name "Roy Orbison" rang a loud bell. However, though Phillips showed a faint but clear interest in what he could make out of 'Ooby Dooby', could Poppa send a copy to Union Avenue so that he could listen to it properly?

Sam was more eager than he sounded. On arrival, 'Ooby Dooby' whirled its little life away on the Sun record player and "my immediate reaction [was that it] resembled some of the cute, bouncy things that were big hits in the big band era, and there wasn't really much of a novelty thing going with rock 'n' roll at the time so I decided, if we could get the proper cut on it, we could probably get Roy Orbison and The Teen Kings before the public. I was very much impressed with Roy's inflection and the way he did 'Ooby Dooby' and I think it impressed me more than it impressed Roy then."[12]

Roy was, indeed, heartily fed up with the gibbering 'Ooby Dooby'.

He'd have dumped it altogether if it hadn't caught on so. It was a millstone round his neck like 'Rock Around The Clock' was to Bill Haley. Already, he was being introduced on stage by this "Big O" nickname that some bright spark of a disc jockey had invented during one of the scattered radio airings of 'Ooby Dooby'. It wasn't as if the wretched record had a hope in hell of being a hit, was it? By the way, has Mr Hollerfield heard from Sun yet?

He had. Could this Orbison and his boys be in Memphis for a remake of 'Ooby Dooby' in three days' time? As the two-car convoy sped the 500 miles towards the ugly, twisting Mississippi, passers-by peered incuriously as the elated young Texans wound down side windows to shout insults at rednecks or thump a beat on the vehicles' roofs as, on wings of song, they roared, faces alight with laughter. Though he had more to get thrilled about, not joining in the skylarks so much was Roy who had to mind his voice.

The merriment died down on the outskirts of Memphis. Slamming the car doors outside the fabled shrine of rock 'n' roll, "In our enthusiasm, I don't guess we looked at how small the place was." About the size of the average hotel bedroom, the playing area in the one-storey building had no acoustic separation. As the equipment was unloaded and assembled, Roy braced himself to let rip over Billy's drumming: "Fortunately, I'd been singing for so long that I could sing with a lot of power."[4] Though the studio was a sophisticated two-track, rather than overdub the voice onto the accompaniment, the second track was used instead for Sun's trademark "flutter" echo – or "slapback" as it was jargonised.

Knowing that the rough edge and driving excitement of King Presley's output had been manufactured in these circumstances, The Teen Kings and Roy were putty in the hands of his hard-nosed *eminence grise* although they soon gathered that, "Sam was like quite a few people who are successful in this business who can't play an instrument, can't sing a lick, can't read a note, can't even whistle."[9] Issuing commands from his glass-fronted booth of tape spools and switches, Sam "wanted everything up, everything fast, everything with all the energy that was possible".[12]

After they'd warmed up with a few run-throughs of 'Ooby Dooby', and the levels had been adjusted, Sam explained how he reckoned the number should sound. This he illustrated with crackling seventy-eight rpm spins of the black R&B originals that he and Elvis had refashioned so sensationally. At this, Roy's hackles rose slightly but he held his tongue. Later, he'd articulate his suspicions that Phillips was "an anachronism. He'd been recording black artists mostly and when he included whites on his label, he'd try to get them to sing like Arthur Crudup. What he meant to say was 'sing with feeling.'"[9]

With an irresolute nod, Orbison returned to the skull-like chrome microphone to forget to be himself. After 'Ooby Dooby' was down to Phillips' satisfaction, just the ticket for the other side was another up-tempo rocker. Roy, however, fancied a ballad for diversity. Dismissively, the man in charge "said, 'No, you're going to sing what I want you to sing. You're doing fine. Elvis was wanting to sing like The Ink Spots or Bing Crosby, and I did the same thing for him, did the same thing for Carl Perkins.'"[18]

Making amends for this little flare-up, Sam selected the disarmingly humble Roy's own 'Go Go Go' from B-side possibilities. Saturated with 'cat" slang, this shuffling two-minute odyssey to find "real gone love to drive a cool cat wild" was notable for Roy's rather ill-at-ease vocal and Billy's quick-witted snare accents. Yet by the time the group repaired to the restaurant next door, their job done, they had to admit that Sam Phillips had done his. You could hardly hear the piano but that crude "cardboard box" drum sound with Jack's bass and Johnny's unadorned thrumming had a danceable urgency that had been absent on the Je-Wel disc. As well as Roy's raw guitar soloing, what would sell 'Ooby Dooby' was the focused drive, the Elvis Presley "feel". You could take or leave the actual song.

In the cold light of the following day, Sam heard little in 'Ooby Dooby' to intimate that The Teen Kings were superior to countless other rockabilly outfits – except, "I knew Roy Orbison's voice was pure gold but I felt he'd be dead inside a month if people saw him." Excluding his misgivings, nevertheless, Phillips set an April release date for 'Ooby Dooby' and hoped for the best.

With the little-loved 'Ooby Dooby' reactivated like a zombie, Roy would now attack it with more venom than it warranted when The Teen Kings re-entered the over-familiar circuit of West Texan high school hops. Fired with the self-confidence of one who recorded for

Sun Records, Orbison no more acknowledged that he might one day be spouting history at a class of wayward adolescents. He was past caring about his own education after the heartstopping strains of 'Ooby Dooby' had poured unexpectedly from a drugstore juke box as he'd been strolling by. On 16 July, 1956, it cracked the pop Hot 100. Then followed a brisk to-ing and fro-ing of telephone messages as Bob Neal, in a quasi-managerial capacity, arranged the group's first tour which would take in most of the South. The wages weren't brilliant but think of how it'll help the record, Roy. While the others simply took their summer vacations early, Roy Orbison threw away his chances of becoming a teacher by quitting college a fortnight before his final exams: "Had I seen any limitations, like, 'You're only as hot as your latest record' or 'What are you going to do when you're thirty?' – had I listened to any of that, I would have cut the dream short."

For fifty dollars a day, Orbison and The Teen Kings would open for Sonny James who was high in the C&W chart; "Singing Fisherman" Johnny Horton – and bill-topping Johnny Cash who, Roy would discover, wasn't always the easiest person to rub along with, having graduated from spirits to amphetamines. During the tour which began, ironically, in a schoolhouse in Charleston, North Carolina, Roy and his Teen Kings, as token hardcore rock 'n' rollers, "danced and shaked and did everything we could to get applause because we had only one hit record".[18] At a stop in Richmond, Virginia – one of Cash's "off" nights – they even stole the show. As 'Ooby Dooby' edged to its high of Number Fifty-Nine, the running order was altered in the newcomers' favour.

When the trip wound down in Memphis, perhaps a greater accolade was the praise heaped upon them by a backstage visitor who'd sauntered across the stage for a short half-time cameo. "Marvellous show!" exclaimed Elvis Presley to a round-eyed Orbison, adding, "Well, I'll tell you one thing: you're that good that I'll never appear on stage with you." This sweet lie came from one who'd "got as much applause as we did just by being announced".[19] Roy would guard as a relic forever the polaroid snapshot taken of himself and the King on that night of nights.

While in Memphis, the group seized the opportunity to sort out a follow-up to 'Ooby Dooby'. In the running was a *risqué* Johnny Cash creation, 'Little Willie Booger' which had much in common with the delicate 'Bugger Boy', a 1954 blues obscurity by Lightnin' Slim. Roy cleansed the Cash song under the more genteel title of 'You're My Baby'. After all, his mother might hear it.

The workshop ambience of Sun also permitted Roy to tape numerous guitar-and-voice demos of the songs that were now streaming from him: "I'd write in the car," he said. "Even when we'd take a break alongside the road, I'd jump on the fender of the wing of the car and play the guitar and sing."[4] Not intended for public ears, these musical sketches were punctuated with errors, hesitancies, microphone pops, impromptu busking and, on one such track, an unscripted "Oh crap"!

The very starkness of certain of these items captured a strange beauty, a freshness at odds with the more unrestrained offerings of the day. In 'I Never Knew', 'Claudette' and 'A True Love Goodbye', there were hints of what Roy Orbison was to become. Not so veiled was the unusual atmosphere of 'The Clown'. If your imagination would stretch to future Beatle John Lennon's 1957 skiffle group, The Quarrymen, performing 'Ticket To Ride', then such was the quantum jump of 'The Clown' which had no commercial precedent or reassuring reference point for Sam Phillips and his assistant producer, Jack Clement. Devoid of discernible "hook" or chorus, this paeon to a heedless love's unconcern, even in embryo, is a haunting melancholia a decade ahead of its time.

Hearing it, Jack Clement had declared, "Roy, you'll never make a ballad singer."[12] Free of Sun's quality control himself, Elvis could appreciate Roy's bafflement at this judgement. The affectionate draping of his royal arm round Orbison's shoulder for the photograph had been the start of a friendship that would last till death. More insecure than conceited by their profession's idiosyncratic exhilarations, miseries and anti-social hours, rock 'n' roll stars tend to stick together offstage as well as on – which is why every pop generation would, by its very nature, throw up an inward-looking privileged clique – an "in crowd".

In with the innermost In Crowd of all, Roy in wonderland spent many evenings loafing about with his new pal. "One night, we went by to pick up Elvis's girlfriend in his purple Cadillac – I think he was making twenty million a year [sic] at the time. When he knocked on the door, the girl said, 'I'm sorry. You're too late,' and walked back in. We all went on to his house and had Pepsi Colas and potato chips. I couldn't believe that some woman would turn down a date with Elvis Presley."[5]

This incident did not belittle Elvis in Roy's eyes. It occurred to him that, for the first time in his life, the plug had been pulled and he'd been sucked into a vortex of events, places and situations that two years before, when he'd finished high school, hadn't even belonged to speculation. Though nobody's fool, Roy was enchanted to be in the King's court; a confidant of the human being, only a year older than himself, who'd been an impossible gauge of teenage escapism and aspiration.

Presley's fame and wealth had afforded unto him a splendid certainty in everything he did or said. America was there solely for his pleasure. He was right and that was all there was to it. Among material prerequisites for Roy and other initiates into his charmed circle, it appeared, was a Cadillac and a diamond ring. Purchasing the former – a white model – with his first and, allegedly, only royalty cheque from Sun was beyond rapture for the bespectacled youth who too long had had his nose glued against showroom windows. More easily than the feckless Elvis, however, Orbison was able to rein a natural extravagance: "Then I got a little bigger [turquoise] Cadillac and a little bigger diamond ring, and then I said, 'That's foolish,' and I stopped."[3]

This was a timely economy for 'Ooby Dooby' was to be the only big seller of his four Sun singles. In its afterglow, a place was found for Roy on a second, bigger tour. While The Teen Kings crammed themselves and their instruments into a second-hand family saloon, the captain of the side would be sharing a hired pink Cadillac with Johnny Cash, Carl Perkins and, a new Sun signing, Jerry Lee Lewis – a piano-pounding fireball from Louisiana. As Roy had done on the previous tour, Jerry Lee would be making all the other acts seem tame via an electrifying stage act.

While "The Killer", as Lewis styled himself, brought the house down, it became painfully transparent that all the fans wanted from the Big O was 'Ooby Dooby', as proved by the less fervent response to its successor, 'Rockhouse'. After a while, he didn't even bother with the new record: "I'd go onstage, and I'd play everybody else's stuff – Chuck Berry's stuff, Little Richard's stuff – then I'd sing my one hit record and get off."

Roy had co-written 'Rockhouse' with another Sun artist, Harold Jenkins – whose backing group was called The Rockhousers. After each found out that the other was composing a piece of the same title, Orbison and Jenkins – who would shortly be assuming the *nom de théâtre* "Conway Twitty" – pooled their ideas rather than argue. The result was not dissimilar to Presley's fourth Sun single, 'Baby, Let's Play House' – though it concerned the subject with which the fading Bill Haley was fast overloading his lyrical canvas: "Rock it in the morning/rock it in the daylight/rockin' through the evening" and so forth. Though a stronger record than 'Ooby Dooby', 'Rockhouse' was too predictable for its sales territory to reach far beyond loyal West Texas.

With this opus not setting the rest of North America on fire, Roy was more often seen on his home turf nowadays. As Claudette was still at College, the couple had taken an apartment in Odessa. Sometimes, they'd enliven the town's glum streets when motorbiking together. Like the Cadillacs, this new pastime had sprung from Roy's Memphis playmate: "It was Elvis who, without knowing it, made me a motorcycling fan. I saw a cycle outside Sun Records studio...somebody told me it belonged to Elvis Presley. I finally managed to get to take a cycle ride with the fellow who bought that machine from Elvis and that was the start of it."[20] After Roy had taught her to ride and bought for her birthday her own machine, Claudette's passion for the sport would last for as long as she lived.

Her spouse might be accosted now and then for an autograph but he wasn't enough of a pop star to be prevented from walking rather than riding to the shop for newspapers and cigarettes. Nevertheless, for a while it seemed like he was never off local television and radio. Outsiders could not be blamed for thinking he was simply flaunting his qualified fame while he was still able. More pragmatically, however, Roy was consolidating local media connections so that, if his rock 'n' roll Big Time was up, a place might be found for him as a presenter or disc jockey. The oil fields would be such an anti-climax after all he'd achieved.

One November evening in 1956 even found him deputising for an indisposed radio engineer at the station in Odessa until five am. Such unsung though skilled tasks weren't exactly showbusiness but they would do while he waited, like Mr Micawber, for something to turn up. Booked for a five song "live" session that night were The Five Bops, a vocal group, who were agape to find none other than the Big O behind the instrument panel. During the small hours, Orbison would also render first aid when the Five's lead tenor, Bill Dees, sustained a minor hand injury when a studio coffee vending machine malfunctioned.

This touching episode was one which had a more than incidental bearing on the futures of both Roy and Bill. Doubling on piano and guitar, Dees was then studying music at West Texas State College. Formed on the campus, The Five Bops moulded themselves on The Diamonds, The Crewcuts and other white harmony groups who plagiarised from black counterparts like The Gladiolas ('Little Darlin'') and The Chords ('Sh-boom'). On a Dot subsidiary, the Five's first single, 'Jitterbugging', was hackled to a Dees composition, 'Unforgotten Love'. This had sold well in New Mexico, even topping the regional chart in Amarillo.

With Dees as main advocate, The Five Bops updated their style to be reborn as The Whirlwinds. In this form, they would be supporting Orbison one night in North Texas when, seconds before showtime, Bill's guitar strap snapped. It was Roy to the immediate rescue with a replacement. Years later, Bill would remind him of this second kindness.

Another snippet from Dees' memory bank was that, several months after The Teen Kings' inaugural date there, The Five Bops had recorded under the affable Norman Petty's supervision in Clovis. Having hit it off more so with the affable Norman than Sam Phillips, Roy would continue to drive "back and forth, on and off"[4] to the Clovis studio throughout his period with Sun. Often accompanied by Johnny Wilson, he would bring song ideas that the more experienced Petty might develop. Though other of Petty's patrons recorded the end-products of these collaborations, the most important recipient in retrospect was Buddy Holly – from Buddy, Bob And Larry – who first visited the studio in 1956. As lead singer, guitarist and founder of The Crickets, Holly was not only to tape an unreleased rendition of 'Go Go

Go', but also would include two Orbison-Petty efforts on his debut LP, *The Chirping Crickets.*

Of these, 'You've Got Love' – written with Wilson – was a medium-paced jollity whose title said it all. The slower 'An Empty Cup (And A Broken Date)', however, was more involved. Though flawed, this ballad betrays both period charm and, like 'The Clown', Orbison's nascent lyrical engrossment with the spurned suitor: "My songs are all about the way I felt personally at one time or another."[2] Stood up, he has been dejected further when his date "drove by with another guy". Nonetheless, piping his eye with one hand and clasping a disposable container with the other, his banal contemplation that "just like this Coke, my love is gone" courts derisive sniggers rather than commiseration.

Roy kept another Petty link-up, 'A True Love Goodbye', for himself. Built round the uniquely circular effect of fingerpicking two guitars, a master of this pleasant, ambling ballad was finished at Sun. Sam Phillips, however, didn't find it fiery enough for release. He made a like judgement on Roy's heavy-handed treatment of 'It's Too Late', fresh from the R&B chart by its composer, Chuck Willis. In a less doleful manner, 'It's Too Late' would also be revised on *The Chirping Crickets*.

Tidy-minded journalists later would propagate the myth that Roy and the fated Buddy had been bosom chums. Look at the similarities. They were both of the same age and social background; Holly's family had even lived in Vernon for a while. Another affinity was their domination of their respective groups. More to the point, both possessed creative talents that made up for other vulnerabilities, not least of which was a deficit of manifest sex appeal.

Nevertheless, the two were only in each other's company on a handful of occasions. The first of which was when The Crickets trooped backstage to pay their respects at the Lubbock stop of that first 'Ooby Dooby' tour. Although Orbison did likewise when Buddy's group – now "Buddy Holly *And* The Crickets" – played Odessa, there was a moment afterwards, and it stuck in Roy's memory, when the light-hearted banter suddenly became feline rivalry. Yes, he liked Elvis too – who didn't? – but 'Blue Days And Black Nights', Holly's first single "sounded just like Elvis. Buddy followed Elvis and they were both tied up in my thinking."[10] A year would pass and Orbison would struggle not to eat his heart out when Holly, blast him, "was a big Number One star, and that was way out of my league. But I continued to record for Sun at the time."[10]

Rubbing salt into the wound, Roy's third release for Phillips, 'Sweet And Easy To Love' was plummeting as The Crickets' 'That'll Be The Day' began its scramble to the top in May 1957. Sam had seemed to use Holly as a prototype on some of Orbison's recordings recently – the most notable xerox being 'The Cause Of It All' with hyperactive slapback bestowing the necessary adenoidal twang. In return, Norman Petty, on Buddy's behalf, had shanghai-ed the Roses, a family of singers, that Roy *in extremis* had imported from West Texas to assist on 'Sweet And Easy To Love', serving him as The Jordanaires did Elvis.

The disgruntled Teen Kings may have regarded the proposal of such augmentation as a slight on their abilities. Furthermore, as Orbison had been identified early on as the group's X-factor, the Sun agreement covered only him, leaving the other four in a ticklish position financially. Fuelled not entirely by Johnny Wilson's frustrated rancour, star and backing group had fragmented. Of the former Teen Kings, Johnny became the rockabilly showman he had so long wanted to be. Under Norman Petty's wing, one of his forty-fives in this capacity, 'Cast Iron Arm' (written with Orbison), became a collector's item. The more phlegmatic James Morrow, however, would be summoned to lend a hand as his old chum's contract with Sun ran its ever more unsatisfactory course.

As well as a moronic but aptly jumpy two-note riff by Roy's new guitarist, Roland James, squawking saxophone from Morrow further gingered up 'Chicken-Hearted', the last official Orbison single for Sun. This had been written by a considerably better-known saxophonist, Bill Justis, who, from the realms of jazz, had been appointed by the busy Phillips as Sun's musical director. With leverage provided when his own instrumental, 'Raunchy', was a huge hit in 1957, Justis was active in mellowing the label's still predominantly rockabilly determination for a populace that was now taking more saccharine sounds to its selfish heart.

This attempted clean sweep reinforced Orbison's perpetual machinations to slow things down a little. Nonetheless, he continued to be thwarted in this by Phillips who, to the end, would insist that, "Contrary to the stories that you've heard, Roy was not displeased at the time with doing the things we did on Sun."

Perhaps this was a misinterpretation of Roy's compliance: "You did everything Sam's way or not at all."[21] In his acceptance of this condition, Orbison was, to his mentor, "one of the easiest guys to work with",[22] as he bottled up misgivings about the endless twelve-bar warhorses he was made to sing. While it was "hard to see what Sam saw in anyone",[10] Roy rocked as hard as he could – even coming on quite fiercely once in a while. In Sun's vaults by 1957 were such remaindered gems as the aggressive harmonica-led 'Mean Little Mama' which begat an adventurous guitar solo. Welding Chuck Berry jangle to rockabilly, more endearingly ham-fisted are 'Domino' and – another with lyrics that looked ahead – 'Problem Child'. With less going for it was his final Sun B-side, 'I Like Love', composed by Jack Clement who, in mitigation, had put several of Roy's own songs before his principal production concerns, Johnny Cash and Jerry Lee Lewis.

The more highly-strung Killer remembered that Roy "minded his own business, stayed in his place...he might come by just to say 'hello', hug your neck real nice and get out of your hair. He was that kind of person. He was a pretty nice guy, wasn't he?"[3] Yes, he was – but he wasn't a rampaging giant of classic rock like you, Jerry Lee. When Roy Orbison's time came, Phillips would recount how he gave him his first big break. Incorrigible old Sam would then concede that, "Roy knew his limitations, and he knew all the time where his forte was – and that was in ballads."[22] His lieutenant, Jack Clement, however, would not recant. Whenever their paths crossed down the years, he'd always ask Roy the same half-serious question: "You still trying to sing those ballads, boy?"

CHAPTER THREE

Sweet And Innocent

Colonel Parker's billion-dollar manipulation of Elvis Presley was the tip of an iceberg that would make more fortunes than had ever been known in the history of recorded sound. All around, the hunt was on for more moneymaking Presleys. Every region of the world seemed to throw up a contender. Off-the-cuff examples include France's Johnny Hallyday and Mickie Most from South Africa. Over in England, Cliff Richard took over from Tommy Steele as poor man's Elvis. Needless to say, these sprouted thickest in the States where the likes of Troy Shondell, Fabian and Ral Donner all mirrored the King's lop-sided smirk, "common" good looks, gravity-defying cockade and hot-potato-in-the-mouth singing.

There were inevitable differences between each Elvis but these were variations on a structure whose regularity was a launch pad for liberal nonconformity within imagined limits. Many thought that Jerry Lee Lewis was simply an Elvis who substituted piano for guitar. That was all they knew. In the rough-and-ready Gene Vincent from Virginia. When Vincent – "The Screaming End" – came down with a bump after his 'Be-Bop-A-Lula' breakthrough, Capitol realised that it was lumbered with the crippled runt of the litter. Yet, despite their finding Vincent and his music objectionable, the label was obliged contractually to cater for his hoodlum following, unreliable in the market place against smoother certainties of the post-rockabilly Elvis sausage factory.

Acuff-Rose had better joy with a pair of quiffed brothers named

Everly. With their delinquent-angel faces, they could be visualised as two Elvises – Elv*i*? Elv*es*? – for the price of one. By 1956, the year it signed The Everly Brothers, the reins of power at Acuff-Rose had passed to Rose's son, Wesley who, in his mid-thirties, was more aware than Fred had been that rock 'n' roll wasn't just another craze that happened to be going stronger than the Jitterbug or the Creep. Witness former C&W paladin Marty Robbins who'd learnt much from a tour of Texas with Presley in 1955. Testing the water with covers of 'That's All Right', Chuck Berry's 'Maybellene' and, like Pat Boone, 'Long Tall Sally', Robbins' conversion to the new regime was vindicated financially when his 'Singin' The Blues', 'White Sport Coat' and similarly bland country-rock fusions charged up the mid-fifties' Hot 100. Acuff-Rose's own Don Gibson – albeit impossibly ancient in his late twenties, and receding to boot also took up the challenge with a not-unsuccessful switch from a hillbilly-cum-honky-tonk style to a vague hybrid of classic rock and country ballad.

Often duetting with Gibson, Nevada-born C&W chanteuse Sue Thompson's conquest of the pop charts with such novelties as 'Norman' and 'Paper Tiger' was only round the corner. Many of her hits had dripped from the fertile pen of John D Loudermilk – also on Wesley Rose's books – whose reputation as a songwriter was to far out balance his modest achievements as a performer. Indeed, his migration from rural North Caroline to Nashville resulted from his composing the big-selling 'A Rose And A Baby Ruth' as sung by his pal George Hamilton IV, and produced by a third native of North Carolina, Fred Foster.

John D's desire to "tell the world how the guy in the filling station feels"[1] was the thrust behind later hits by such diverse artists as The Chordettes, Bobby Vee, Frank Ifield and Jerry Lee Lewis. In the mid-sixties, The Nashville Teens would bear much the same mutually advantageous relationship to Loudermilk as Manfred Mann would to Bob Dylan. Loudermilk's golden year, however, was 1961 when he notched up a world-wide smash off his own bat in 'Language Of Love' – whose chorus, incidentally, centred on his burbling "ooby dooby dooby doo" *ad nauseum*. Moreover, that was also when his 'Ebony Eyes' shifted a million for The Everly Brothers.

This duo – christened Isaac Donald and Philip – had been born into the music business and thus had been incorporated into their singing parents' Mid West radio shows almost as soon as they were weaned. In May 1956, nineteen-year-Don and his younger brother auditioned for Wesley Rose. As the brothers' severe close harmony and clanging left-handed guitars filled his office with half-hidden clues of what lay ahead, Wesley pretended nonchalance as his father would have done. Inwardly, however, he was yelling, "Klondike!"

Cajoling label boss Archie Bleyer – who hadn't been immediately impressed – to chance Don and Phil on his Cadence outlet, their new manager grubbed round his filing cabinets for a commercial vehicle with which to present them for public consumption. At RCA Victor's Studio B in Nashville, The Everly Brothers would tape 'Bye Bye Love' from Felice and Bordleaux Bryant. Within an incredible month of its release in March 1958, it would be high in all three chart categories.

Next up was 'Wake Up Little Susie' whose banning by some radio stations for its "suggestive" lyrics probably assisted its topping of the Hot 100. This innocent opus of inadvertent flaunting of small town mores welded to a rock 'n' roll beat typified the forceful but romantic essence that would keep Phil and Don in hits for another decade.

Their own compositions didn't yet sound like hits so there was a constant rummaging through demo tapes and manuscripts as well as critical listening to the efforts of hopefuls who sang into the middle distance beyond Wesley Rose's desk. This musical treasure hunt became especially urgent when the third single's paltry apex of Number Twenty-Eight suggested to fans that The Everly Brothers were fallible. By early 1953, another Bryant number, 'All I Have To Do Is Dream', was earmarked as the next A-side. All that was needed now was a strong coupling that, as often happened, might register in the charts on separate sales as, say, The Coasters' 'Young Blood' had on the back of 'Searchin'' the previous summer.

The search ended at the unlikely source of a warm-up act at an Everly Brothers bash in Indiana. Having been reduced to borrowing money to get there, a weary Roy Orbison was angry with himself for leaving behind the demo recordings that he intended pressing on the prize exhibits if they should speak to him. Not a natural hustler, he melted into the background, smoking quietly on a window ledge. Desultory backstage chatter amongst the Everlys and others on the bill polarised on the aggravating question of what to put on the B-side of 'All

I Have To Do Is Dream'. Turning round, Phil Everly asked Roy if he had any tunes. He wrote a bit didn't he?

With all eyes on him then, the self-effacing Texan almost shook his head to slough off the hushed butterfly concentration. Instead, he heard his voice croaking, "I've just got one." Clearing his throat, he stubbed out the cigarette. Then he lifted up his Gretsch semi-acoustic and started chugging quavers. A deep breath and into the line "I've got a brand new baby and I feel so good..." and he was in the throes of the one that rhymed "get", "met" and "pretty little pet" with its title.

Glistening with embarrassment while the asinine words and three simplistic chords hung in the air, he blinked at his feet as 'Claudette' died away. An exclaimed "Yeah!" broke the silence. Orbison with enquiring eyebrow glanced up at the nodding, smiling hubbub. Because of past disappointments, he was bemused when, before departing, the Everlys got him to dictate the lyrics and chords to 'Claudette' which were jotted onto the cardboard top of a shoe box. After all, they'd already turned up their noses at demos that Buddy Holly had deigned to send them. Expecting nothing, Roy was astonished when "the next thing I know, Wesley Rose from Nashville's calling me in Memphis at Sun Records, telling me to sign this contract for the song 'Claudette' that The Everly Brothers were going to record – they actually already had recorded it."[2]

The great Rose's communication filtered through to Orbison down in Odessa. Theoretically, he was still tied to Sun but, "I'd sort of quit recording – Sam had released a couple of songs that I didn't think he should have, so I sort of retired."[2] With Claudette now pregnant, twenty-two seemed a good age for a one-hit wonder to settle down. Other than rare and unremunerative expeditions like the one to Indiana, Roy had re-entered the trivial round of parochial bookings at venues where he'd always gone down well – though there were still supports whenever a big name came to Texas. Looking forward to the past, even awareness of worth in the teeth of ill luck and bad advice no longer fed hope. Soon would come a day when he would be able no more to retime the truth and, with a certain logical blindness, imply that he'd Hit The Big Time with his meagre 'Ooby Dooby' flush of 1956. The white Cadillac he'd bought with the proceeds was less shiny than it had used to be. Maybe the El Paso Natural Oil Company would give Roy his old job back. He could still perform semi-professionally at weekends although, "I lost all interest and for seven months I just ambled around. No, I didn't do a thing, except to think."[3]

This 'Claudette' windfall with The Everly Brothers would allow him to "amble around" for a while longer. On the strength of it, there might be an avenue for not so much expanding as consolidating his status as a rockabilly entertainer. The only barrier to proceeding with Rose's proposal was the "very likable and affable"[2] Sam Phillips who, like Michaelangelo claiming credit for his apprentices' work, "wanted part of the song, and we had a three-way conversation. Wesley said, 'Why do you want Roy's money?', so Wesley sounded great and Sam sounded like he was a...wanted a little too much, so I left then. I left Sun."[2]

Sooner than anyone could fancy, Phillips would be repackaging every Sun track on which Orbison had ever breathed – "even just with me and my guitar, so it seemed that after I really did do well in the business, they wanted to cash in on it."[2] While Roy shuddered inside, all the forgotten Ooby-doobyings of his flaming youth – including the "crap" try-out of 'Claudette' – would surface as frequently as rocks in the stream for the next thirty years.

For all the shifty manoeuvres, his former protégé nonetheless found it in him to admit, "I owe Sam so much."[4] Incorrigible and self-glorifying, Phillips half-believed the prodigal would return. In 1961, a wealthier Roy "went back to the studio to pay my respects. Sam just looked at me, smiled and said, 'You'll be back.' His brother Judd was in the same room. He just looked at me, rolled his eyes and said, 'The hell he will.'"[4]

During the haggling with Wesley Rose, the composing of the majority of Orbison's Sun recordings came to be attributed to Phillips for, other than monetary – "he didn't even pay union rates!"[4] – and repertory incertitudes, Sun "had no publishing outlet, so all of us just had to leave".[4] In this respect, Roy for one landed on his feet with Acuff-Rose which had become a huge publishing and management concern. The drug-induced passing of its major source of revenue, Hank Williams, had been a body blow but, taking stock, the company and its affiliations would be occupying four addresses in Nashville alone by 1957. Moreover, its president's grey eminence would arouse, even then, enough supplication for that ordinary mortal Wesley Rose to be styled "the uncrowned king of Nashville".

Sure enough, such fawning reverence ensured that Rose was unconscious victim of innumerable derogatory *bons mots* in rival offices of "Music City USA". Its symphony orchestra a mere sideshow, Nashville was – and is – the Hollywood of country music with, in the words of Buck Owens, "songwriters under every rock". [5] Rapidly saddened then hardened by curt brush-offs, unanswered letters and unreturned calls, the more thick-skinned of these would-be Loudermilks would continue plying their taped, dotted and in-person wares round tree-lined Sixteenth Avenue. An erstwhile residential area, this Tin Pan Alley of Nashville had no high-rise glass towers in the late fifties but in its environs were clotted music publishing firms by the score – most of them hand-in-glove with more than a smattering of record companies and studios within spitting distance.

In connection with the merchandising deals, franchises and estimates of Sixteenth Avenue would be downtown excursions by talent scouts to view the human goods displayed nightly on nicotine-clouded stages in truckers' bars and honky-tonks – the true heart of Nashville. More upmarket were joints like Tootsie's and Merchant's Lounge along the city's Broadway, nicknamed "Paradise Row". Always there was an outside chance of a rags-to-riches leap onto the hallowed boards of the weekly *Grand Ole Opry* – which was to the country entertainer the same as Everest to a mountaineer. Once your name was embossed on the garish billboard screaming across the brick facade of Ryman Auditorium's world of cowboy suits and rehearsed "sincerity", the only other way was down.

That the *Grand Ole Opry* prohibited drummers from defiling its sacred stage until well into the fifties illustrated the rigid formality that both the commercial dictates of Sixteenth Avenue and the conservatism of the Country Music Association of America had imposed. It was as if country music couldn't be recorded in any other way or with any other musicians than that self-contained caste who, as few of them could read music, could improvise the orthodox "Nashville sound" from a notation peculiar to city studios. The Nashville sound rested on its originators' close knowledge of each other's work through playing together as sidemen at the *Grand Ole Opry* and in countless daily record dates. Afterwards, they might unwind in late night jam sessions at Ronnie Prophet's exclusive Carousel Club.

Some of these craftsmen made records of their own. Among the brightest stars in this inward-looking firmament were Chet "Mr Guitar" Atkins, Floyd "Mr Piano" Cramer and Boots "Mr Saxophone" Randolph. As well as scoring in the country charts, these three had first refusal of virtually all Nashville studio sessions until well into the sixties.

In a dramatised film biography in 1979, "Buddy Holly" loses his temper during an ill-fated Nashville session in 1956. As well as suffering a 'That'll Be The Day' syncopated with a corny swirl of fiddles and steel guitars, "Holly" has been forbidden to play his own electric Fender by a producer who treats him as an unseasoned hick. Rock 'n' roll, you see, was not considered a natural adjunct of country but a nigger-inspired heresy. No-one was purposely unfriendly but, unless he toed the line, there was no place in such a closed shop for any rockabilly rebel from West Texas.

More amenable a West Texan than the mercurial Buddy, Roy Orbison in 1958 was open to careers advice from troubleshooting Wesley Rose. Since its writer's extrication from Sun's clutches, 'Claudette' in The Everly Brothers' brisker hands had netted over one million sales. At Number Thirty on *Billboard*, Orbison's song – with his name mis-spelt on the label – lagged way behind 'All I Have To Do Is Dream' but the figure on his mechanical royalties cheque for 'Claudette' would be the same as the Bryants' for their chart-topping A-side.

As if all his birthdays were coming at once, another Orbison ditty backed Jerry Lee Lewis's 'Breathless' which stood at Number Seven. Unable to leave anything alone, the Killer had so warped the lyrical gist of 'Go Go Go' that "Down The Line" became forever the accepted title of what had graced the flip of 'Ooby Dooby'. Even its composer would one day re-record it under this new name.

With these undercover achievements under his belt, Roy "made enough money to move to Nashville and it set me up for about a year".[2] Orbison's gradual migration to the Holy City 600 miles away was not, however, a matter of glib spontaneity. Brought to his knees as he had been by the music industry, Roy kept his options open after enlisting as a house songwriter at Acuff-Rose. Renting a pied-a-terre in Nashville, he nevertheless worked mainly from home in Odessa.

Within a few years, with internal sources of new material and their own publishing companies, The Beatles and other self-created beat groups would give the institutions of Tin Pan Alley a nasty turn. Prior to this semi-purge, however, the jobbing tunesmith was an indispensable staple of the record business. In New York's Brill Building, there was even a songwriting "factory" where such stars-in-embryo as Carole King and Neil Sedaka won their spurs churning out assembly-line pop for the masses.

Like any self-employed worker, Roy Orbison disciplined himself to a strict routine. Generally around eight am, he would "sit down and say, 'I'm going to write a song and I don't get up again until I've written it' – not hard when you know you can do it but I didn't find it like that in the beginning."[6] After tuning his guitar for the day's labours, "The title is my starting point and you must have one that conveys the meaning. Ideas come from anywhere."[7] By early evening, he'd usually had enough.

When he'd accumulated sufficient product, he might submit demo tapes – just guitar and voice as with Sun – for assimilation by Wesley Rose. Now Roy's business manager, Rose would then endeavour to place the items with suitable artists. If in Nashville himself, Orbison would overcome misgivings about visiting prospective customers to sing the number there and then. Nothing he wrote then was as negotiable as 'Down The Line' or 'Claudette' had been, but he ticked over with country-pop songs for Sue Thompson, Kris Jensen and other singers on Acuff-Rose's roster. From the company's new London branch came Orbison-penned singles for Gene Thomas and future Eurovision Song Contest winners, the Allisons – one of Britain's "answers" to Don and Phil. His confidence boosted by this distant syndication, Roy put offerings the way of bigger fish like Burl Ives – international entertainer since the thirties – and Patsy Cline, country queen of the heartbreak ballad who, it was said, could "cry on both sides of the microphone".[8]

One day, Orbison was attempting to sell a song to Hank Cochran, former partner but no relation to Eddie Cochran, a multi-talented Oklahoman Elvis. After Roy had finished, Hank reciprocated by trying to interest the mildly surprised Texan in one of his own.

This mistaken assumption that he was still a recording artist was one of several of late that had given Orbison pause for thought. Each morning, his shaving mirror would tell him that he'd never be Elvis Presley but, as he explained to Wesley Rose, "Once the singing bug's got you, you always come back."[3] Wistfully, he'd drink in travellers' tales from The Everly Brothers and Buddy Holly about touring countries that would always be outlandish and unreachable to a backroom songwriter, however content and prosperous. He was their age but, while they'd made inroads in hit parades all over the world, Orbison singles hadn't even been released outside North America, though an EP – extended play – record, *Hillbilly Rock* containing four Sun tracks had leaked to Britain in 1957, and thence to obscurity. With an inner ear cocked to the far-off roar of the crowd, Roy insinuated to his manager that it might do no harm to put out a belated follow-up to his Sun swansong, 'Chicken-Hearted', lost to the deletion racks for over a year. Loudermilk still made records, didn't he?

Orbison was no Mr Universe but Rose conceded that, yes, he could sing – and in the pop universe that counted for something. The four Sun singles hadn't excited him tremendously but, not wishing to alienate this promising songwriter, the Uncrowned King of Nashville said he'd see what he could do. Starting at the top, Wesley sounded out Elvis Presley's label, RCA Victor. As he'd anticipated, the recording manager of its Nashville operation – who happened to be Chet Atkins – was glad to oblige such a prominent provider of chart fodder. This consideration loomed large when Atkins agreed to try out Wesley's boy on a couple of forty-fives.

"Mr Guitar" had pulled some bold strokes recently. Promoted from backing guitarist to Presley's co-producer in 1958, Atkins had given this piston-hipped *nouveau vague* his head in the arrangements of 'One Night', 'A Fool Such As I' and others from the once incompatible motherlodes of country and R&B. Furthermore, he'd seen fit to foist on RCA Charlie Pride, a negro C&W artist which, in those less enlightened times, was tantamount to a contradiction in terms.

By his own admission, however, Mr Guitar was "a little square but it helps to be that way".[9] Partly because he'd breathed the air round Elvis, Atkins was regarded as a console Svengali. If he took you on, you'd stand a fair chance of Making It as long as you would "keep your mouth shut and listen to the musicians. They know what it's all about. Of course, you've also got to know a good song from a bad one."[10] His involvement with dramas like 'Heartbreak Hotel' aside, thirty-five-year-old Chet as producer leaned towards lightweight tunes with jaunty rhythms as road-tested in the charts by RCA's own Perry Como, Kay

Starr – and, more to the point, Jim Reeves as typified in the harmless bounce of his mid-fifties smash, 'Bimbo'. With 'Ooby Dooby' to go on, Atkins saw no reason for deviating from this rule when plotting this Orbison youngster's two sessions at the Victor studio on Seventeenth Street and Hawkins.

In later years, Roy would confess being "too much in awe"[11] of Atkins to have spluttered "I'd rather not, sir" when presented with 'Seems To Me' and 'Sweet And Innocent' – as innocuous as their titles imply – to sing for his maiden RCA single. The perpetrator of 'Seems To Me', Bordleaux Bryant's initial impression of the new signing was as "a timid, shy kid who seemed to be rather befuddled by the whole music scene. I remember the way he sang then – softly, prettily but almost bashfully as if someone might be disturbed by his efforts and reprimand him."[12] In an unimagined future, many of those supercilious session players under the calm and familiar baton of Mr Guitar would be dancing as this gullible and awkward youth whistled but, out of his depth in 1958, Orbison was indistinguishable from any other merely competent vocalist under the aegis of a big shot producer. Even Bryant, in retrospect called it "the turkey of the season", but so lacking in conviction was Roy on 'Seems To Me' that Gordon Stoker from the celebrated Jordanaires – hired for backing four-part harmony – was instructed to sing along in unison out of microphone range behind the timid songbird's left ear.

After 'Seems To Me' bit the dust, Bryant's next effort for Orbison – the Frenchified 'Jolie', a distant cousin of 'Jole Blon' – was demoted to B-side. More absolutely discarded were John Loudermilk's run-of-the-mill 'I'll Never Tell' and Roy's own 'Double Date' – on which a buddy steals Roy's girl. On a hunch, Atkins took a risk with another Orbison song, With its rapid-fire couplets and tension-breaking tacit, 'Almost Eighteen' was an improvement on 'Seems To Me'. However, what might have been a fiery if derivative rocker was emasculated by its squeaky-clean and gutless instrumental precision topped by the chinking of Mr Piano.

Questioning his producer's competence in channelling his abilities towards the pop market, Orbison found an ally in Don Gibson who likewise felt that Atkins' fixed ideas did him no favours. Kicking against these widely-practised commercial methods, Gibson's own more ponderous stylistic wilfulness would be summarised in the titles of his biggest hits – 'Sea Of Heartbreak' and 'Lonesome Number One' – which, if doom-laden and woebegone in content, were neither particularly sentimental nor marred with lip-trembling pathos. Big-eared, chubby and eight years Roy's senior, Don Gibson's music and individuality were so concordant with his own artistic frustrations that Orbison would be. turning regularly to the Gibson songbook as a monk to the Bible.

Gibson's standing with RCA in early 1959 was a deal more assured than his admirer's when, during the firm's customary board meeting in New York, it was decided after a single hearing to waive the option on the third Orbison single. As if poor sales for 'Seems To Me' and 'Almost Eighteen' hadn't been enough, the most Chet Atkins could conjure up next for this Roy *schmuck* was a depressing little trudge to "the blue side of town" entitled 'Paper Boy'. It may have helped if Chet could've got him to burst into tears on tape as Johnny Ray had threatened to do.

At the post-mortem in Acuff-Rose, artist listened quietly as manager hit the roof. Bitterly, Wesley Rose dissected RCA's executive body. He railed about its short-sightedness, its mental sluggishness, its cloth-eared ignorance. Damn it, 'Paper Boy' had "hit" carved all over it – ask Chet Atkins – and RCA had passed it up. No men of vision left, that's the trouble. Even if he had to dial his index finger to a stub on the phone, he'd set up a new contract for Roy right now.

Before that outraged afternoon was out, Rose would prove true to his word. Picking up the receiver in the Washington office of the newly-launched Monument label was one whose will to succeed was stronger than that of any salaried RCA time-server. A key protagonist in Roy Orbison's next and greatest bout of success was the chap who, Rose remembered, had done wonders with Loudermilk's 'Baby Ruth' song for George Hamilton IV in 1956. Without mincing words, Wesley Rose wanted to know if Fred Foster had "ever heard of Roy Orbison, and I said I'd heard 'Ooby Dooby' and maybe 'Rockhouse'."[13] Lending a sympathetic ear to a rose-tinted version of how come Fred had never heard any of Roy's RCA sides – "I don't want Roy on RCA if they don't believe in him,"[13] snarled Rose – it was suggested that Orbison could be an even better proposition on Monument where everyone – ie Foster – fired on all cylinders.

Fred Foster was the scion of a line unrepresented by direct musicianly forebears. Nevertheless, his father's craving for music was such that one season's cotton crop from the family farm in the Appalachian foothills was sold to buy an Edison wind-up phonograph for his vast record collection. Mrs Foster might have preferred a more practical investment – like a station wagon – but this Jack and the Beanstalk episode would fade to affectionate memory following her husband's untimely demise in 1946 when Fred was fifteen.

Flying the nest two years later, young Foster was sweating it out as a curb manager in the Hot Shoppe, a fast food drive-in in Washington DC, when he scraped acquaintance with the shoppe's most flamboyant diner, night club owner Billy Strickland. Through Strickland, Fred came to put words to melodies from music publisher Ben Edelman. Their first effort, 'Picking Sweethearts', was recorded in 1953 by The McGuire Sisters, a white vocal group who specialised in watered-down covers of rhythm-and-blues hits for the pop charts.

Giving Foster a greater incentive to chuck in his rotten Hot Shoppe job was what resulted from his supervision of a recording session for Jimmy Dean And The Texas Wildcats, a combo then resident in the city's Covered Wagon bar. Although he'd never produced a record before, it was thanks to Foster that Dean and his Wildcats gouged a wound in the C&W Top Ten.

Fred's path became clear. Within months, he'd talked his way into a record promotion post with Mercury. Scrambling up the executive ladder, he transferred his allegiance to the less confining ABC Paramount in 1955. Though officially a regional promotion director, Foster would bring to the label talent he'd discovered on his beat from the East Coast to Texas. Among these *ultra vires* A&R finds were George Hamilton IV and, from New Orleans, Lloyd "Mr Personality" Price who would become one of the best-known R&B stars of the fifties.

Married with children who wanted him home more often than his interstate journeyings would permit, Fred collected his cards from ABC for a desk job heading the pop department of J & F Distributors in Baltimore. This settled period ended in the spring of 1958 shortly after a confrontation with Walt McGuire, New York sales manager for London Records. In the midst of McGuire's finger-jabbing tirade about falling profits in the Maryland territory, Foster interpolated patiently that out-of-date London artists like warbling David Whitfield and "Forces Sweetheart" Vera Lynn had been drowned in the rip-tide of rock 'n' roll.

Stung by this stark truth, the New Yorker threw down the gauntlet with a door-slamming, "I'd like to see you do any better, Mr Foster."

Buoyed by Foster's life savings, Monument opened for business. In September 1958, the shoe-string operation took off with a reworking of the traditional 'Done Laid Around' – retitled 'Gotta Travel On' – sung by former Texas Wildcat guitarist, Billy Grammer. Percolating to a pop Number Four, 'Gotta Travel On' enabled Fred to set up another office in the Nashville suburb of Andersonville. Two more releases grazed the charts for Monument, and its owner was wondering where the next hit was coming from when Wesley Rose's call came through. Roy Orbison "never embarrassed Fred by bringing it up but I got the feeling he thought he was signing Warren Smith – Wesley told him that I'd cut 'Ooby Dooby', and Fred may have thought he said 'Rock And Roll Ruby'. We all have genius after the fact."[4]

A self-taught producer who could locate middle C on a piano, Fred Foster wasn't a genius musician as he'd be the first to admit. He knew what he liked though. Unlike Chet Atkins and even Don Gibson, he had little to unlearn in his quest for a new angle whereby country would meet pop in a manner acceptable to an audience then biased against one or the other. The answer was as likely to be found in this Roy Orbison as anyone else.

The responsibility for choosing Roy's debut on Monument, however, was not Foster's. Before signing any formal agreement, Wesley Rose – still piqued about 'Paper Boy' – had one stipulation: "I want you to duplicate the session Victor turned down because I think it's good. After that you can do as you please."[13] For this postscript to the RCA era, it made sense to solicit the assistance of Chet Atkins – who'd also played on 'Gotta Travel On' – and book a three hour session at the same studio.

With the cancelled master as a useful demo, Foster and Atkins gingered up the paper boy's declamation that Roy and his baby were through, with a fat inter-verse trumpet section and Chet's own echo-chambered arpeggios. For the B-side, another go at 'Double Date' was unworkable so, for want of anything better, 'Paper Boy' was partnered with some country clowning exhumed from Orbison's days with The Teen Kings in which "We had this imaginary bug we would throw on each other – and where it hit you, you had to shake."[15]

Deadpan, he outlined 'With The Bug' to Atkins, Cramer and the other 'Almost Eighteen' veterans who found him the same acquiescent shrinking violet. Roy's coyness this time may have been aggravated by a tardy arrival by aeroplane from Texas for this, his first meeting with Fred Foster.

Rather than plant a Gordon Stoker behind him, the ever-inventive Foster came up with a solution so simple that Atkins wondered why nobody had thought of it before. Referring to Roy as he would an amplifier or drum kit, Fred suggested that, to enable this soft singer to be heard above the musicians, why not place his microphone behind some sort of barrier where it would pick up far less of them. After the engineer had homed in on an acoustically compatible corner, "We put a coat rack in front of him and covered it with coats and blankets, and I couldn't see him. Out of that came the 'isolation booth'. They reckoned that that was the first time that was done here in Nashville."[13]

The taping of 'Paper Boy' might have altered studio procedure forever – and, as a side reaction, alleviated Roy's painful self-consciousness. However, despite a favourable review in *Billboard*, Wesley Rose wasn't yet able to thumb his nose at RCA. 'Paper Boy' had created, nonetheless, enough of a stir to jog a few disc jockeys' memories when Orbison's next one came out.

While 'Paper Boy' bubbled under the Hot 100, way above was 'Three Stars' by a Tommy Dee. This purported alias for John D Loudermilk may have been assumed to preserve some self-respect for, lucrative as it was, 'Three Stars' was one of these bilious "tribute" discs that capitalise on a celebrity's death.

Dee's whimpering told of the elevation of the Big Bopper – JP Richardson – to "new fame and fortune" in heaven but, though its narrative extended to the also deceased pop star Ritchie Valens, 'Three Stars' may not have inched to Number Eleven had not Buddy Holly perished in the same four-seater plane crash on 22 February, 1959. Before they'd even wiped away the tears, the moguls of his record company had been forced to meet the demand kindled by the tragedy. Rush-released while the corpse was still warm was Holly's 'I Guess It Doesn't Matter Any More'. With a string section taking what had once been the lead guitar part, this was an enormous hit resuscitating a flagging career.

Roy Orbison had hardly known Buddy Holly. All the same, that fame had cost so dear was a sobering thought for Roy in his obscurity. In the first instance, for a while after Buddy's accident – and after hearing, at a party, a chilling account of high altitude engine malfunctions from Elvis Presley – Orbison had "sworn that I would never use US charter flight again unless it was to get a member of my family to hospital in an emergency".[16] More than this short-lived sacrifice, it confirmed what was already a fundamental philosophical tenet of Orbison's. To rationalise triumphs and tragedies in his own life, he would "take the edge off anything that is supposedly super and, in the same way, with anything that affects you adversely – have a sort of balance, an in-between, as opposed to just stepping aside. You must continue doing things that you normally do. Whatever it is, continue and then everything comes out fine."[17]

Mitigating his flop records, for example, was a then-happy marriage to Claudette, his muse and doting mother of that little rascal, Roy Duane. A by-product of the modest acclaim for 'Paper Boy' was a more promising date schedule. The number of bookings that had once signified a month's work had become a week's. This meant that Claudette wouldn't operate the vacuum cleaner until the early afternoon when her husband woke. Roy's snoring-off of an increased accumulation of late nights also necessitated the abandonment of his daytime songwriting rota.

One major benefit of Roy's becoming a nightbird was that – apart from the baby squalling now and then – household distractions were minimal in the graveyard hours. Conditions in the young family's cramped apartment had been such that an irritated bard would be driven sometimes to "go outside and sit in the car and write, so that was a lonely experience...I suppose it was a lonely area. There wasn't much to do there."[2] As it always would, the cinema provided solace whenever Roy hit a writer's block, and it was while passing an Odessa drive-in in the autumn of 1959 that Joe Melson spotted the Orbison Cadillac.

Since the advent of Elvis Presley, there'd been no looking back for twenty-four-year-old Joe. With the sundering of the Fannin County Boys, his championing of rock 'n' roll soon became audible to his family and their neighbours. Backed by The Cavaliers, the singing guitarist's cavortings before the microphone became a common sight in the clubs and high school hops of mid Texas. The former Fannin County Boy's repertoire was now invested with an even bigger shot of rhythm-and-blues; much of it taken from the "shooby-doo-wah" school of black vocal groups. With guileless fervour, the likes of The Five Keys, The Pelicans and The Harptones would never shrink from stretching beyond their vocal compass. Neither did Joe Melson who was also bold enough to insert a few of his own compositions into the set.

If a pop combo then attempted anything other than the familiar, dancers would be inclined to either sit it out, visit the bar or go to the toilet. Normally, the last thing anyone wanted to hear was a home-made song. However, one local impresario, Ray Rush, observed that some of Melson's originals were drawing more than passive attention from the clientele. Largely through Rush's machinations, Melson and The Cavaliers' 'Raindrops', their most appreciated crowd-pleaser, was released on a Texan label. The altruistic Ray was also the mutual friend that brought Joe Melson to Roy Orbison.

When the introduction was made in the Orbisons' living room, there was no instant rapport. Jovial and open-handed Joe was put off by his host's rather stand-offish manner. As if in a brown study, the so-called Big O didn't look at you when you spoke to him. In the thick bi-focals he'd never worn when stirring the nation with 'Ooby Dooby', Orbison sat dumpily with his wife, quaffing nothing stronger than cola. Far from the Sun wildman Melson had half-expected, the depth of depravity for Roy, it seemed, was twenty filter-tips a day. He brightened up slightly when Melson complimented him on his singing but the evening wore on with little more from Roy than polite platitudes, nodding agreement and a puffy smile when Claudette mentioned to Joe that she liked 'Raindrops'.

Four months later, Roy wound down his car window at Joe's tap. Close up, Joe perceived that it was the lemonade bottle lenses in front of the flickering amblyopic eyes that had made Roy seem miles away last time. Over a coffee after the film, Joe then understood that the Big O's supposed aloofness was nothing other than diffidence. When you got him on his own, he was quite chatty. He even cracked jokes. Furthermore, it turned out that Roy liked 'Raindrops' too and, "He thought that if I could write a good song and he could write a good song, we might write a great one together."[18]

No great one would be written immediately. There was no music-lyrics delineation between the functions of Melson and Orbison as there was between teams like Bacharach and David or Gilbert and Sullivan. More often than not, one or the other would have, say, a title, a riff, maybe an entire chorus from which a song could grow. Cudgelling a red-eyed, unshaven objectivity on some such doodle, they'd tinker into the night on guitars that sometimes might as well have been tennis racquets. The sun would often rise on the two dozing over their instruments. Becoming close friends, they developed a restricted code whereby an utterance unfunny to anyone else would have Roy and Joe howling with hilarity on the carpet and waking the baby. Among their private criteria of quality was "trying to get the mood of the song and the feel of it, the right lyrics. Then we'd play it in the daytime to see if it held up."[15]

Now that 'Paper Boy' was over and done, management and record company were drumming their fingers for the next Orbison single. In November 1959, Roy in Nashville sang four possibilities to Fred Foster. 'Pretty One', a mellow ballad from Roy alone was almost-but-not-quite; too much like Presley's 'I Was The One'. 'Blue Avenue'... hmm, save it for an LP, if we ever make one. 'Raindrops'? Not bad. what else have you got?

The fourth choice it was. From Roy's title, 'Uptown', Joe had devised a blues-derived strut accordant with lyrics about a bell hop coveting some Mr Big's floozy. Pinioned by a swatting snare drum, 'Uptown' bore a resemblance to Eddie Cochran's 'Teenage Heaven' but it was nearer to the raucous urban blues contrived in the studios of Chicago – though Roy's restrained drawling was a generous dose of country.

In Nashville, if accompanying harmonies did not belong to The Jordanaires, then most likely they were emitted by choristers led by Anita Kerr, a less ubiquitous mainstay of the "Nashville sound". Enhancing the Anita Kerr Quartet's skittish doo-wopping on 'Uptown' was boogie continuo by Mr Saxophone and Mr Piano. Though otherwise merging more with the backing singers, an innovation most prominent in the latter half of the record was a string section.

The worm hadn't turned completely but Roy's more convincing singing at the 'Uptown' session betokened his greater say in the running of the operation. Prodded by Joe Melson, he'd "wanted to use violins, and since I'd had such a rough time at Sun trying to get what I wanted, I was really ready to fight for violins, and Fred Foster said, 'Okay, no problem.' Then I think maybe it was all the flavouring and the special musical things that happen on my records came out of my hunger. I'd wanted to do that for a long time and wasn't able to."[2]

With this unprecedented and determined glint in his artist's eye, Fred Foster had touched a metaphorical cap and scuttled off to confer with the gifted Anita Kerr who was equally at ease writing string arrangements for both the Nashville Symphony and department store muzak. Scoring for 'Uptown' would be simple enough, "But she didn't know if we'd be able to find too many string players in Nashville. It just wasn't being done then."[13] Chasing round, Anita Kerr came across four violinists who could sight read and were available – two from the city orchestra and a couple of music students.

Bill Porter and Tony Strong, the engineers at Victor's two-track studio, did what they could with double-tracking and reverberation to fatten this sparse endowment. It wasn't as stratospheric, however, as the denser accompaniment pioneered above the Mason-Dixon line earlier in the year by The Skyliners, The Drifters and, while in New York, Buddy Holly. Strings now were gnawing at songs as much as saxophones and guitars did.

More conventionally, the Nashville violinists fairy-dusted 'Pretty One' which was a more reliable sketch of future direction than its A-side. Taking a leaf from steady Don Gibson's book, Roy would never stoop to simulating despairing sobs as Johnny Ray almost had, and an obscure New Orleans singer, Edgar Myles, actually did at having 'No-One To Love Me'. Needing only to digress into a hitherto unrealised falsetto, Roy Orbison could concoct the same sense of submissive devotion for his "lovely, unfaithful pretty one" without sounding pathetic.

CHAPTER FOUR

The Crowd

Enough to hold on hoping, 'Uptown' left a tide mark at Number Seventy-Two on *Billboard*'s pop chart. Though this was twenty places behind 'Ooby Dooby' – four years old and wretched – no more was Roy Orbison either a one-hit wonder or backroom songwriter assumed at twenty-four to be "past it". Indeed, he looked forward to maturing into "a middling singer, you know – comfortably off".[1] With a backlog of a few more like 'Uptown', he'd be in a favourable negotiating position for lucrative and respectable night club work – residencies maybe, rather than a thankless slog of one-nighters in back-of-beyond dance halls, gyrating and rolling on his back as the Ooby Dooby man.

With more application than ever, the Orbison organisation – star, co-writer, manager and record producer – scrutinised the Hot 100 because "if a lot of people have put the records in the charts, there must be something about them. So I always listen carefully and then find out why it's popular. It's no good getting bitter and saying so-and-so's record shouldn't be there."[2]

Clogging the ether of spring 1960 was pop at its most harmless and ephemeral; doggerel to be hummed, whistled and imperfectly sung by the milkman over a few weeks while the powers that be prepared another ditty by reworking the same precept from a slightly different angle. It was especially common in the early to mid-sixties in America to follow a hit single with records that sounded similar.

That was why former chicken-plucker Chubby Checker Twisted like a man possessed for two years. Hot on the heels of another Philadelphian singer, Len Barry's breakthrough with '1-2-3' in 1965 came his 'Like A Baby' which regurgitated all the salient points of its lightweight predecessor. Even in Britain as late as 1974 when martial arts were all the rage, Carl Douglas zipped in sharpish with 'Kung Fu Fighting', muscling in three months after this chart-topper with 'Dance The Kung Fu'.

Dance craze records making the charts usually mean stagnation in pop. This was certainly the case in Britain at the dawn of punk but worse was the hiatus from 1960 to 1962 with its chain of variations on the Twist, and inconsequential but maddeningly catchy assembly-line drivel. 1960 alone threw up Brian Hyland with his 'Itsy-Bitsy Teeny-Weeny Yellow Polkadot Bikini' which he'd never live down, as well as Perry Como's 'Delaware' which tortuously name-checked every State in the Union: why did Cally phone ya?

Most of the fiercest practitioners of fifties classic rock were either dead (Buddy Holly, Eddie Cochran), jailed (Chuck Berry), disgraced (Jerry Lee Lewis), in holy orders (Little Richard) or otherwise obsolete. The Everly Brothers were a year away from enlisting as marines when Elvis Presley was demobbed a sergeant and "all-round entertainer'; his taming epitomised by Italianesque ballads and infrequent self-mocking rockers as if obliged to humour his old following while smirking at those of Frank Sinatra's "Rat Pack" who'd guested on his homecoming television spectacular from Miami. With the King of Western Bop's capitulation to showbusiness proper, the grabbing record industry's mopping-up operation demanded the isolation of what it saw as his more palatable, all-American aspects. These would be components of a model on which to groom legions of smooth-running ciphers.

The hit parades of North America – and, by implication, everywhere else – became constipated with insipidly handsome boys-next-door; all doe-eyes, hairspray and bashful half-smiles. Their forenames and piddle-de-pat records matched – 'Swingin' School' from Bobby Rydell, Johnny Tillotson's 'Jimmy's Girl'. If they faltered after a couple of Hot 100 entries, queuing round the block would any number of substitute Bobbies, Jimmies and Johnnies like stock Hollywood chorus girls hoping to be thrust into a sudden starring role.

In this twee morass, there were few sparkles. Bobby Darin scored with a finger-snapping translation of Brecht and Weill's 'Mack The Knife', while the brothers Everly's lovelorn bluegrass polyphony still cut through with 'Let It Be Me' and 'Cathy's Clown'. Tamla Motown, a promising black record label from Detroit manoeuvred its first fistful of signings into the charts in 1960 while Ray Charles and Fats Domino, without compromising their rhythm-and-blues determination, were yet very much *Billboard* contenders. These and the throat-tearing assaults on old piledrivers like 'Way Down Yonder In New Orleans' and Kid Ory's 'Muskrat Ramble' by the aptly-named Freddie Cannon only validated Roy Orbison's argument that "whatever is the dominating factor of the day, its opposite extreme is never completely submerged, and is always represented to some extent".[3]

One turn-of-the-decade musical seam noted by Orbison was mined profitably by Jim Vienneau, a young producer based in Nashville. Later taken on board the Orbison ship of state, Vienneau's speciality was overblown melodrama of disaster and torment. Exploiting the public's morbid fascination with the Grim Reaper were the likes of Jody Reynolds' 'Endless Sleep' (though the girl is saved), 'Teen Angel' by Mark Dinning – which spent a fortnight at Number One in March 1960 – and Ray Peterson's car smash epic, 'Tell Laura I Love Her'. To a lesser degree than dance crazes, a proliferation of "death discs" was seen by some pundits to expose periods in pop of overall creative bankruptcy.

'Tell Laura I Love Her' even prompted the desperate reply 'Tell Tommy I Miss Him' from a Marilyn Michaels. Another "answer" record was Jeanne Black's 'He'll Have To Stay' to Jim Reeves' 'He'll Have To Go' – in which the Bimbo Boy dials a girlfriend when she and his rival are entwined on the sofa. High in the pop charts as these were, their country-and-western undercurrent of guilt, infidelity and loss had much in common with the death discs, and had been anticipated already in pop. Apart from specific songs like the unhappy 'Danny' (a *King Creole* out-take) and The Drifters' 'There Goes My Baby', the "beat-ballad" or "rockaballad" as it was sometimes known was pioneered by, and became central to the work of certain artists. Among these were Conway Twitty (whose 'It's Only Make Believe' was prototypical), Don Gibson – and Roy Orbison, some of whose recordings with Sun can now be seen as dry runs for the sixties. The contrition of 'I Never Knew', for example, was resurrected for 1963's 'Falling'.

In The Wink Westerners' repertoire had been the fanciful 'Dream' from a Fred Astaire musical. Though this was composed in 1944 by Johnny Mercer, a more distinguished antecedent was the work of French poet, Gerard de Nerval whose suicide in 1855 may have been related to confusion arising from his artistic investigation of the dream as a bridge between reality and the supernatural. Not quite so earnestly highbrow or self-immolatory were those who used the dream motif to sell records in the middle of the twentieth century. Released by RCA in 1959 were 'Afraid To Sleep' and 'Sweet Dreams' by, respectively, Chet Atkins and Don Gibson – both artists who were esteemed by Roy Orbison. That same year saw Bobby Darin chart-riding with 'Dream Lover' while Johnny Burnette cracked it in 1960 with just plain 'Dreamin''. On his third album, Roy would pay respects to the other side of the disc that established him as a songwriter in a retread of 'All I Have To Do Is Dream'.

From the elements then present and from his and Joe Melson's hard-bought artistic dossier came Orbison's pedantic transition to pop stardom. An astrologer might have deduced that he was a typical Taurean in his astute expansion of another's idea – for it was Melson who devised the "dum-dum-dum dummy-doo-wah" vocal counterpoint from which emerged 'Come Back To Me, My Love', which addressed a girl who had died on her sixteenth birthday. This song was among many presented to Fred Foster in Nashville during a short-listing for the next single – which took the best part of an autumn 1959 fortnight. 'Come Back To Me, My Love', thought Fred, was too much like the up-and-coming 'Teen Angel' but he liked Joe's dummy-doo-wah bit which reminded him not so much of the extraordinary background chanting of black vocal groups as the gentle close harmony of the white boy-girl Fleetwoods who he'd seen in Washington. They'd just wended their way to Number One with 'Come Softly To Me' which began with a "dum dum-dummy-doo-dummy-doo-bee-doo".

Another offering from the Melson-Orbison catalogue was one that had already exhausted three provisional – and unoriginal – titles. The verse of 'Cry'/'Why'/'Young Loves' boasted a lengthy *rubato* melody with the phrase "only the lonely know the way I feel" beginning its short chorus: "So I suggested we drop the verse, take the vocal figure out of 'Come Back To Me, My Love' and insert it between the lines of 'Only The Lonely'." Adhering to this executive brief back in Odessa, Melson proposed that a falsetto should end the final, crescendoed eight bars: "Joe wrote a good bit [of 'Only The Lonely'] and he had some of it when we started even" recalled Roy. "I remember [rehearsing] one day and it was sort of heading up and I just went with it...for a baritone to sing as high as I do is ridiculous. It only comes from the fact that I didn't know what I was doing."[4]

The composers were as unsure of the outcome as the other participants when the 'Only The Lonely' session shifted into gear. Potentially the bitty song – or medley – was as trite as any Bobby-Jimmy piffle what with the tinkling piano triplets, the bright string clichés and the rhyming-dictionary lyrics which covered the old ground of romantic bust-up and consequent heartache. There was even a lift from 'There Goes My Baby'. None of this mattered necessarily. These days you could get a hit with any sort of crap.

To this unappetising brew was added transforming ingredients. After an age of grim acquiescence, Roy found his voice at last. No more the Sun hillbilly cat or RCA goo merchant, he unfurled a rich, supple purity that, without plumminess, grafted a *bel canto* eloquence onto 'Only The Lonely' that invested it with a hitherto unrealised maturity of gesture. By the same instinct that governed street corner clusters of youths singing for their own amusement, operatic pitch and breath control were Roy's without years of carping tutorial and tedious exercise. He'd fallen on a sound reserve that was generated not from his throat but deeper within. Like a fisherman's tall tale, media hyperbole would extend Orbison's tonal range to an impossible six octaves. Though his vocal daredevilry grew with succeeding records, "My octave range isn't extremely wide but what I do have, everything is solid and useful." Even when his untrained diction verged on slovenliness, it only reinforced endearing idiosyncrasies whereby, in the opinion of no less than Duane Eddy, if others attempted to "sing the songs that he sang, they didn't have the same raw power and the same sound that he created...when you thought he'd sung as high as he possibly could, he would effortlessly go higher and finish up with a big finish and it was wonderful."[6]

More subliminal than the way Roy told it was the augmenting of the Anita Kerr Quartet's dum-dumming with the edgy sibilance of Joe Melson who agreed that, though a silk purse had been made of 'Only The Lonely', it might be more profitable all round if – rather than risk it with Roy's name on the label – it served as a useful demo in a campaign to persuade a major artist to record it. Five months of peddling, however, came to nothing. Elvis, for instance, couldn't be bothered to rise from slumber when Roy with tape in hand called at Gracelands, while The Everly Brothers, having found their feet as composers, more courteously passed it up.

"I don't know – what do you think?" was the spirit that pervaded Monument's unleashing of 'Only The Lonely' by Roy Orbison which infiltrated the crowded wavelengths of North America as 1959 dissolved into 1960. There it nestled uneasily among the likes of 'Robot Man' by Connie Francis and the novelty 'Alley Oop' from the Hollywood Argyles. On the air too were more comparable challenges in 'Lonely Winds' by The Drifters and Don and Phil's 'When Will I Be Loved'.

Thus encroaching on public consciousness, 'Only The Lonely' sneaked into the Hot 100's low seventies – where 'Uptown' had peaked – and seemed poised to possibly equal 'Ooby Dooby'. Then an avid surveyor of *Billboard*'s tabulations, imagine Orbison's exhilaration when the next week it shot up thirty places: "So I knew what was to follow."[7]

Threatening Connie Francis' chart dominance, Roy Orbison arrived at Number Two. Unlike callow Gene Vincent whose gladness had come too fast, "I was fortunate that I had been playing and singing for thirteen years when success came. It touched me deeply but it didn't make me crazy."[8] Concurrent with its four month harrying of the US Top Twenty, 'Only The Lonely' also splintered hit parades world-wide, actually clambering to the top in both Australasia and – after a sluggish start – Great Britain where only the latest from Elvis could drag it down.

He couldn't retire on it but suddenly there were more dates booked than Orbison could ever keep. Summoned from the ballrooms, Roy made his national television debut on *American Bandstand*, broadcast from Philadelphia, whose purpose – according to its clean-cut presenter, Dick Clark – was "to reflect what's going on early enough to make a profit on it". As the new sensation hadn't even a passing resemblance to Presley, and was, therefore, more perishable than any Bobby, it was prudent to cash in quick by shunting Orbison into punishing coast-to-coast package barnstormers that could drag on, on and off, for up to three months. Friday was some kitsch palais on the Bronx; Saturday, the local boy would make good at Texas State Fair. Because of the vast distances and flight connection variables, he acquired later a tour bus with fitted bedrooms, TV and telephone to more comfortably hurtle across the continent.

Those who knew noticed that the onstage Orbison had cast aside the ill-at-ease hip-shakin' shufflings of the fifties. Though rock 'n' roll wildmen were outmoded, neither did he go in for Bobby-type scripted grinning and inoffensive playfulness. His future stage act did not take hold with the same *fait accompli* jolt as had the new voice but, even on *American Bandstand*, he gave 'Only The Lonely' no help whatsoever beyond just singing and thrumming its four chords, letting it fend for itself "rather than by selling it with a lot of gesture and body movement. I'm not a super personality onstage or off. I mean, you could put workers like Chubby Checker or Bobby Rydell in second-rate shows and they'd still shine through but not me. I'd have to be prepared. People come to hear my music, my songs. That's what I have to give them."[9] Never again would his self-respect be corroded by garish Ooby Dooby capering anymore – not when he might yet fulfil an unspoken ambition "to do a show of just my own material".[6] While still pandering to his audience, so far he could rely on the three Monument A-sides plus 'Claudette' and soon the new single, 'Blue Angel'.

As would be the cases with Len Barry and Carl Douglas, a law of diminishing returns would apply to Orbison whose 'Blue Angel' was actually more substantial a song than 'Only The Lonely'. But so similar in arrangement was it that it paid but the most fleeting call on

Billboard's Top Ten. With a title taken from a Don Gibson number, 'I'm Hurtin'' battled to an unobtrusive Twenty-Seven while barely registering anywhere outside America. "Let's not start changing immediately" had been Fred Foster's counsel, and so the falsetto was transposed and the melodramatic circumstances shifted. 'Blue Angel', for instance, had suitor Roy comforting a girl still carrying a torch for her previous lover (a scenario later re-enacted by The Beatles in 'Baby's In Black'). Like snatches of kindergarten babble, "dum-dum-dum-dummy-doo-wah" mutated to "sha-la-la-dooby-wah-dum-dum-dum-yepyep" then "dumby-dumby-dum-ooo-yay-yay".

Rather than sticking with the devil they'd just met, maybe the alternatives should have merited more consideration. Perhaps because none were Orbison-Melson concoctions, their use as A-sides were regarded as a regression. 'I'm Hurtin'' was backed with a routine but not unattractive re-run of Gibson's 'I Can't Stop Loving You' but a greater departure from format was 'Blue Angel' coupling, 'Today's Teardrops' whose composer, a Connecticut teenager named Gene Pitney, "was surprised to hear Roy do it. I don't know if I could picture anyone who would do 'Today's Teardrops' but there were some I couldn't imagine doing it.'"[10] Sticking strictly to the multi-tracked demo, Orbison's voice was even speeded up mechanically to more precisely adapt Pitney's dentist's drill whinge on a piece that owed much to Buddy Holly's frenetic 'Rave On'.

Gene and Roy's paths crossed but twice in twenty-five years. On the last encounter – at Nashville airport in the seventies – "We said 'hello' and laughed about it because promoters would never have us out at the same time as it would be cutting into the same audiences."[10] Stereotyped – as Orbison would be – as a purveyor of woe, Pitney likewise put in a generation's hard graft on the road, staggering his sixties winning streak in foreign sales territories, thus postponing an undignified demise at home. Another victim of the same passion and vintage was Del Shannon, a square-jawed hunk from Michigan with a trademark abrupt falsetto. Stating his intent with 'Runaway' in 1961, he continued a best-selling exploration of small town soul-torture with the ilk of 'Hats Off To Larry', 'Little Town Flirt' and 'Two Silhouettes'.

They had professional ups and downs but all in this triumvirate, when their individual moments came, had accumulated sufficient music industry experience to outlast the prettiest Bobby, without jumping too heavily on passing bandwagons. Never was there a Twisting Orbison, a psychedelic Shannon or punk Pitney. All three had big voices, understated image and cautious business acumen. Although each made unwise decisions over the years, they alone accepted self-contained responsibility for them. While advised by managers and other payroll courtiers, Shannon, Orbison and Pitney were no corporation marionettes. Indeed, they maintained an intense and often unwelcome interest in every link of the chain from studio to pressing plant to marketplace.

In 1961, Roy was anxious about his sixth Monument single. Losing his grip on the Hot 100, he was objective enough to realise that, "Most of the time, an artist is the last person to know what is best for him. It doesn't follow that a composer should sing his own songs."[11] This was why in the running for the next A-side was the self-explanatory 'Love Hurts' from the pen of Bordleaux Bryant. Though they recorded it later for a long-player, 'Love Hurts' was another likely smash given a thumbs down by Phil and Don Everly since they'd discovered composing royalties. Roy's became the definitive treatment of this mournful pop standard which might have been wasted had it B-sided any lesser song than 'Running Scared'.

Once more, born loser Orbison found himself the other man in an eternal triangle. He'd win this one but his victory might have only been Pyrrhic, on account of the quivering hopelessness in Roy's most impressive performance on record thus far. More demanding and high-pitched than any he'd ever tried was the ending of 'Running Scared'. Despite a pep-talk from Foster, Orbison puffed several fretful cigarettes as, in the still filling studio, Anita Kerr's choristers chatted idly, violinists tuned up, amplifiers buzzed into life and horn valves fluttered and slid prelusively. During the now customary fortnight's preparations for each single, "It came down to a simple matter of finding the right beat" recalled Foster. "I asked him if he knew Ravel's 'Bolero' and he said he did not." With this foreboding rhythm as the pulse, the allotted hour of recording time got under way with Bob Moore's band call. Gaining confidence behind the coat stands, Roy did what he imagined was a passable take within twenty minutes. He'd swerved into falsetto for that nerve-jangling *coup de grace*, but since sound technology wasn't yet advanced enough, the engineer had been unable to catch it on the console. Roy would have to belt it out louder. Either that or the orchestra had to play a self-defeating touch quieter – which clearly wasn't on. Another try and Fred seemed pleased even if Roy clearly wasn't. "We've got a good one," reasoned the producer, "but I guess we could re-do it. Just go for broke, Roy." Two minutes after the tape rolled again, even the most grizzled session player was stunned when, from his hiding place, the singer reached that apocalyptic G sharp with his natural voice. A re-take was out of the question.

As well as a cut that everyone concurred was more promising than 'I'm Hurtin'' had been, so too was established a blueprint to which the team would revert for most of Orbison's best-loved songs for the next four years. Whether rejected lover or romantic martyr, Roy's ominous narrative stripped of superfluous dum-shooby-wah nonsense, would build from apprehensive muttering to ultimately overpowering anguish, the gradual interpolation of each instrumental section as the lament progressed contributory to the thrilling tension. "He used such intricate, beautiful melodies," enthused the catalytic Foster. "He brought sort of a baroque, classical style to pop music."'[2]

In the spring of 1961, however, all Fred knew was that, with 'Love Hurts' and 'Running Scared', he had a record that – if there was any justice on the airwaves – would restore his reputation as well as Orbison's. With acetates in attache case, he flew to Chicago to conduct market research round this key territory's radio stations. At WIND, the last port of call, Howard Miller – then the mid West's king disc jockey – said that if Foster left the white-labelled waxings, he'd spin both and take calls from listeners to gauge preferences. During a fifteen-minute ride to the air terminal, Fred learned the result from the taxi radio: hands down, it was 'Running Scared'. They'd never heard anything like it.

The Windy City's verdict proved to be correct as the rush-released 'Running Scared', in with a *Billboard* bullet on 10 April, shot to the top of the Hot 100 before the month was out, ensuring that its perpetrator's twenty-fifth birthday was unusually auspicious. As with

'Only The Lonely', this feat was repeated to varying degrees throughout the world.

Monument could afford then to declare its independence of ABC Paramount and, with no middlemen taking a cut, press and distribute its own product. Furthermore, to paraphrase 'The Ballad Of Jed Clampett', the next thing you know old Roy's a millionaire – but, as he had long understood, showbusiness was a fickle mistress, ready to fling him back to Ooby Dooby oblivion at the drop of a seventy-eight. With this worrying psychological undertow, Orbison had started investing unadventurously but providently in middle range real estate. In this modest bracket had been the Orbisons' first home in Nashville, unpretentious without either the obligatory swimming pool or trophy room for the breadwinner's disc awards. "You may not believe this," gasped his fan club secretary, "but Roy likes the simple life. He gets all the excitement he wants just shopping for groceries with his wife."[13]

Prosperity did not alter instantaneously or totally this uncomplicated ritualism. Roy might not have been too upset if he'd been condemned to return to the safer anonymity of straightsville or worse: "If I had to go to prison or was shipwrecked, and I had a guitar, I would go on singing."[2] Travel refined him but part of Roy Orbison would always be a pipe-and-slippers watcher of American football on TV. Though he acquired a taste of spicy Indian food, he always preferred steak and mushrooms. As his fame necessitated longer and longer spells away, he grew to value more than ever "just being home with my wife and boys. I have a lot of fun with them. And, frankly, I just enjoy getting on some loose rough-and-tumble lounging clothes and relaxing."[4]

Often the anti-social hours of his profession would turn night to day, causing him to "relax" until breakfast in the late afternoon fuelled him for composing into the small hours. Otherwise, inspiration would manifest itself when it was least desired. 'Running Scared' had been initiated by a newspaper headline glimpsed by Roy on a flight to New York. Song fragments would materialise in hotel lounges, chattering backstage passages or when sinking into velvet blue oblivion: "I'd written a couple of songs in my dreams but I'd thought they were someone else's."[5] Against such heavy-lidded discomposure, a notepad and biro lay beside the bed.

Wherever it came from, the raw song – just voice and guitar – would be transferred onto a domestic tape recorder for elaboration when demos were tried at either Acuff-Rose or, now he could afford it, Orbison's own studio: "I generally write the basic bones of the song then leave it for two to three months. And if they still hold up, have some value...then we think we have something and rework it finally."[1] Sometimes he would write at the speed of a train of thought, "But there are other occasions in which I sit brooding for hours – and absolutely nothing comes."[15] With the unfettered conviction of the naive, there were no advance drafts or agonising for weeks over a lyric or chord sequence: "All my best songs took only half an hour to write."[7] Into these were blended a pot-pourri of virtually every idiom Orbison and his collaborators had ever absorbed – Mexican, rockabilly, light classical, Zydeco, Western Swing, The Drifters, Don Gibson – you name it. Unconcerned with the quasi-mathematical dos and don'ts that traditionally afflict creative flow, there were only habits ingrained since the Fort Worth defence plant singalongs on which to fall back, "Though I'm sure we had to study composition or something like that at school, and they'd say, 'This is the way you do it,' and that's the way I would have done it, so being blessed again with not knowing what was wrong or what was right, I went my own way...so the structure sometimes has the chorus at the end of the song, and sometimes there is no chorus, it just goes but that's always after the fact – as I'm writing, it all sounds natural and in sequence to me."[4]

As with "Cry Guy" Johnny Ray and the surfing Beach Boys, Orbison's initial handful of hits cemented him in place forever as a specialist in one particular style. Over a quarter century later when he volunteered to sing a selection of a tendential George Harrison B-side, the ex-Beatle felt he had to "bung in a sad bit for Roy".[16] Like Chubby Checker would always be Twisting, Roy's rut would be grief-stricken ballads – even if closer examination of the same often revealed a happy conclusion to emotional traumas – or, at least the hope of one. Like Bob Hope, Roy sometimes got the girl. When he didn't, he usually faced desolation with dignity and plaintive sadness rather than self-pity: "Like 'Cryin'' – I didn't mean that song to be taken as neurotic. I wanted to show that the act of crying for a man – and that record came out in a real 'macho' era when any act of sensitivity was really frowned on – was a good thing and not some weak...defect almost."[7]

Orbison and Melson were, by 1961, ceasing to write to order. Generally, items were registered with Acuff-Rose who these days weren't so much canvassing as distributing to supplicants material the pair felt were unsuitable for Roy. While they never spawned any massive money-spinners like 'Yesterday', 'Moon River' or even 'Claudette', there were over 100 of these remaindered Orbison-Melson compositions recorded by other artists including one by the longest serving Bobby of them all, Bobby Vee.

Perhaps the last commissioned work, 'Cryin'' developed from 'Once Again', earmarked for Don Gibson. From a casually crooned phrase by Joe, the title became 'I Am Crying'. That very instant, a mental flash of an old flame, willowy and heartless, reared up before Roy. Though it had taken its cue from Gibson's – and, once upon a time, Orbison's – country-and-western stylistic resolution, the emerging result could not be exiled from pop. Even if it would be fifth in an unbroken line of melodious morosities, it was far enough removed – slower, more fragmented – than 'Running Scared' to warrant inclusion on the next venture to the Hot 100 interior.

In case the masses couldn't tolerate a lachrymose Roy, 'Cryin'' – the 'I Am' docked as "too country" – was yoked with the infectious rhythm-and-blues bounce of 'Candy Man' which betrayed a carnal side of Orbison hitherto unsuspected by most of those diary-scribbling, self-doubting adolescents who'd latched onto 'Only The Lonely' as some kind of anthem. Now their blue angel unveiled a laconic snarl on 'Candy Man' in which a crunching rhythm was overlaid with interaction between belligerent electric guitar and slashing mouth organ. This iconoclastic opus was the brainchild of two odd New York bedfellows, Beverley Ross and Fred Neil. The former's walk with destiny began with 'Lollipop', a vacuous 1958 chartbuster for The Chordettes, while Neil, a frustrated pop singer, was instead to surface as a Greenwich Village cult celebrity, best known as the writer of 'Everybody's Talkin'', theme to the Oscar-winning *Midnight Cowboy*.

'Candy Man' prowled the US Top Forty for two months but

swallowed dust way behind its vinyl companion which, proving moonlight and love songs were never out of date, cried all the way to Number Two. "They're therapeutic," explained the artist of this and his other *cris de coeurs*, "When people hear my songs, they realise they're not in such bad shape after all."

'Cryin'' had been the only Orbison composition passed by Fred Foster with no prescribed alterations. In the studio, weeping violins, wobbling xylophones and minatory tom-tom tattoos would detail a sound picture of one who, after short-lived relief, fought to keep his misery in check when breathing the air round its still tantalising source. Enhancing 'Cryin'' further were some of many minor tracking and miking experiments that Foster imposed on all Orbison's Monument output.

In later years, Roy would acknowledge that the musically unlettered Fred "was the perfect patron for a young artist because his attitude was, 'Here's the canvas. Here are the paints. Get on with it.'"[5] As George Martin would for The Beatles, Foster functioned as Orbison's sounding board, editor and fixer, head-to-head in the control booth with "the greatest talent I ever worked with"[2] while the session crew awaited instructions.

By 1961, the favoured accompanists for Orbison records were – nicknamed by Foster – the "A" team of drummer Murray "Buddy" Harman, Floyd Cramer and, dependant on needs peculiar to each piece, a pool of three lead guitarists – Jerry Kennedy, Hank Garland and Gray Martin – anchored by the subordinate rhythm fretting of Ray Edenton. Whatever the personnel, the fixed general supervisor was Bob Moore whose double bass throb was often supplemented by Harold Bradley's new-fangled Framus electric. With the audio synthesiser still but a twinkle in Doctor Moog's eye, human augmentation to this instrumental bedrock required musical scores which, as Roy could barely sight-read, had to be notated – often laboriously – by Moore or Bill Justis as the composer dah-dah-dah-ed: "I always always felt each instrumental and vocal inflection had to be special...I'd spend almost as much time on those as I'd spend on the song itself. Looking back on it now, I feel I was blessed much like the masters, I guess – the guys who wrote the concertos. I'd just have it all in my head."[5] With finance now less of a restriction, the sparse quartet of violinists roped in for 'Uptown' could be expanded to an orchestral string section of up to twenty. Roy's "good luck charm", Boots Randolph – "I'd pay him even if he didn't play"[14] – would head the brass and woodwind if used.

Because the acoustic separation hinged in the early sixties on primitive *ad hoc* measures involving coat racks, the danger of leakage – not to say voice-fretboard coordination – precluded Roy's playing guitar on his recordings. Besides, never would he claim to be a genius instrumentalist. "Sufficient, I suppose," estimated a later member of his backing group, "rhythm and a bit of lead. Technically, he wasn't very proficient – though his guitar was superb."[18]

The six-string most associated with Orbison of the twelve he would own was his black semi-acoustic Gibson but this had superseded an expensive red Gretsch Tennessean – "But it wasn't much of a guitar so I took a rubber hammer and knocked the neck off and was going to put another on but it got to be a real job so I had some professional help and they got another neck for me. Then they put steel pick-ups in, and we sprayed it black and it was a new creation and a great guitar. The Japanese wanted to make copies of it. So I let them have it and never got it back: no royalties, no guitar, no nothing."[19]

That he could shrug off such misplaced trust was an accurate barometer of Roy's grip on the indulgent reality of the pop star suddenly rich. In common with Elvis, money was no object if the Orbison entourage wanted to watch a cinema film in the middle of the night. The building's proprietor simply had to state a price for re-opening at two am for a private viewing. If merely peckish in the sort of diner where you had to order a full meal, Orbison would satiate his appetite with the soup before directing the waitress not to bother with the other courses, just bring the bill for them. Biting back on his annoyance with one singularly intransigent New York restaurateur, Roy stalked out to return within the hour, having bought the place for the stark pleasure of sacking his aggressor. If such free spending was mentioned in gossip columns, it used to be accepted – even lapped up – by fans as the prerogative of glamour.

There was much bowing and scraping in one London showroom when a salesman's scornful remark about pop singers having too much money led the offended Orbison to reconsider the purchase of a Rolls Royce limousine. Roy's obsession with automobiles became such that, "If he saw a vintage car he liked on the road, he'd chase it and make the owner an offer he couldn't refuse."[8] A Lord Montagu in microcosm, he'd accumulated by 1966 antique vehicles enough to deliberate the founding of a museum in Houston: "Maybe my old car mania will end up like my diamond rings. Those rings just get bigger and bigger so I couldn't carry them round on my little finger anymore." Housed either outside on asphalt or in one of his three-car garages, the Orbison collection ranged from a rickety 1916 Ford to the tarnished splendour of von Ribbentrop's staff Mercedes.

The acquisition of the executed Nazi ambassador's property afforded piquancy to the self-improving Texan's continued study of contemporary military history in the pages of such set works as Shirer's *Rise And Fall Of The Third Reich* and the four-volume memoirs of Churchill. Not strictly leather-bound interior decorating either, these and other books were to fill the library of the opulent ranch-style family home to be built on a tree-shrouded 11,000 acre plot overlooking Old Hickory Lake in the postal district of Hendersonville. Although habitable by 1961, the planned extensions and structural idiosyncrasies that would more than double its value would take ages, calculated the eager and futuristic architect engaged to facilitate the construction of such as the cavernous music room, the waterfall for the entrance hall, the living room swimming pool, the hydraulic lift to the beach where Roy would go angling or pilot his speed boat.

At the touch of a button, their father could amuse Roy Duane and his younger brother Tony, born in 1962 by winging his radio-controlled model Spitfire high over the lake. This toy was the *pièce de résistance* of a squadron of miniature aircraft worth a small fortune. Of his and Claudette's more adult pastime of motor-biking, he enthused, "It's a thrill, a pure joy – and a health factor."[20]

To furnish the more immediate needs of stomach and household, Mr and Mrs Orbison would journey more serenely by Volkswagen to shops in Hendersonville, a township whose municipal pride reflected that of Nashville, the "Music City" twenty miles to the south-west for, as well as its public holiday in honour of Jim Reeves, once its most renowned addressee, Hendersonville was also birthplace in 1918 of Eddy Arnold, another of RCA's paladins of sweetcorn.

On either side of the Orbisons lived Johnny Cash – who was assuming Hank Williams' crown as both entertainer and drug abuser – and, an older acquaintance from Texas, Bob Luman who had crossed over to the pop charts in 1960. Despite a persisting tendency not to plug country-and-western on pop radio, Johnny Horton, Skeeter Davis and Jimmy Dean would also notch up entries in the Hot 100. Yet living and recording in the environs of Nashville was not an automatic qualification for corresponding placement of a pop record on C&W stations' playlists – as the eventual exclusion of The Everly Brothers, Brenda Lee and Conway Twitty demonstrated. They – like Jerry Lee Lewis and Elvis – were thought to have somehow reneged on their roots by an unremittent wooing of a more generalised pop consumer.

Apart from a one-shot duet with Emmylou Harris in 1980, not once did Roy Orbison ever make the country chart. However, though his had been the city's first major record success that was explicitly pop, the Nashville *crème de la crème* were not as derisive of Orbison as might be imagined. After all, he had served under godhead Chet Atkins; chosen his pickers from the "Nashville sound" hard core and, of his songs, had admitted always "that they are derived from and influenced by true country music".[11]

To an amused cheer, he got away with performing on a Nashville stage in a mickey-taking cowboy outfit. Indeed, it didn't seem strange to Hank Snow, Skeeter Davis and Bob Luman when Roy joined them on a tour of Canadian music fairs. At the Winnipeg stop, a son of a local journalist's path became clear. Inspired by Orbison's act, nineteen-year-old Neil Young would carry its contradiction of enjoyable depression to absurd lengths with the coming of the "Woodstock Generation" in the later sixties.

Perhaps it was through his father's Fourth Estate eminence that young Young got to see the show because – like Roy's cowboy suit bash in Nashville – most of the Canadian venues were semi-private functions in which music was incidental to the wheeling and dealing of each exhibition centre's promenading entrepreneurs. Consequently, the entertainers' approach to their tasks was less intense, almost like an escape valve from the presumptions of a more interested audience. At one or two of these revues, onlookers were neither seated nor silent as the bands played virtually in the round, bereft of curtains and *son-et-lumière*. Competing against the stadium's other attractions, it was necessary for singers to address the passing crowd. Disquieted by this, Orbison picked the brains of his musicians for some ad lib one-liners: "So we got together some really corny things like, 'I've just flown in from England and my arms are tired' – that kind of hick joke." Informality is frequently a breeding ground for clowning. Prior to Orbison's entrance, his group cranked out fifteen minutes of instrumentals "and the drummer did all the gags. Then Roy came out and did exactly the same lines. We were falling about and he's looking round and wondering what's happening."[18]

Chuckling along with such pranks against himself, Orbison proved an amiable, considerate employer – one who'd stand a round for the crew, smiling quietly at dirty jokes and monotonous accounts of the previous night's carnal antics. Usually he confined himself to a mere tolerant observance of human folly but a calamitous evening in a Las Vegas casino resulted in Orbison's renouncement of roulette – as he had denied himself spirits after that first and only youthful slug of whiskey.

As principal asset of what was now grandly titled "The Roy Orbison Show", he was above petty jealousies, and could lend warm and generous encouragement to backing musicians. Enlisted in January 1962 to strum chords underneath John Rainey Atkins' lead guitar was Bobby Goldsboro, a Floridian just turned twenty-one, in whom Roy perceived much of his former self. The onset of puberty had found Goldsboro looking for an opening in pop but, while an undergraduate at Auburn University near West Point, he'd been heedful enough to both keep up with his studies and freelance on guitar with various combos working clubs in and around the campus. His exhausting but exciting three-year apprenticeship in the bespectacled Texan's employ was to have a lasting, beneficial effect. In hotel rooms and backstage passages,

Goldsboro would tinker with tunes and rhymes, often seeking the guidance of the easy-going Orbison who was impressed enough to co-write with his hireling. Two Goldsboro-Orbison numbers – 'Stand By Love' and 'Baby's Gone' were even recorded by Gene Thomas, a British vocalist.

That such a liaison could form was indicative of Joe Melson's growing disenchantment with the ratio between his role in the wayfaring Roy Orbison Show and its negligible rewards. When his brief spot was announced, he'd bound into the spotlight to rattle off 'All Shook Up' or similar, plus his own latest single be it Phil Everly's 'What's The Use' or, from his and the main event's portfolio, 'No-One Really Cares'. Both titles too aptly summarised Joe's diminishing hopes of a hit record in his own right and, therefore, extrication from being part of Roy Orbison. One bitter freedom from his partner was that the economics of many future ventures – especially those beyond North America – excluded all Roy Orbison Show stalwarts bar the star himself. He'd use a pick-up band and be supported by local heroes.

Orbison's first steps on foreign soil were during a whistle-stop trip to Australia in spring 1962. Concerts in Melbourne, Sydney and Brisbane – with Down Under's "answer" to Presley, rough diamond Johnny O'Keefe – culminated with a slot on the national television broadcast, *Bandstand* among whose regulars was a trio of brilliantined, dentigerous brothers called The Bee Gees.

Nearly as preordained as his bi-annual bouts of flu, visits to Australasia invariably added inches to the Orbison waistline. No longer the college pudding he'd been in the fifties, he was, nevertheless, too self-conscious of his figure to wear jeans. However much his weight dropped, the most flattering cameras could only rarely hide the penumbra of a double chin, the puffy jowls, the doughy complexion. Like gawky Buddy Holly before him, Roy's soft-focused features *sans* spectacles would adorn the initial cache of record sleeves. Even when encircled by encroaching shadow on one EP cover, no photographic miracle made Roy's face his fortune.

Jerry Allison's advice to his deceased Buddy was then practised by Orbison: "If you're going to wear glasses, then really make it obvious you're wearing glasses."[21] Offsetting Roy's amorphous paleness would be a huge pair of black hornrims. Mothballed forever were the seedy-flash rockabilly duds of yore. Instead, Orbison garbed himself in sombrely tailored suits, plain shirt and slim-jim tie. Never coy about his marriage and children or a liar about his age, still he retained, as a French correspondent put it, "*toute les characteries d'un employe de bureau*".[22] Corroborating this observation, Roy had once commented, "I'll probably be on the administrative end of the business in about three years. I'll have plenty to do."

This level-headed forecast would forever be held in check by the unexpected longevity of the unprepossessing Orbison's performing career. On Elvis Presley's recommendation, Tommy Steele had caught Orbison's act well before it was seen in Britain. After the instrumental intro, the proclaimed "Mister Roy Orbison" strolled centre stage to begin a tentative 'Only The Lonely'. Appearing to Steele "like a mechanical mole, I sat and hoped that he wouldn't be great – he couldn't be looking like that – but he was. Once into the lyric, he had me – the rhythm and the tune all added to the magic of the moment."[24] Belying the off-stage Orbison, the stoic deliberation evoked by the hits accentuated the introspection of one so bound in tragedy that every hypnotic utterance seemed to have been wrenched from his very soul. So "gone" was he that a fire in one theatre's stalls was no distraction: "It wasn't gallantry or anything but I could concentrate on my performance and forget the smoke."[25]

Thrown together on an aeroplane flight, Roy and Georgia soul shouter Otis Redding had mulled over the feasibility of cutting an album together, even bestowing it with the provisional title *Big O: Black And White Soul*. That a project like this could be contemplated seriously was because Orbison too was a soul singer. The scarcity of instrumental breaks might have obliged him to remain close to the microphone but Roy's stationary stage persona was as contrived as Redding's hammy exhibitionism. Yet beneath these trappings, both artists went further than simply putting on the agony beneath the proscenium. Even after years with his name in lights, Roy would never assume that he would be acclaimed automatically. Never delivering less than his utmost, "I'd always wait until I reached 'Only The Lonely' before I stopped being a bundle of nerves."[25]

Symptomatic of Orbison's diffidence as well as his dowdiness and meagre teen appeal, the picture fronting his second LP showed not a portrait of the artist but a theatrical mask in keeping with its title track, 'Cryin''. Geared for the singles market as most pop stars were until the close of the decade, albums containing a best-selling forty-five could still do well – in the States especially – even if short on needle time and padded with previously released B-sides, forgotten flops, hackneyed showbiz standards, stylised "originals" and, sometimes, time-consuming instrumentals. Some were driven to copies of rivals' current smashes as was Johnny Tillotson with 'Only The Lonely' and Bobby Vinton with 'Cryin''. Roy lent a more assured attack to three Everly Brothers hits, even rearranging 'Bye Bye Love' for a fuller production incorporating *pizzicato* violin arpeggios – translated across the Atlantic as 'Stringbeat' by Adam Faith who tore up the British charts using this conceit.

Collections of separate selections – often programmed haphazardly – rather than rounded entities in their own right, albums *circa* 1962 merely chased singles as a display of an artist's "versatility", with no real cultural value. Good looks and vibrant personality could render fans uncritical enough to digest frankly sub-standard produce. This may explain why – in an age when some would schedule as little as six weeks gap between albums – Orbison's steady one per year from 1961 to 1963 testified to quality rather than commercial pragmatism. Nonetheless, only a greatest hits compilation in 1966 would earn him his first gold disc in this field.

Like everyone else, Roy looked to his Hot 100 entries as chief selling point. Though the albums were stuffed with old chestnuts like 'Cry', 'My Prayer' and 'Beautiful Dreamer', these had been nurtured in hick dance halls over the years stretching back to The Wink Westerners.

Rather than these regurgitations – however imaginatively dispatched – Orbison leaned more on his and Melson's efforts as well as those of other professional songwriters such as, again, Gene Pitney ('Twenty-Two Days') and Lee Pockriss whose made-to-measure 'House Without Windows' was an improvement on his 'Itsy-Bitsy Teeny-Weeny Yellow Polkadot Bikini' for poor Brian Hyland. Wesley Rose waded in with 'No-One Will Ever Know' which fused the story line of 'Cryin'' with a familiar bolero beat – while Joe and Roy re-wrote the atrophied 'Come Back To Me, My Love'. There were similar recycles as well as the recording of image-gilding titles like 'Blue Avenue', 'Loneliness' and Kitty Wells' 'Lonely Wine' – in which Roy's tipsy musings may be seen as a sequel to 'Wedding Day', a saga of a jilted bridegroom and the nearest Roy-as-recording-artist would come to lip-trembling pathos. By contrast, 'Sunset' and its companion piece, 'Nightlife' – which lived in its stalking horn riff – have Roy rubbing his hands in anticipation of a tryst beneath the stars. Probably too risqué (and under-produced) for a single, was his captivation by the wanton 'Gigolette'; Roy's transition from forewarned pleasure-seeker to beguiled victim insinuated by a seductive fiddle *obligato* and swirling Latinate melody.

Back to the mundanities of the Hot 100 on which his income would always depend, it was not with his own song that Orbison first dabbled in the symbolism of dreams. It was with Cindy Walker's upbeat 'Dream Baby' that he would equal 'Cryin'' in units sold. 'Dream Baby' also broke the pattern of plodding vinyl misery that has hounded Roy since 'Only The Lonely'. Mooning over his dream baby, his eventual happiness is by no means guaranteed but he's egged on by a skittish girlie chorus and packing-case snare drum in an accompanying cauldron more subtle than the ballads in its instrumental deployment – rasping saxophone, for example, intruding only on the coda which, for once, fades rather than climaxes. On Nancy Sinatra's smash of 1966, 'These Boots Are Made For Walkin'' is evidence that her producer had listened hard to the overall sound of 'Dream Baby' – notably its introductory double bass and jogalong acoustic guitar.

However efficacious in the charts it was, the very use of a non-original as an A-side ratified further erosion of Roy and Joe's professional relationship. Prompted by family commitments and unabated disgust at the shabbier depths of the music business, Melson withdrew gradually from the Orbison cabal. Still the best of friends with the increasingly less available Roy, Joe endeavoured to keep in touch.

He left when Roy's second career peak began its downward spiral as 'The Crowd' trudged into only the lower reaches of the Top Thirty.

With its martial tempo, stop-start arrangement and reiteration of the hackneyed old grandiloquence, it was a deterioration in quality, let alone sales, and a reminder of how great 'Running Scared' had been.

This breath of stale air commenced a wrestling with vocational stimulus for Orbison who – not replacing Melson – would search for thirteen months before finding gold again. Bound to four singles a year both by contract and the dictates of the time, his coterie decided on a pot shot over Christmas 1962 with two sides penned solely by Roy: 'Working For The Man' which harked back to Sam Cooke's back-breaking 'Chain Gang' of 1960, and 'Leah', a stand-by "death disc". After much um-ing and ah-ing, two finished masters from the Melson era had been put in cold storage – a rather languid item entitled 'Blue Bayou', and the anachronistic 'Lana' which, like Bobby "Boris" Pickett's 'The Monster Mash' that same season, substituted euphonium for bass guitar.

A few months earlier, a John D Loudermilk B-side, 'Darling Jane', had concerned a honeymoon couple drowning. Laughable though it was with its convoluted rhyming and off-hand angst, it was not unlikely that – also published by Acuff-Rose – 'Darling Jane' may have sparked off the abundantly superior 'Leah'. 'Working For The Man' was technically the top side but, deservedly, it was superseded for the slight chart honours by the tear-jerking 'Leah' in which floating marimbas, pattering tenor drums, a ghostly choir and the drawn out *morento* of Hawaiian guitar encapsulated both the sub-aqua dissipation of sound waves, and the ambivalence of a pearl diver's nightmare and his sweetheart's unspecified but watery doom. In the death, it was Orbison's vocal outpouring in the keening one-word chorus that intimated that yearning for the lost Leah was too deep for satisfactory verbal articulation. 'Leah' would be in Roy's set at the last concert.

'Working For The Man', however, wouldn't be. "Rather mediocre" was the conclusion of one reviewer, "pounding beat and very little else."[26] In retrospect, this seems harsh for, though not Roy's best, this jumping, modernised cottonfield holler – enhanced by apposite grunts and moans – is still quite danceable and, in less than two-and-one-half-minutes, condenses the soap-opera complexities of a labourer's homicidal hatred of his tyrannical paymaster which is tempered by the love-struck attentions of the latter's daughter which the overworked hand intends to exploit in an intended takeover bid.

This diversionary tactic of a single spread itself thinly enough to shift eventually one million copies without actually breaching America's Top Twenty – though, of all his records, it was the one that first struck oil for Roy in France. Yet for all that, the less than spectacular showing of these last two forty-fives signified that, unless Roy Orbison received another 'Running Scared' godsend, a career as "a middling singer" might be beckoning still.

CHAPTER FIVE

Distant Drums

If Roy couldn't come home, then a home of sorts came to him. More often than not, he'd be arm-in-arm with Claudette when he stepped off a plane. After 1963, flash bulbs would frequently catch Roy Duane too, clasping Mummy's hand and proud of Daddy's celebrity. Shielding the lad from the nicotine clouds, rude words and late nights of the road, Claudette preferred to commute occasionally to her husband's places of work from some central point. For his second British tour, for example, the Orbisons decided on a Victoria Embankment apartment within a stone's throw of all the sights – St Paul's, Big Ben, Westminster Bridge and our wonderful policemen. You don't see many Bloody Towers back in the ol' US of A. For the very purpose of his soaking up historical London and her browsing round the shops, Roy engineered a few uninterrupted free days before the first show on 28 September, 1963.

During his first round-Britain trek but three months earlier, Roy's exhilaration when a Spitfire zoomed above the tour bus had bemused John Lennon, a singing guitarist with one of the other acts. Boredom may have set in had Lennon accompanied Roy to the Imperial War Museum where the American wandered for hours, lost in wonder at this Lancaster bomber nose section or that Volksturmmann rifle mechanism. He splashed out on the inevitable vintage car to be shipped back to Hendersonville but time restrictions and wishful thinking forced several disappointments: "I would have loved to see

Sir Laurence Olivier in a play; I intended to visit the Tower of London; I wanted to visit a big car factory...but most of all, I would have liked to have met Sir Winston Churchill – just for the pleasure of shaking this great man by the hand."[1]

This endearing naivety was indicative of Orbison's captivation by Britain. Beneath the stock it's-wonderful-to-be-here vapouring, his love affair with these islands overruled even monetary *realpolitik*: "I can earn three times the money I make in England by just carrying on working at home...by the time all the expenses are paid and I've paid the band, it's not worth all that much to me."[2] There was also the cold and rain; the overpriced lard and chips in flyblown wayside cafes with no public toilet; the toyland currency; the unfinished motorways; only two television channels and, except in the poshest lounge bars, no ice in your Coca-Cola. What Yank couldn't help but adore the place? Female traffic wardens called you "love"; cigarettes could be purchased in ten-packs, and pubs were more than just places where guys got drunk. From the bluster of the States, Roy would always look forward to Britain's more sedate pace of life.

Sometimes, he'd cross Britain up to three times a year as he did in the twelve months from May 1963. However, unlike such dissimilar Anglophiles as PJ Proby, blues pianist Champion Jack Dupree and actress-singer Marsha Hunt, it was not in the less financially vulnerable Orbison's long-term interest to make Britain his home. Besides, with the young architect putting the finishing touches to their dream home in Tennessee, Claudette's appetite for travel was evaporating.

Unannounced in the reception area of Mayfair's Westbury Hotel, Roy Orbison had given his debut public performance in the United Kingdom free of charge. On an unseasonably cool June afternoon in 1962, he and a pick-up group had run through ten numbers – including, naturally, both his latest single and most recent hit – in front of a few score of those fan club members who'd disentangled themselves from their usual daytime commitments, plus pockets of journalists still around after the press reception in the Americanised establishment's Mount Vernon room. Like attending a Decca Records award ceremony for easy-listening maestro Henry Mancini later that week, Orbison's "impromptu" concert was part of a public relations strategy to be employed on other occasions during his European business trip with manager and producer to view market conditions and meet major distributors: "It's one of my ambitions within the next two or three months to really consolidate the world market for my records."[3]

Prior to his appearing there regularly, apart from 'Only The Lonely' and 'Dream Baby', Roy's forty-fives did less well in British chart terms than at home. 'I'm Hurtin'' even missed completely while 'Working For The Man' died its death after only one week in the Top Fifty. However, it was in this minor sales territory and jumping-off point for more lucrative continental killings that Roy found an audience that would support him unswervingly through a decade of hits and into the subsequent nether-world of cabaret. Bar the remote Elvis, Orbison came to command the most devoted British following of any American pop star – and would be the only one to top the UK charts during the fifteen months after Presley's 'Return To Sender' was dislodged by Cliff Richard, his principal English "answer". Both Elvis and Cliff would be shovelling out a greater proportion of potboiling ballads and musical films of cheery unreality when confronted with the rearing monster of Beatlemania and its aftermath.

Rather than similarly beating a calculated retreat from the pop mainstream – or adjusting his style towards ersatz Merseybeat – Roy "did very much what I like to call 'my truth' or my real thing and not follow or get thrown by whatever comes along. I thought maybe in 1964 I could have been swamped by The Beatles and people but it turned out the other way round and I was voted Number One male vocalist in 1965" – in a British music press popularity poll. Unnecessarily he added, "The Beatles were Number One group."[4] In March 1964 – month of the first ever all-British Top Ten – Associated Television contracted Orbison to headline two *Sunday Night At The London Palladium* spectaculars and, for a record-breaking fee, his own forty-five minute *Roy Orbison Show* in the autumn.

Pop is an erratic business in which the most arbitrary isolations can prompt changes affecting the whole course of an artist's career – a sore throat at an important audition; Brian Epstein turning up when you're valiantly over-running because the main attraction hasn't sobered up yet; a top disc jockey flipping his lid over the B-side of your record, and spinning it into the charts. In 1965, Dave Berry – a vocalist from Sheffield – suddenly found himself the Presley of the Flatlands after a comparative flop at home became Holland's biggest selling disc ever. That same year, PJ Proby's fall from grace was precipitated by his too-tight trousers splitting from knee to crotch during a second house at Luton Ritz.

Variables as bizarre as these intruded upon Roy Orbison's professional life too but his profound success in Britain cannot be explained away so tidily. Other than a relatively small hard core uncritical enough to buy before listening, whether Roy's records sold or not depended – with one debatable exception – almost entirely on their commercial suitability, though he sustained and often increased interest in his output by constant touring and scrupulously plugging each current release on television and radio. In an age when he and his peers were only as big as their latest single, it was binding on Roy to balance cash amassed in the hit parade with his self-picture as a creative artist. Later and less well-loved singer-songwriters would be able to convince their fans that *Top Of The Pops* excursions were trivial tangents to their main body of work on albums. At least Roy was no such snob; in the mid-sixties, he couldn't afford to be. Plugging 'Borne On The Wind' on the BBC Light Programme's *Saturday Club* was all part of a day's work.

The acceptance of Orbison as an honorary participant in the British beat boom was partly because, as Alvin Stardust – then "Shane Fenton" – admitted, "None of us could sing but some got the breaks and some didn't."[5] One of the few exceptions was Ray Phillips of the Nashville Teens who, during the group's season at Hamburg's Star Club, won frauleins' hearts with his note-for-note facsimiles of 'Cryin'' and 'In Dreams'. He and others such as elegant Colin Blunstone of The Zombies and Cliff Bennett, leader of The Rebel Rousers were all deprived of the acclaim their abilities deserved , blurred as they were by integration into bands that lacked "image". One whose backing combo faded away the moment he sniffed success was Welshman Tom Jones – a favourite singer of Orbison's. Like Roy, he was blessed with a most professional projection, flexible vocal command and a certain steady consistency – "squareness", some would say – that wasn't effeminate or subversive like some of these blasted long-haired guitar groups. Moreover, the likes of The Beatles and Rolling Stones "couldn't sing": not "real singing" like Roy Orbison.

Though this intimates that Orbison was idolised only by older pop consumers disenfranchised by the Big Beat, he was also a songwriter who scorned onstage ostentation and therefore merited the respect of both ducktailed Rocker and backcombed Mod.

Predictable as he became – and, to many, irritating in his later refusal of encores – none could complain about the quality of the performance. It was like expecting a racing bike for your birthday and getting one. "He didn't have to introduce any songs," reminisced one of his British musicians, "because he'd confidently be aware that they would know and the reaction to each was always the same with the initial burst of applause that would then subside, and he'd wait for that to die down and he'd say no more than 'thank you so much' or 'mercy'! And if he did introduce the next song, it'd be no more than, 'Here's a song...' Lack of verbal contact seemed to add to the nature of the performance."[6]

A crucial supplement to the introspective Orbison persona were the striking Ray Ban Wayfarer sunshades he was obliged to wear for the first time onstage on the opening date of that first British tour: "I found myself getting photographed, and when the pictures went around the world, everyone commented on my [sun] glasses. From that day, I decided to stick to them. When I don't want to be recognised, I take the dark glasses off."[7] With a gimmick as distinctive as the Beatle fringe, Manfred Mann's beard and Johnny Kidd's eyepatch, further UK visits brought gradual refinements of this image. Out went the bank clerk threads; in came five-inch Spanish heels, high-waisted *calzonera* pantaloons and puffed-sleeve jerkins. Apart from intermittent medallions and his gold wedding ring, every sartorial detail – socks, watch-strap, buttons – had to be bible-black. Sometimes he'd sport biker gear – though leather made him sweat. Of course, it is incumbent upon any entertainer to take heed of his public image. However unintentionally, Roy – who leaned towards green garments off-duty – had stumbled on one that worked and, "Once you become successful, you don't want to change anything too drastically so I sort of stuck with all that, but it wasn't anything I designed."[7]

Roy's mid-sixties stage act in its full flowering was as foreordained as James Brown's cloak-laden Grand Exit or Screaming Lord Sutch's cartoon horror. After the master of ceremonies' build-up, you'd hear a lone guitar strumming the 'Running Scared' bolero as the curtains parted with the spooky deliberation of a dream's slow motion. On a stage lit only by tiny amplifier bulbs, a pencil spot would fade in round the central microphone. A murmur would arise, swelling into unacknowledged hero acclamation. This wasn't television or an LP sleeve mug shot: veiled in flesh but impenetrable, the Big O was actually there. Embarking on the first verse to only his own fretting, this weird cynosure of all eyes would seize possession as the boards filled with light and the orchestra assumed form behind him. Clustering towards the front might be fascinated Quant-cropped dolly-birds for whose bolt-upright boyfriends Roy Orbison did not represent a threat. A good few of them would also hasten up the aisles to gape at one who was as erotic as a favourite uncle.

Because he was neither sexy nor sinister, you didn't mind your girlfriend signing letters "Orbisonly yours". He was the sombre side of Freddie Garrity's coin. For all the smash hits they clocked up, both were four-eyed and unglamorous. Although 'Dream Baby' had once been in The Beatles' *modus operandi*, Freddie's was one of the few acts at Liverpool's famed Cavern Club to include Orbison numbers. Nevertheless, though he was as "professional" and thoughtful of the paying customer as Roy, the trouser-dropping chief show-off of Freddie And The Dreamers was never as dignified in the teeth of the hooliganism ever present on the package tours. Orbison even kept his cool when "someone leapt onstage at Newcastle and whipped his specs off. He was at a bit of a loss. It's a severe loss of part of the image, isn't it? So he went off and got another pair. He made no comment on it. He just took it as part of the index of possibilities of what might happen."[6]

While deploring the Geordie souvenir hunter's conduct, this travesty of legitimate admiration may be seen as an attempt to penetrate the mystique that Orbison generated for the ordinary British fan. What's he like? Is he blind? Albino? Does he never talk to anyone? What's with the black outfit? What is he like?

Building on Roy's monochrome precedent, later "Men In Black" such as Lou Reed (who pioneered black male lipstick), the seedy

Stranglers and ghoulish Dave Vanian of The Damned tended to effect a sullen, moody intensity offstage too. The more conservative fan was delighted to discover that Orbison did not live the part; the brooding aura vanishing as soon as he ambled into the wings after the final bow. Smiling indulgently, he let a giggling Marianne Faithfull remove the famous sunglasses in one backstage corridor encounter because, "I've always wanted to see what he really looked like."[8] He didn't mind a bit when a snap of this "unveiling" – as Marianne called it – was splashed across *Melody Maker* in February 1965.

Back in 1962, however, Roy Orbison had been the one least likely to garner such coverage in six months', let alone three years' time. When his maiden British tour was under discussion, promoters Danny Betesh and Peter Walsh – who was to name his Surrey home "In Dreams" – were so dismayed by their subject's homely looks and staid demeanour that they questioned whether a television slot beforehand wouldn't damage both ticket and record sales. Echoing this "*quieta non movere*" argument, impresario Tito Burns would "never forget my feelings on seeing Roy's photo after agreeing to present him here in Britain. After all, this was the era of the good-looking boys like Cliff and here was, let's face it, an older person wearing tinted spectacles singing slow, sad songs and, I understood, didn't move a muscle onstage."[9]

At the Westbury Hotel press shenanigans, even when posing for snaps without his specs, there was, indeed, no escaping from it: the boy looked a square. It wasn't just the Jodrell Bank ears, weak chin and hair slicked back in a smarm – he'd compounded it by owning up to being married with children, for Gawd's sake. Furthermore, he acted neither sullenly nor brashly in his dark business suit: no jive talk, no prima donna tantrums, no good copy. He seemed more like a manager than heart-throb pop sensation: "I had a contract to sign...and decided that I might as well sign it in London, fix up a few details and take a look round the British market."

"I shall cut a record especially for the British market," he promised. "It will be very near the C&W style but will be tempered to your taste."[3] Words are cheap. Orbison had noticed that, as in North America, Ray Charles was in vogue again, having shelved his jazz-gospel fusions to chance an arm with the first of his *Modern Sounds In Country And*

Western albums which ran a stylistic gauntlet from Ted Daffan via Hank Williams to The Everly Brothers. While Roy was in London, its promotional single – a revamp of Don Gibson's 'I Can't Stop Loving You' – was racing to the summit of Britain's chart where, after a fortnight, it would be unseated by Frank Ifield's seven-week reign with a C&W arrangement of 'I Remember You' with a yodelled selling point.

For want of a better description, Orbison had been branded a country-and-western exponent by British reporters and, in the light of current trends, it seemed prudent not to gainsay them. "The guitars of C&W could mean a lot here,"[1] he conjectured. "You don't seem to have the kind of rhythm groups that we have in the States – and I'm sure that is what the kids want: strong, beaty rhythms that make them jump."[3]

Nobody in the plush Mount Vernon room that summer's day could foresee that native British "rhythm groups" would be jumping up the hit parade in unimagined abundance. However, with 'Please Please Me' almost a year away, solo stars, both from and taking their cue from America, still dominated the charts. In some cases, the late fifties "Somebody and the Somebodies" dictate still held, differentiating between "featured singer" and faceless backing combo. This was the case with Brian Poole And The Tremeloes who earned a footnote in history as the ones Decca chose on New Year's Day 1962 instead of The Beatles.

Though their failed Scouse supplicants were to be grabbed to teeth-gritting effect by arch-rival EMI later that watershed year, one consolation for Decca high command would be the continued licensing arrangement with key US record companies through the London-American subsidiary whose roster embraced the cream of top-selling US pop. This included Roy Orbison who thought the deal with Decca so satisfactory that, even when he eventually switched labels in the States, a special clause would be inserted in the new agreement whereby he would remain on London-American in the UK. During that exploratory visit in 1962, for example, there had been no raised eyebrows when Fred Foster, attracted by a new British system of recording strings, suggested a session with Roy at Decca's West Hampstead studio – maybe during this British tour, whenever that would be.

Whilst in London, Foster had also engaged a new assistant to handle British affairs from Monument's Nashville office. Among former EMI secretary Janet Martin's qualifications for the post had been her co-founding of Roy's British fan club. Among her new duties was excusing to the press her idol's recent poor showing in the UK Top Fifty: "He was very disappointed about 'The Crowd' and 'Working For The Man' not making it, which ended his big run of chart success in Britain. He has some theories about why this was so. 'The Crowd' he thought too fussy while in 'Working For The Man' he reasoned that the lyric was too complicated."[10]

Popular with the Orbison children and a frequent guest at the unfinished Hendersonville mansion, Janet noted with patriotic pride that, in one room there, a corner was set aside for memorabilia and keepsakes from British well-wishers. Roy also subscribed to the London music press which normally he would study as a stockbroker would a shares index. Still procrastinating about returning to tour, he "inadvertently picked up this [British] magazine. It said, 'Highlight of the evening was Del Shannon's version of Roy Orbison's "Cryin'" or "Running Scared".' Or both. So I got to thinking that if he did that well with my songs, I might do as well if I came over."[11]

Three weeks' worth of dates were pencilled in for October 1962 but no such undertaking proved feasible as Orbison – especially with 'The Crowd' peaking at a humble Number Forty in summer – was not considered powerful enough box office to headline alone. No available British performer was judged to be an adequate co-star and, after negotiations for soul crooner Sam Cooke and then Carl Perkins petered out, Orbison and his investors elected to wait a crestfallen while longer.

Transferred back to England in early 1963 to reorganise the fan club, Janet Martin was thrilled to report that Roy was "mighty relieved about the success of his current release, 'In Dreams'" which actually crept fractionally higher in Britain than in *Billboard*; its five month chart run matching that of 'Only The Lonely' in 1960.

Suddenly he was back on form, having shaken the curse of either looking to other writers for hits, or his own composing efforts being consigned to British bargain bins after indifferent sales. 'In Dreams' had been conceived "half asleep and my thoughts were still racing when that whole introduction just came to me. I thought, 'Boy, that's good. I need to finish that. Too bad these things don't happen in my dreams.' I woke up the next morning. Twenty minutes later, I had the whole song written."[12] On vinyl, it eased in like an off-the-cuff strummed lullaby to, perhaps, the infant Tony. However, breaking into an agitated *moderato*, 'In Dreams' was to be no soothing children's favourite like The Chordettes' 'Mr Sandman' from 1954. After a "magic night" of unconscious reverie, the deranging pallor of dawn brought only the agonising reality of the departed lover, conveyed beyond words by Roy's despairing falsetto coda.

'In Dreams' relegated Cindy Walker's exotic 'Shahdaroba' with its snake charmer *ostinato* to the B-side. On the rebound, a heartened Orbison – again, without Joe Melson – penned the follow-up, 'Falling', which was likewise coupled with a Walker flip. As much of a holding operation as 'Blue Angel' had been after 'Only The Lonely', the remorseful 'Falling' likewise wasn't as big a hit as its predecessor but was a hit all the same. As demonstrated by Jim Reeves' posthumous Number One with it three years later, the blood-and-thunder B-side, 'Distant Drums', may have been a bolder but more effective choice.

'Falling' charted shortly after Roy had embarked on that long-awaited British tour. Fresh from The Top Ten, he no longer needed a Cooke or Perkins to guarantee profit. It had been arranged for Orbison – replacing his disinclined friend, Duane Eddy – with his supporting programme to open at Slough's Adelphi theatre on Saturday, 18 May. Second on the bill, so Janet Martin informed him by transcontinental telephone, were The Beatles. "I had never heard of The Beatles," reflected Roy, "and it seemed to me at first like it was just a rehash of rock 'n' roll that I'd been involved with for a long time, but what it turned out to be was these four guys, their particular spirit...putting out rock 'n' roll as they saw it and it turned out to be very fresh and full of energy and...vitality. So I recognised it at the time."[13]

Once the Beatles had been "just a rehash of rock 'n' roll" and would always remain in artistic debt to the trailblazing sounds created in the studios of Norman Petty, Sam Phillips and, more recently, Fred Foster. Of 'Please Please Me' John Lennon recalled that, in its downbeat lyric and nascent slowish tempo, "It was my attempt at writing a Roy Orbison song."[14] The faster version that was the making of The Beatles also raked up Orbison in its flights of falsetto.

Aspects of the Orbisonian dialectic were felt too in such post-Beatle British hits as Dave Berry's 'The Crying Game' and the equally tearful 'Juliet' from The Four Pennies. The most exquisite record any incarnation of The Moody' Blues ever made, 'From The Bottom Of My Heart' took the musical mountain climbing of 'Running Scared' and 'In Dreams' half a step further by swelling over three minutes from muttered *sotto voce* to wailing horror movie crescendo. A different cue from Roy's 'Borne On The Wind' was also taken by John D Loudermilk for his 'This Little Bird' a 1965 high-flyer for both The Nashville Teens and Marianne Faithfull.

Even when furthest from their English grammar school interpretation of American pop, traces of Orbison lingered among the sitars, electronic collages and drug-dazzled vision of The Beatles' later work – as exemplified by the melodic melancholia of 'She's Leaving Home' and the nothingness-to-eternity structures of such as 'A Day In The Life' and 'Happiness Is A Warm Gun'.

The Moptops of 1963 had surfaced as self-assured but unpretentious Liverpool lads, still slightly bewildered by their sudden fame. On the Orbison expedition too were Gerry And The Pacemakers, then on terms of fluctuating parity with their fellow Cavern dwellers. To be introduced by mahogany-toned interlocutor Tony Marsh, the all-styles-served-here fare was completed by stand-up comedian Erkey Grant, balladeer David Macbeth and baby-voiced Louise Cordet. These small fry were accompanied during their allotted ten minutes each by The Terry Young Six who kicked off the proceedings fronted by hip-shakin' vocalist Young.

The remainder of the Six – which included Barry Booth on keyboards and, on bass, future Shadow John Rostill – were also responsible for backing Roy Orbison who, they had heard, expected his musicians to follow precisely the scores notated by arranger Bill Justis for his records. Low opinions by other Americans – albeit bad workmen blaming their tools – prompted The Great Man's desire to "arrive about a week early and rehearse with my backing group until I'm satisfied".[10]

Roy's schedule was such that this worthy intention became

impractical. The best he could manage was a swift run-through in the late afternoon using the Slough Adelphi's house sound system amid a clutter of cables, guitar cases and Ringo Starr's yet unassembled drum kit. In the dusty half-light beyond footlights still being tested, the newly-arrived John Lennon and the odd road manager looked on as the star turn tuned his Gretsch Tennessean from Barry Booth's purring electric organ. A feedback squeak from a nervous amplifier launched a pleasantly unproblematic rehearsal. Items that Roy had inserted into the set lately that The Terry Young Six didn't know were picked up with minimum instruction. Instead of an imperious martinet who'd bust your ass if you played a bum note, the Six found their new employer "very easy-going. I don't know why we should have felt in awe of him but his material was solid and interesting to work. He had the quality that I don't think in those days was that common. He just turned up with these songs – some of which, we'd made ourselves acquainted with prior to his arrival – and just dived into the rehearsal situation."[6] Roy was especially impressed with academy-trained Booth for whom the occasion in retrospect was recalled as one of these Momentous Encounters.

Afterwards, as the Six cleared a space for The Beatles' more pristine equipment, another Momentous Encounter could no longer be postponed. In his dressing room, the jet-lagged American had barely sat down when Lennon – now joined by his manager, Brian Epstein – asked if he'd got a minute. It was like this: "They said, 'How should we bill this? Who should close the show? Look, you're getting all the money, so why don't we (The Beatles) close the show?' I don't know whether that was true or not, whether I was getting that much more than they were. It wasn't that much – and the tour had sold out in one afternoon."[15]

No-one could pretend that Roy was the foremost cause of this quick profit. The Fab Four's 'From Me To You' would be a Number One fixture for the duration of the tour. Just before shrieking pandemonium would greet even Tony Marsh and his attempts to keep order, backstage The Beatles were presented with a Silver Disc for this, their third single, by Gerry Marsden with whom they would be slugging it out for UK chart suzerainty for the rest of 1963. Two months earlier, The Beatles had served Orbison's poorly-received compatriots, Tommy Roe and Chris Montez – also attended by Terry Young's sextet – as they would be serving him within the hour. John, Paul, George and Ringo were still a few months short of becoming a national treasure via *The Royal Variety Show*, but it, nevertheless, made sense for the last scream-rent chord of their 'Twist And Shout' signature tune to signal the final curtain and their escape to a ticking-over back-alley limousine. In their new broom wake, the more insipid Bobbies and Jimmies from post-Presley America couldn't get arrested in Britain now. Within a year, Frank Ifield would also be in supper club obsolescence.

Aware of the chasm into which even he might plunge, Roy in the murk behind the plush Adelphi curtains steeled himself to face facts before someone else's audience. Into the bargain, he felt vaguely uncomfortable in the prescription sunglasses which were all he had to shield his eyes since mislaying his clear spectacles on the aeroplane to London from sunny Alabama where he'd played the previous night. Over there, they would have just finished lunch by now.

Opening with – what else but – 'Only The Lonely', Roy Orbison had a walkover. While the Terry Young boys sight-read or not behind him, all he had to do was stand his ground with his black guitar and sing. Apart from a tapping heel chord changes and rare directive nods for the band, his only other gesture was whipping out a harmonica for 'Candy Man'. Another up-tempo concession to the evening's most prevalent mood was trading "heys" and "yeahs" with the audience in a 'What'd I Say' which he took down easy to work the tension up again to raving panic. This was quelled with a plaintive 'Cryin''. Of his bigger hit rockaballads, he was required to reprise 'Running Scared' mid-set while the sustained cheering – rather than screaming – after the 'In Dreams' valediction was such that a relieved Tito Burns at the back of the hall bore witness that "after thirty minutes – he was booked to do fifteen – we still couldn't get The Beatles on. This was the first time I'd seen a standing ovation in Slough."[9]

Thus was set the pattern not only for the three weeks that he had to precede The Beatles but also for subsequent nationwide jaunts throughout the golden age of British beat. "He'd slay them and they'd scream for more," sighed Ringo. "In Glasgow, we were all backstage listening to the tremendous applause he was getting. He was just standing there, not moving or anything."[16] At one venue, a writer's-cramp-inducing 600 autograph books were left for Orbison to sign. Even when his record sales began their downward spiral in late 1965, he could still work that old magic without obvious effort, enough to disconcert any beat group, chart-riding and frantic, on the same bill.

"The nice thing with Roy," recounted Gerry Marsden, "was that when they got American stars over, they used to do a big thing of supplying them with a car. Roy, God Bless him, said, 'No, I don't want a car: I want to travel with the boys.' We'd have sing-songs on the coach – it was good fun. Roy had this very, very extraordinary ability for doing three to five octaves with his voice which we all tried to do and it made us speak strange for days after singing his songs – but they were nice songs to do."[9]

Marsden is said to be prone to viewing his past sometimes through rose-coloured lenses but this anecdote typifies the underlying good nature of British pop's most optimistic period. Roy's initiation into its spirit began in Slough when, "I remember Paul and John grabbing me by the arms and not letting me go back on to take my curtain call. They [the audience] were yelling, 'We want Roy. We want Roy,' and there I was, held captive by The Beatles [who were] saying, 'Yankee, go home.' So we had a great time."[5]

Flattered to be told of a favoured Liverpool musicians' watering hole named The Blue Angel, Roy also enjoyed chatting about music with that first touring party's Scouse faction. As the "Nashville of the North" held more C&W bands than anywhere in Britain, The Pacemakers and Beatles were lay experts on the genre's obscurer trackways. Among numbers common to many Merseybeat groups were 'Beautiful Dreamer', 'Money', 'What'd I Say', and 'Sea Of Heartbreak', all of which passed through the Orbison repertoire too.

Some new song ideas were also tossed around, but the laugh-a-minute ambience of tour bus and artists' bar circumscribed serious composition – though Roy, as always, continued to revise and develop any such flashes of inspiration in hotel suite seclusion. Persistent jet-lag aggravated his inclination to oversleep – a trait he shared with The Beatles' lead guitarist, a ponderous youth called Harrison: "George and I missed the bus a lot. They left without us. We slept in."[17]

George's group, Roy considered, were pretty rough-and-ready "but they had the magic there",[11] and, as for Gerry, "I think that monster smile would sell him before they even heard his voice."[18] Marsden's advancement in North America would be surprisingly sluggish but, in a matter of months, The Beatles would spearhead what has passed into myth as the "British Invasion" of the States by beat groups, an eventuality predicted by Orbison after he touched down for some Californian ballroom dates that June, with English screams still ringing in his ears.

As the US music industry had long regarded British pop as merely the furbisher of nine-day wonders like The Tornados or Acker Bilk, few believed him. Two who did were Del Shannon and Gene Pitney, both of whom had also had first-hand experience of the pop pestilence enrapturing the Limeys. Like Orbison, these two had not been found wanting by Britain's beat-crazy teenagers either. Del and Roy had first met in England that previous tumultuous month. Comparing notes, Shannon revealed that a break in his UK itinerary had allowed him to book a London studio for a crafty cover of 'From Me To You' to steal a march on The Beatles before they hit America. Through breathing the air round The Rolling Stones, Pitney would be shortly entering the British Top Ten with a ballad written by their Mick Jagger and Keith Richards.

Evidence of Roy's fascination with British pop would never be as practical. Nonetheless, if his new-found friends were criticised, he would charge to an unexpectedly ruffled defence. His rejoinder to some sour remarks by *American Bandstand* mainstay Len Barry was, "I hear he said some things about The Beatles and the Stones. If he's really that all-knowing, he should be able to tell us if there's life on Mars and when and if there's another world war coming. I just don't think he's qualified to say things like that."[19] This outburst could be justified by Roy's better informed overview. Not only was he enchanted by world-wide smashes such as The Searchers' 'Needles And Pins' but he was also startlingly in the know about the most unbeknown items like 'Why Did You Bring Him To The Dance' by a Coventry quintet, Peter's Faces, though "I don't know who Peter is – or his Faces – but they sure sound good to me."[20]

In their emotive vocabulary, both this disc and 'Needles And Pins' drank from the same pool as most of Orbison's hits. However, dislocation of love was a much more negligible facet than anticipated in Roy's 'Blue Bayou' which, coinciding with his second British tour of 1963, barely rippled *Billboard*'s Top Forty while gushing to Number Three in fair Albion. Stimulated by Joe Melson's drive through the Arkansas fens in 1961, 'Blue Bayou' had no precedent in the Orbison canon. Considered too risky for a single then, it was too intriguing to bury on a long-player.

Largely through Roy's necessarily lengthy absences in foreign climes, and an understandable indolence whenever he could snatch a few days at home, his partnership with Melson had all but fizzled out by the late summer of 1963. Fresh out of new material, he blew the dust off 'Blue Bayou'. For insurance, it was coupled with a straightforward rockin' re-run of 'Mean Woman Blues', a Jerry Lee Lewis B-side from 1957. In America at least, this caution could be excused by the elevation of 'Mean Woman Blues' into the Top Five but it is 'Blue Bayou' that more piquantly activates memory banks. Not another Himalayan ascent like its two chart forebears, a low-dynamic, jogalong verse-chorus format is undercut by a lazy harmonica and wordless female vocal harmonies in counterpoint to Roy's close-miked homesickness for a sleepy pastoral haven where there's always nothing doing.

In view of the increasing spectrum of Orbison's travelling life in the Swinging 'Sixties, 'Blue Bayou' was only more poignant. Zig-zagging round the world in the torpid warmth of jet, limousine, train and luxury coach to strange towns, strange venues and strange beds, even "days off" were often filled with photo calls and interviews. Caught off guard by sales abruptly picking up in France, he'd have to drop everything in the middle of a tour of the Philippines to wearily mime the track that had done the trick on *Tele De Bois Et Ages Tendres* in Paris before dashing back to the interrupted far eastern campaign.

In a trunk call to Hendersonville, he'd enthuse that, of all the places he'd been so far, he'd got the softest spot for Britain, adding – so he informed one newshound – "Believe me, I say in all sincerity that I cannot wait to get back in September with my good friend, Bob Luman."[20] Not doubting her husband for a second, Claudette was there when The Sons Of The Piltdown Men – a renamed Terry Young

Six – piled into the instrumental prelude on that September first night – once more at Slough's Adelphi. For subsequent Beatles tours, the Six had been supplanted by Sounds Incorporated after some beery unpleasantness involving Lennon. Under this cloud, the group had all but disbanded when, to back Orbison again, a five-piece amalgam of ex-Young veterans and bass guitarist Danny Thompson (later of Pentangle) to be coalesced by Roy's American drummer, Paul Garrison, was pulled together by Barry Booth who, as Orbison was discovering, was worth his weight in gold. Another familiar British face at that Saturday afternoon soundcheck was that of Tony Marsh who would be officiating for a supporting cast, featuring The Searchers, Freddie And The Dreamers, and Brian Poole And The Tremeloes. In a land where nearly every town and shire was now supposed to have a "sound", these acts represented, respectively, Liverpool, Manchester and Essex.

Originally, Roy was to have headlined an all-Merseybeat rival troupe, already under way, with Billy J Kramer, The Fourmost and Tommy Quickly. As with The Beatles, these were all Epstein clients so Roy's choice of even a Terry Young Six without Terry Young might have been among factors causing the change of plan. Moreover, the substitution of the doubtful Tommy Roe for the sonorous glory of Roy Orbison would be less intimidating for Epstein's second division chartbusters.

While Roe counterpoised Orbison, The Fourmost's opposite number was Freddie And The Dreamers whose act was centred critically on getting laughs. A comedy element was also present in the recorded works of Poole and his group. Therefore, it was to be expected that the mile-consuming camaraderie this time was even more uproarious than with Gerry and The Beatles. A poker-faced Tony Marsh assured the American contingent that passports had to be produced by aliens wishing to enter Scotland. With all such documentation safe with Claudette in the London flat, a tense Roy, Bob and Paul fidgeted as the coach hurtled from the previous night's stop in Blackburn to the Glasgow Apollo. At a border pub, the landlord – going along with Tony's jape – demanded passports from any foreigners among the drinkers. "Gee, Roy, what're we gonna do?" moaned Luman.

A Glaswegian policeman on traffic duty outside the Apollo was victim of some high jinks springing from Orbison's known hobby of collecting uniform cap badges – a pastime he shared with Elvis Presley. With a communal kitty as prize, points were awarded according to the various stages of gaining possession of a stranger's headgear from first accosting the wearer; initiating a conversation about the hat; removing it and, for the maximum allocation, bringing the hat to the other players who would then explode with laughter. A turbaned Sikh had been the hardest nut to crack but Barry Booth did well to cajole the Scottish constable into Roy's dressing room to surrender his badge in exchange for an autograph for his daughter.

A less elaborate remedy for the tedium of the road was Freddie Garrity's fondest recollection of the tour. Freddie had blown most of his first big royalty cheque on an E-type Jaguar three times the price of his humble abode in a Manchester suburb. With time to kill before the performance at that city's Odeon, he invited Orbison round for a meal: "So he came to this two up and two down like on *Coronation Street*...and he owns a ranch with all these acres of land and I served him salad. He had these lovely songs and a great voice, and I just liked the guy."

After much persuasion, another Orbison admirer consented to close the show for the last six nights. On 10 October, Brian Poole's rendering of The Contours' 'Do You Love Me', having fought off a rival version by The Dave Clark Five, had toppled The Beatles' 'She Loves You' from Number One. With 'Blue Bayou' about to slip, the relinquishing of his bill-topping supremacy for the second time in five months made sense to Roy – so long as he still got paid as per contract. Overwhelmed, Brian – shy and over-modest offstage – wasn't happy about lording it over one who he, Freddie and The Searchers, revered as a Grand Old Man. Roy hadn't yet turned twenty-eight.

Brought into Brian And The Tremeloes' vexing backseat discussion about a suitable successor to their chart-topper, the venerable Orbison suggested and then played 'Candy Man'. As a two-year-old B-side, it would be unknown to those consumers unacquainted with pop before 'Please Please Me'. In a backstage alcove the next day, Poole asked to hear 'Candy Man' again. Taped immediately the tour finished, Brian and his group's cloning of the Orbison arrangement was put on frustrating ice by Decca in favour of the lacklustre 'I Can Dance'. When

The Teen Kings, 1956: (l-r) Billy Par Ellis, Roy Orbison, James Morrow, Johnny Wilson and Jack Kennelly

A Monument publicity shot, 1959: no photographic miracle could make Roy's face his fortune until spectacles became part of his public image

A Decca reception for Roy: (l-r) Fred Foster, President of Monument Records, Ted King, Roy Orbison, Don Moss, Brian Willey, Johnny Stewart and Robert Fleming

Roy and Claudette Orbison at an awards ceremony at London's Westbury Hotel

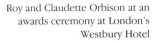

An aptly pensive moment on the Brian Poole tour, 1963

Springtime in London, 1964: Roy recalls musical times past with Norman Petty

Of the twelve guitars he owned, the one most associated with Orbison was this black, semi-acoustic Gibson

On UK TV's *Ready, Steady, Go* in August, 1964

GAUMONT THEATRE
IPSWICH
ROY ORBISON and
THE WALKER BROTHERS
2nd Performance 8 0 p.m
SUNDAY
APRIL 24
CIRCLE 15/-
E18
No ticket exchanged nor money refunded
THIS PORTION TO BE RETAINED

John Walker's assertion that "being on a bill with him has brought fantastic luck to other artists" came true when, mid-tour, the Brothers' 'The Sun Ain't Gonna Shine Anymore' topped the charts in 1966

April, 1967: after the death of Claudette, English nanny Dorothy Cook was hired to look after the Orbison children

Roy as "Johnny Banner" finds another use for *The Fastest Guitar Alive*, 1967

In a London recording studio, in July, 1968

Orbison's increasingly longer absences from the family home contributed to his and Claudette's brief divorce in 1965

Roy feels the too familiar symptoms of writer's cramp

"It was Elvis who made me a motorcycling fan": after Roy had taught her to ride too, Claudette's passion for the sport would last for as long as she lived

Orbison's obsession with automobiles became such that "if he saw a car he liked on the road, he'd chase it and make the owner an offer he couldn't refuse"

Rescue workers remove the body of Roy Junior from the burned ruins of the family's house in 1968

Barbara – the second Mrs Orbison – and Roy pose with his and Claudette's surviving son, Wesley

Roy and his new family outside their Bavarian-style chalet in Hendersonville

With co-writer Bill Dees at Roy's home

In March 1977, the Big O appeared in iconoclastic white attire

The class of '55 thirty years later: (l-r) Johnny Cash, Jerry Lee Lewis, Roy Orbison and Carl Perkins

Bruce Springsteen bolsters his position with a credible influence

Roy adjusts a thoughtful microphone at a press conference, 1988

Roy created the aura of a fresh sensation through *Mystery Girl*, its spin-off hit single, 'You Got It' – and his membership of The Traveling Wilburys supergroup – and as a guest on UK TV's *The Last Resort*

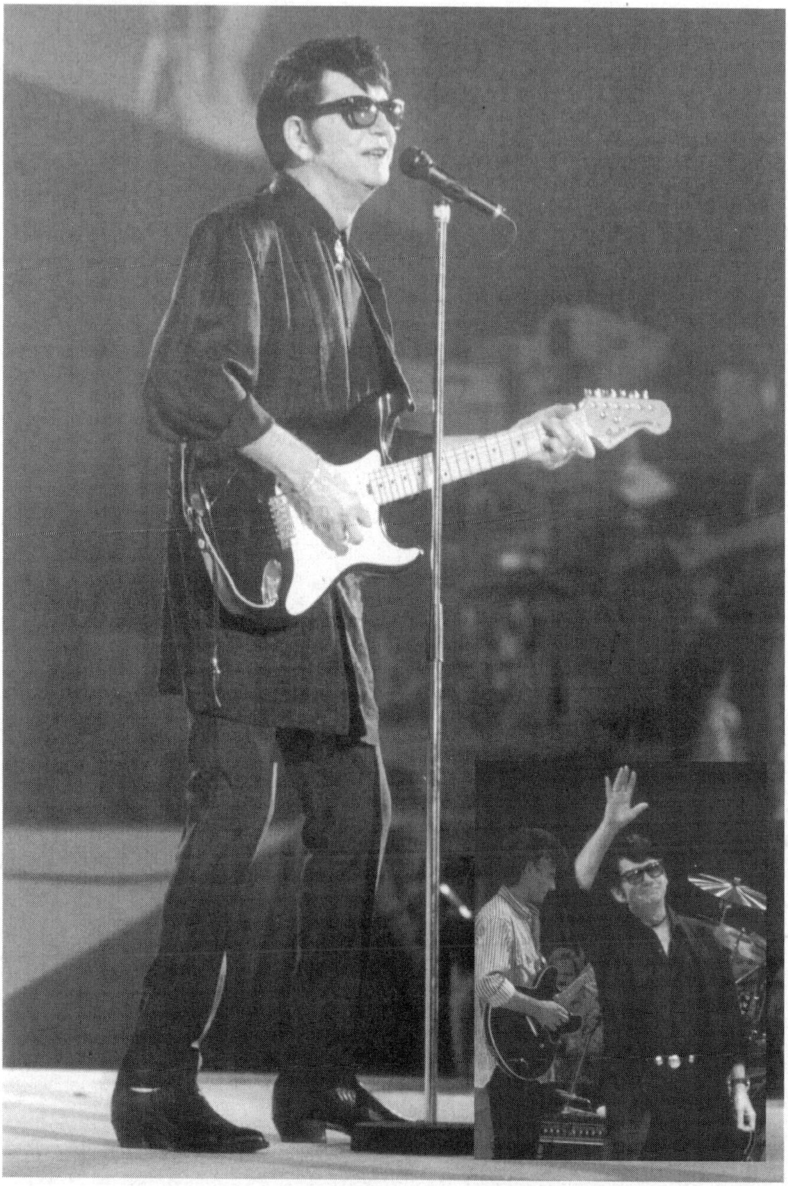

Main picture: towards the end, he became quite chatty on the boards before grinning, waving and vanishing into the wings forever. Inset: "Goodnight" – Roy's last concert in Akron, Ohio, 4 December, 1988 – two days before his death this stopped short of the Top Thirty, out came 'Candy Man' which restored Poole and The Tremeloes to the higher reaches of the charts. As instigator of their good fortune, Roy also lent moral support when the group – about to record 'Someone, Someone' (their last Top Twenty entry) – sought the practical approbation of Roy's old colleague, Norman Petty who had supervised the original version by The Crickets.

Roy's current producer was also in London, keen to try out this new method whereby, rather than trusting a solitary omni-directional microphone slung above the heads of a section numbering up to twenty, each individual string player would wear "a neck mike which made a tremendous recording sound – and this was the thing Fred Foster wanted for Roy' Orbison."[9] Thus spake Ivor Raymonde, musical director for the session that yielded 'Pretty Paper', Orbison's only single with a Yuletide theme – and the sole Willie Nelson composition to breach the British Top Ten. Roy's approval of this chiming sob-story in waltz tempo, after a demonstration in a hotel room, gave Nelson's bank balance a vital shot in the arm since the destruction of his Nashville house by fire forced his move back to Austin. Possibilities of a Nelson-Orbison songwriting team were, therefore, precluded by geography though the pair cobbled together 'Summersong' which boasted an arresting instrumental preamble reminiscent of Stravinsky.

In 'Pretty Paper', Roy was projected into the midst of seasonal jollity to observe Christmas shoppers ignoring a roofless beggar – the sort who would gravitate at dusk to the shelter of the Embankment, near Orbison's spacious *pied à terre* chosen because of its indoor swimming pool. Though the rush-release of 'Pretty Paper' caught the December "sell-in" in the States, "the tapes got fouled-up on their way over here, so it couldn't be issued in Britain. We had to have something, so we decided on 'Borne On The Wind' – though I didn't expect it to do very well."[21]

Backed with a workmanlike 'What'd I Say', this stop-gap effort was the first fruit of Roy's collaboration with Bill Dees, a bond that was to prove more productive than any either participant had known before. Since the sundering of The Whirlwinds, Dees had retreated from the limelight to try his luck as a full-time tunesmith in Nashville. With Joe Melson unwilling to face another moonlit mile, Bill gladly took his place in Orbison's growing nomadic retinue – which, by 1964, catered for two respective trios of violinists and backing singers.

After one show, Dees trailed along to a party to which his co-writer had been invited. Made to feel that he had somehow gatecrashed, he slipped back to the hotel where grief for a drowned friend flooded his thoughts. The skeleton of 'Borne On The Wind' was tangible on Roy's return in the graveyard hours.

In its juxtaposition of other-worldliness and pulsating Spanish-Mexican canter, it was a refinement of those windswept 'Johnny Remember Me' console inventions pioneered by the formidable English producer Joe Meek. An aetherial chorale layered a rhythmic thrust, action-packed with rumbling tom-toms and alternating piano glissandos and ascending inversions. Way above, Roy soared and fluttered the chorus before swooping into the galloping bridge and a sweep of violins. Under-rated by both its composers and the public, this careering drama – not deemed worthy of release in the States – flitted briefly into Britain's Top Twenty. In February 1964 spring came late, and 'Borne On The Wind' was driven yelling to its shelves on the deletion rack.

CHAPTER SIX

It's Over

Confiding to a scribbling journalist that, "I have such a tight schedule that if I take a vacation, I can feel the work going by," was Roy Orbison bragging or complaining? Certainly he was leading what the economist might call a "full life". As well as his British expeditions, within the space of two years from 1963, his globe-trotting encompassed extensive touring of Australasia, the Far East and Europe. There was also a trip to South Africa which, with its apartheid policy reminiscent of Texas in the mid-forties, had also been used as the film location for the Jim Reeves vehicle, *Kimberley Jim*, with hardly a liberal eyebrow raised in those days.

Immortalised in song by her husband, Mrs Orbison was warranted a second-hand celebrity. Gripping Roy's arm proprietorially, she wandered an earth less and less eye-stretching. Brussels resembled a cold Fort Worth – the same comparison holding between the British Midlands and Tennessee. A luxury hotel in Canberra was just like one in Johannesburg: the Coca-Cola tasted exactly the same. At each capital city, the couple would split like amoeba – he to go through his paces in a monotony of concerts; she to her own devices with a cheque book and room service.

How then could Claudette possibly be bored? She couldn't be homesick either with at least one of the children and, more often than not, her father-in-law along for the ride? Softening her drawl at reception desks, she'd still be stung by the muffled tittering of those to whom wealth was second nature. With the switchboard relaying greetings, complimentary tickets and invitations from loud-mouthed showbusiness periphery, how could she be lonely? At parties where she'd pass a dozen famous names along a single staircase, she was more irked than out of her depth. In the powder room, a Quant-cropped gold-digger with sooty eyes and wasp waist would actuate inane dialogue with Claudette, congratulating her on hooking such a well-heeled pop star of a man like Roy Orbison. As travel had brought Claudette souvenirs without wisdom and fatigue without stimulation, so Roy's fame elicited flattery without friendship.

An additional incentive for her stepping off this facile roundabout was that – with only a few alterations to go by April 1965 – the new house on Old Hickory was no longer an unserviceable no-man's-land of rubble, planks and coffee-swilling artisans who knew not the dignity of labour. After being a stranger in his own home for most of his life, Tony could now leave his grandparents' care in Texas. The only impediment to this restoration of family stability was father's job. Ten days in New Zealand – a month in Canada – six days' television in the Netherlands – a weekend in Cyprus – "This means I don't get much time with my family and they are looking forward to me spending three or four weeks at home from the end of October."[2] The sound of his engine dying on the gravel outside would signal one more deliverance from the treadmill of the road as, from another time zone, a voluptuously weary Roy would drop his cases in the hall, hand out the presents and tramp upstairs for some shut-eye, dumping his travel-stained clothes on the bedroom carpet.

Admitting that he was "not very good at just sitting around",[3] he would be shuttered away for hours in the music room, making sense of and extrapolating song fragments born on his travels. If distracted by household noise, he'd repair with guitar on back seat to Nashville and his office at Acuff-Rose. When these outstanding snippets out of the way, he might listen to how Roy Duane was progressing on guitar and, more recently, piano. When he'd had time, Roy had used examples from his own repertoire to show his son enough fretboard chords for the eight-year-old to stun his sire with a soprano rendering of 'Cryin'' as well as some precociously original compositions.

Freeze-framed in a backstage photograph with his parents and The Beatles, starstruck Roy Duane's ambition to follow in father's footsteps had been kindled further by the Beatlemania sweeping America. The four fellows who'd patted his head in Slough were omnipresent on TV. At the apogee of their large scale re-run of British beat delirium, they'd have five records in the US Top Ten – and Roy Duane's dad was their friend: "I talked with them on the phone and invited them to my home where they would be guaranteed no publicity but, in their own humorous way, they replied that they weren't interested if there was no publicity. Anyway, I hope to catch up with them when I'm next in England."[3] He did indeed when they arrived at his twenty-ninth birthday party in the basement of Quo Vadis restaurant in London's Soho, having been forced – as their host had been – to enter by the fire door to sidestep the fan bedlam that had hailed every limousine drawing up at the front entrance.

Dad could raise riots without their help too. The cornerstone of the Irish showbands that dominated that country's music scene rested on the pop end of country-and-western. This ranged from the sentiment of Jim Reeves to Frankie Laine's cowboy drama, punctuated with rockabilly and singalong evergreens by the likes of Ned Miller and Guy Mitchell. It was small wonder then that, having coalesced many of these preferences, Roy Orbison's six ballroom dates in the Emerald Isle in October 1963 – immediately after the attentive silences and considered ovations on the Brian Poole tour – roused undiscerning screams from frantic girls, deaf to warnings about rushing the stage to clutch at this four-eyed throwback to the fifties. Thrice, authority stopped the show as PA columns toppled and an astounded Orbison was mauled. Here at least, he was the kind of pop star you *did* mind your colleen liking.

For static Roy to induce such libidinous commotion, however rarely, hammered home to Claudette that time hanging heavy from one concert to the next wasn't only killed with hat contests and sauntering round museums. As *omerta* was to the Mafia, a tacit vow of silence concerning illicit sex persisted among troupes of roving minstrels. A strong motive for any red-blooded lad to become a pop singer was that, no matter what you looked like, you could still be popular with young ladies Look at spindly Freddie Garrity or Ringo with his nose. Look at Roy Orbison. It is distressing to report that some musicians used to take things a bit far and, well, consort with a certain type of female admirer: "scrubbers" they were called then.

Occasionally, fan letters less demure than the "Orbisonly yours" sort would not amuse Claudette as they sometimes did her husband. Fêted wherever he went, he may have had requests to meet girls in the romantic seclusion of a backstage prop cupboard but there is scant evidence to suggest that Roy was ever unfaithful to his wife. After figuring out what hour it would be in Tennessee, he would telephone her every day without fail from whatever region of the globe his work had taken him.

Of hard drugs, Orbison remained "uninformed. I was invited to an LSD party recently...I wasn't even tempted."[4] Among his few indulgences on tour were the old ones. During a two-day British stopover in 1964, he sat through two showings of Hollywood epic *The Fall Of The Roman Empire* a couple of hours after a vast sum had changed hands for a 1939 Mercedes-Benz 300 with a mahogany dashboard to be shipped back to Hendersonville.

For all his exemplary behaviour, Roy was no universal aunt. As long as they were punctual and efficient on the boards, he was tolerant – even sympathetic – towards the vices of backing musicians. However, he was drawn into the ensuing ribald mirth at his drummer's frustrated tilting for the downfall of Marianne Faithfull's knickers throughout an entire three-week tour.

If any of his boys were below par through no fault of their own, Orbison proved a considerate boss. Having plucked Barry Booth from the Sons Of The Piltdown Men, Roy's concern about a throat infection contracted by the Yorkshireman *en route* to a show in Dawson City on the Yukon was such that "he plonked me into a hospital in British Columbia. They did a date and I got some massive jabs and stayed overnight and they came back and picked me up."

The most hair-raising part of Booth's initiation into Orbison's service was when the non-arrival of a work permit meant that, "My first entering of the States was illegal. I had to secrete myself in a car boot – albeit a generous one – under a blanket." For the next three years, Barry would function on the road as Roy's keyboard player, musical director and confidant.

He would also introduce Orbison to the gastronomic raptures of Marylebone's Divan I Am, an Indian diner haunted by Booth when a Royal Academy of Music student. Later, a photograph of Barry and his distinguished guest would adorn the restaurant's menu card. An Indian dinner lasting hours was among newer diversions favoured by Roy at a time when most square meals served in Britain after ten-thirty at night were foreign. He was also sighted on more than one occasion feeding himself in the Italian trattoria in Soho which had replaced the fabled 2 I's coffee bar where the likes of Tommy Steele and Cliff Richard had been discovered. Picking at a Huddersfield snack bar dish without enthusiasm, he mused, "These boys in their early twenties, their digestion can take it. I'm conscious that I'm getting too much fried food."[5]

During that same March 1965 conversation, he mentioned that he'd been home only two months of the previous twelve, and that "This business takes years off your life and I know, even though I keep myself fit, that I'm going to have to slow down in the next year. I doubt whether I'll ever take a tour like this again."

A man so busy is apt to be an inattentive spouse. True enough, he'd undertaken this most recent and seemingly endless slog round the world to pay for the palatial spread in the pines of Old Hickory. Absent when Claudette's third labour began, he lamented, "Nashville is full of people like me. They don't often see home. When they do, they like to stay in it. There isn't much social life, except among the wives."[5] Appreciating too well what an ordeal of conviviality his job could be, Claudette was tolerant when her overworked man didn't want to go out much. Nonetheless, she hoped he might unwind a little, talk to her and enjoy their brief leisure with the new baby, christened Wesley.

Instead, keeping his odd hours, he'd insist he was "compelled" to compose as he disappeared to the music room or Acuff-Rose. Before midnight recording sessions, he liked "to see at least six hours of films before I begin. It freshens my mind. If there is nothing good on at the local cinemas, then I watch them on television. We have full-length colour films on Fridays, Saturdays and Sundays so I always try not to get booked on those nights."[6] To his tired wife, he didn't seem to be trying all that hard anymore. At times, he acted as though she was there only to provide refreshments and hand him packs of duty-free Gauloises while he frowned over contracts or scrawls of chords and words.

One of the house's interior designers had become Claudette's most frequent companions as she grew accustomed to life without Roy. Good-looking and amusing, this young bachelor would squire Mrs Orbison to the ski club, coffee mornings and stuffed-shirt suppers. Discontented as her "*cavaliere servante*" he quickly grew impatient of always meeting her in public. So far, she had resisted being alone with him.

Hunched over guitar and tape recorder with or without Bill Dees, or surrounded by papers and cigarette smoke, it scarcely occurred to Roy that there was a limit to wifely loyalty and affection. He'd provided her with everything she could possibly want, hadn't he? Neither of them were lusty teenagers in Odessa any longer but he still loved and respected the mother of his boys. Twenty-four-year-old Claudette's frank nature would not allow her to remain silent about her increasing disinclination to play Joan to Roy's Darby – but too soon would come his hand-squeezing departure for Nashville airport and another distant stage.

He'd been home on 25 June the previous summer when an English journalist rang with the intelligence that the follow-up to 'Borne On The Wind' had knocked former Cavern cloakroom attendant Cilla Black from the top of the charts. "At a time when British artists are all-powerful in their own country," began the measured reply, "I regard the attainment of Number One position in Britain as the high spot of my career."[2]

The premonitory 'It's Over' hinted that perhaps Roy was not unprepared for some confessional outburst from Claudette. Disarmingly described as "a ballad with a lush arrangement",[7] a strummed C major chord was the merest preamble to the bald utterance, "your baby doesn't love you anymore", and the snare drum rataplan that ignited an artistic statement that was the embodiment of Roy's oft-quoted remark about packing as much poetry and philosophy into a two-minute single as possible. Though counteracted by cunning details like off-guard bars of two-four and castanet clacks, 'It's Over' is almost bombastic in metaphor. However, Orbison in control advances on its falling stars, weeping rainbows and lonely sunsets with the grace of a fencing master, amid flurries of cinematic strings, murky horns and anguished wailing choral headwind. A suicide note set to music, it reaches boiling point as trees claw the moon. Then he slumps into a forlorn void before the next and final explosion. The bleak apotheosis of the 'Running Scared' tension-building blueprint, 'It's Over' – like its subject – stood alone.

From the apocryphal period between Melson and Dees, the musical climate of its B-side, 'Indian Wedding' had many precedents. Evoking images of tomahawk-wielding redskins dancing round a campfire in the approved fashion, its pulsating tom-tom beat had figured previously in Hank Williams' 'Kaw-Liga' – later recorded by Orbison – and, both from 1960, Johnny Preston's 'Running Bear' (composed by the Big Bopper) and Larry Verne's comical 'Mr Custer' (covered in Britain by Charlie Drake). In 'Indian Wedding', however, the matter-of-fact account of how the newly-wed Yellow Hand and White Sand were united in death was a glance back at the drowned 'Leah' who was also remembered in the high-pitched construction of Yellow Hand's "wedding song".

For this bit, rather than dual-track the harmony, Roy had been joined at the microphone by Bill Dees. So interchangeable were their voices that the co-writer actually took the lead in the chorus of 'Ye Te Amo Maria', a gauche love refrain which rode on the back of 'Oh! Pretty Woman' which, four months after 'It's Over', was the only Orbison record to top the charts both in Britain and at home.

'It's Over' had been predominantly Roy's baby but it was with 'Oh! Pretty Woman' that Bill Dees came into his own: "We'd just begun about six in the evening," Roy recalled. "What you do is play anything that comes to mind, and my wife wanted to go to town to get something. I said, 'Do you have any money?' And Bill Dees said, 'Pretty woman never needs any money.' He said, 'Would that make a great song title?' I said, 'No, but "Pretty woman" would.' So I started playing the guitar and he was slapping the table for drums. That was the conception and by the time she got back – which was about forty minutes – we had the song."[8]

Subjected to Fred Foster's quality control, the pay-off line – "she's gone and walked away from me/but there's other fish in the sea" – was thought "too negative". Revised, the shameless vision of loveliness parading past lonesome ol' Roy not only proffers him a second glance but – good grief! – also slinks seductively in his direction. Maybe disillusions will result – she's his long-lost sister or a transvestite – but, for one incredible moment, our wishful hero is ahead when the number ends. Not only just as in 'Running Scared' or to his cost in the arms of corrupt Gigolette, he's actually picking up a bird with no strings attached.

There were twinges of desperation in the doleful "middle eight" section – Bill's idea – and the teasing coda, but the re-entry of Jerry Kennedy's swaggering eight-note guitar riff revived Roy's confidence. It improved his bank balance too by outselling all his other records. The unseating of 'Oh! Pretty Woman' from the top, however, precipitated a restless farewell from the charts. As 'Only The Lonely' had bid him welcome in 1960, 'Penny Arcade' – with almost mathematical symmetry – would wave him out of sight in the dying weeks of 1969.

Only teetering on the edge of the Top Thirty in Britain and doing even worse in America, 'Penny Arcade' would see Roy off with a chart-topping bang in Australia. That most of his singles in the later sixties scaled the Australasian Top Twenty with ease while struggling elsewhere may be ascribed to the lasting impact of his tour of the continent in January 1965. He'd been second-billed to the resounding violence of The Rolling Stones of whom an Illinois newspaper had just written, "You walk out of the amphitheatre after watching The Rolling Stones perform, and suddenly the Chicago stockyards smell good and clean by comparison." Derided so by adults as Presley had been, naturally they were as rabidly worshipped by the young.

In the teeth of his toughest test to date, Orbison recreated much the same tumult as he had upon preceding The Beatles in 1963. Following his act nearly two years later in God's Own Country, Mick Jagger – outrageous and frenzied – was still able to whip up the screeching rabble but the reaction would be more subdued sometimes than he had come to expect. Towards the last night in New Zealand, a half-serious Jagger "proposed that I sing the worst record that I'd ever made, and I said that I'd be happy to if he did the worst record he'd ever made. So I went on and I figured that 'Ooby Dooby' was the worst...so I sang it. Then they went on and I watched the performance but they didn't do their worst record...but there was a little gathering afterwards and, in lieu of their not doing their worst record, they gave me a silver cigarette case. 'From The Rolling Stones to Ooby Dooby,' it's inscribed."[8]

More constructively, Jagger and his songwriting confrere, Keith Richards, had logged the snare-hi-hat bash that spurred the guitar *ostinato* as 'Oh! Pretty Woman' unfolded. Combining the same percussive unison and an eight-note riff would be the epoch-making '(I Can't Get No) Satisfaction' that the group recorded in Los Angeles that May.

Via the Far East, Orbison plunged next into a headlining British tour, having supplemented his six-piece band with a native flautist and female vocal trio, The Three Quarters. Purposely untroubled by usurpers of the Beatles-Brian Poole persuasion, there were, nonetheless, some very competent vocalists in support. Leader of The Rebel Rousers, Cliff Bennett of West Drayton could tackle updated American rhythm-and-blues without departing far from its over-riding passion. Like him, the next band on – Birmingham's Rockin' Berries – were bathing in the afterglow of a solitary hit. Though it was sugared with conscious comedy, the Berries closed their act with their cover of The Tokens' 'He's In Town'. This throbbing sob-story in the 'Running Scared' mould was sung almost entirely in pleading Orbison-esque counter-tenor by rhythm guitarist Geoff Turton.

Unperturbed by pretenders, Roy as usual gave 'em nothing that hadn't made the charts for him – including the latest entry, 'Goodnight', and the postponed 'Pretty Paper' – which had restored him to the Top Ten as Britain slept off 1964's Christmas dinner. Because he was the undisputed star this time round, *de rigueur* screaming mayhem was unloosed as each smash hit cadenced – especially when he let out the lecherous gurgling growl that, previewed in 'Mean Woman Blues', had been resurrected for 'Oh!

Pretty Woman' to become as anticipated a vocal gimmick as Frank Ifield's burdensome yodel.

More a household name than the others, Orbison would be recognised across a wayside eaterie's formica table whenever the tour's fifty-seven seater took a break. Pestered for autographs, he'd sign and smile for the most irruptive fan. Back on the coach, Cliff Bennett noticed that, "Roy played poker at every opportunity." Stakes of up to a fiver curbed the participation of all but the most expert gamblers in days when a ten bob note (fifty pence) was thought an adequate consolation prize in a television quiz. It surely restrained the less than immortal Untamed who, glad to open the show with ten minutes of R&B, were never certain that they'd sleep in proper beds that night. Some of Roy's American musicians – announced as "The Candy Men" – were placed in similar doubt when their poker-faced employer pulled the old Scottish passport lark on them.

Though they too joined in the fun, everybody close to Roy Orbison knew that an uneasy press wouldn't keep quiet for long. During the hiatus between the final date of the tour and facing the TV cameras on 7 March for his three-song part in *Sunday Night At The London Palladium*, Roy – uncharacteristically extrovert no more – confirmed rumours that he and his wife, once considered to be ideally matched, had parted: "Very few people were in on it. Divorce is something you don't rush out and shout to everyone."[9]

The decree nisi had been accorded to Mr Orbison in Tennessee on the all-embracing grounds of "cruelty". Undeniably, it had hurt when – before Claudette could tell him herself – a "friend" spilt the beans about her and the interior designer. What had been a light-hearted flirtation on Mrs Orbison's side had taken a dangerous turn. Roy was incredulous but did not erupt with anger. Gently, he implored his wife to help him grasp what it all meant. Thinking aloud with the same questions coming up again and again, he seemed to be groping for some reason that would explain and excuse her conduct. He was still searching when he drove off with his pride smarting to another faraway soundcheck, leaving Claudette wondering whether divorce would mean her losing the house.

A less personal estrangement would take place later that turbulent year as the expiry date for the Monument contract loomed nearer. After meeting with representatives from every major record label and rubbing his chin over their bids for Orbison – hot property then – Wesley Rose coolly informed Fred Foster that to even qualify to re-sign Roy, "I would have to guarantee him a million dollars – which had never been done for an American pop artist at the time; that I'd have to guarantee a minimum of twenty prime time TV appearances, and also offer him a movie contract. I told him I didn't have a movie studio and that, as far as television appearances were concerned, after all these hits, Wesley would have no problems getting them himself. None of this went down too well."

Rose was more unhappy about executive washroom whisperings concerning Monument's financial difficulties – though the company would survive into the seventies. Next there was a dubious criticism that Foster wasn't recording enough Acuff-Rose material. To add injury to insult, Wesley Rose was now occupying the central chair behind the console. As he'd done when The Everly Brothers reached their optimum moment in the charts, Rose took over as *de facto* producer when 'It's Over' on the way down from the top collided with 'Oh! Pretty Woman' on its way up. While Rose directed operations on '(Say) You're My Girl' – his client's first serious flop since 1962 – Fred Foster bit his tongue and left quietly.

The more tidy-minded would attribute Roy's fall from the charts to this *coup d'etat* but, although world sales for 'Goodnight' had been respectable enough, it was a real comedown when compared to even 'Pretty Paper', never mind 'Oh! Pretty Woman' – Orbison's final million-selling single. Against the maelstrom that was 'It's Over', 'Goodnight' seemed pallid despite a plangent finale. However, in its singer's longing for his untrue woman, it – and, less so, its flip side, 'Only With You' – can only be heard today as a snatch of autobiography. It lends credence to a remark about "hopes for a reconciliation" by Roy to his father minutes before marching from the London Palladium's star dressing room to emote 'Goodnight', 'Cryin'' and 'In Dreams'.

There seemed little hope of kissing and making up in the remaining months of 1965 when, taking the children, Claudette –

insisting that, "I never really wanted to leave him"[10] – went home to mother in Houston. Meanwhile, her ex-husband resumed his disturbed sales campaign with renewed urgency as the slight '(Say) You're My Girl' was given a rough time in the summer charts. It was, nonetheless, a courageous – or foolish-release. Sniffing round his best mate's former girlfriend to a samba shuffle, Roy takes a breather during a plink-plonk piano solo before cutting in for the cha-cha-cha ending.

Perhaps the new deal with Metro-Goldwyn-Mayer would bring an improvement. Not only was it worth a reputed £800,000 but the best fringe benefit was the promise to make Roy a film star as Paramount had Elvis. In 1964, Orbison had expressed interest in composing soundtracks and – as far-fetched afterthought – directing. After all, he was quite a film buff. During the Beatles tour, he'd spoken with quiet pride of "going to three different cinemas in a day and [seeing] more than a dozen films since I came to England. I think *Fifty-Five Days In Peking* impressed me most."[6] His liking for this allegorical retelling of the Boxer Rebellion showed an intelligent rather than intellectual passion for the cinema that was not extended to its *avant-garde* extremes.

On the look-out for an acting opportunity in 1965, "I was offered only singing spots in movies but, through going along, building contacts and getting to know people in the business, I got what I wanted in the end."[11] A script for a moral-studded western in which the male lead was a spy for the South in the Civil War was found; shooting to commence as soon as a sufficient gap appeared in Orbison's taxing schedule. How about September 1966?

For a start, films were incidental to his main purpose. Also, MGM had him down for forty songs per year, and he'd have to unload some of them on a new album before 1965 was out. Theoretically, the new company allowed greater artistic freedom and promotional budgets that would result, hopefully, in rapid sales animation. Trade figures already signified that, though forty-fives were still going strong, there was a burgeoning market for albums these days – ones that didn't give short weight as had the throwaway *Orbisongs*, a Monument patchwork of A-sides, B-sides and tracks arbitrarily extracted from earlier LP.s. Issued to squeeze revenue from 'Oh! Pretty Woman', it and its kind were cheapskate anachronisms now that The Beatles with their *Help!* soundtrack, Bob Dylan's *Bringing It All Back Home* and even *Session With The Dave Clark Five* – all containing no time-consuming musical bilge – were each showing that the age of codswallop long-players built round a hit single were numbered.

In this respect, 1965's *There Is Only One Roy Orbison* was his first true album as a worthy product in its own right. Approaching thirty and in no position to take hits for granted, this new horizon seemed to be superficially a contingency plan for Roy to make headway as a "quality" entertainer. Excuses offered for singles by Tony Bennett, Al Martino and their syrupy sort being in the bargain bin was that they were "too good for the charts", a plea conveniently forgotten when, in 1966, Frank Sinatra was suddenly at Number One with the schmaltzy 'Strangers In The Night'.

Despite the lilting cocktail piano, a noticeable shying away from falsettos and growls, and the selection of Bob Montgomery's semi-standard 'Big As I Can Dream', *There Is Only One Roy Orbison* was no *Songs For Swinging Lovers*. However, apart from the jarring 'Sugar And Honey', it was a bedsit rather than a dancing album. More cohesive than, say, 'Lonely And Blue' or the cash-in *Orbisongs*, a crisper sound also marked the defection to MGM's more advanced studio facilities. "Overdub" and "drop-in" pocked the jargon of head engineer Val Valentin as Roy sang on a separate and retractable track to an accompaniment which could now, if required, feature the Orbison guitar.

The hero of the hour, however, was Bill Dees who, either alone or with Roy, composed the only five new songs in a programme of twelve. There'd been much delving into the Orbison-Melson file for items given originally to other artists as 'I'm In A Blue, Blue Mood' was to Bob Luman – as well as recourse to non-originals like Chet Atkins' 'Afraid To Sleep'. Such backsliding tended to occur when Orbison "was unhappy or discontented and I couldn't eat, I couldn't sleep, I couldn't communicate, and I certainly couldn't write a song."[12]

This writer's block did not prevent more than a little soul-baring to infiltrate *There Is Only One Roy Orbison*. Most blatant was a punchy 'Claudette' with Roy spitting out every word. More subliminal were interpretations of 'Two Of A Kind' – from Bob Montgomery and Earl Sinks' Clovis backlog – and Melson's 'If You Can't Say Something Nice' – presumably about Claudette.

On the back cover, Orbison was pictured astride one of the three motor-bikes that once had been his and Claudette's to ride together. Now he rode alone like the freewheeler in the album's promotional single, 'Ride Away'. Indifferent rather than celebratory of his bitter freedom, he zooms into a prairie sunset soaked in violins Though couched in romantic allusion, the lone rider – not surprisingly – is looking for a bit of frivolity. There were plenty of pretty girls after a bit of frivolity too.

Possibly because the brake had been applied to the old monumental operatics, 'Ride Away' furthered the wane of Roy's hit parade fortunes. It really might have been "too good for the charts".

Fred Foster did not share this opinion: "There's an old saying over here – 'Don't disturb a winning combination' – and he and I obviously were a winning combination, and I think while getting adjusted to a new producer or producers, his writing suffered. Whether or not it was because he was then the possessor of the biggest contract ever given an American artist at the time and he lost his incentive, I don't know. I don't think he even knew what happened but he started doing things that, to my mind, weren't prudent things to do to build his career."

The next item to be cast adrift on the vinyl oceans, 'Crawling Back', bolstered this supposition in an industry where sales graphs are arbiters of success. It coasted to the brink of Britain's Top Twenty but, where it counted, 'Crawling Back' only dithered for seven weeks around the middle of the Hot 100. An outline of some poor, uncomplaining fool always coming back for more tranquil abuse of his solemn infatuation, it was a perfectly reasonable song of its kind but the comparative failure of 'Crawling Back' was due to too much subtlety. Acoustic arpeggios had replaced the cruder Gibson "drang"; instead of sawing bows was *legato* fairy dust. The half-crazed howler of 'It's Over' was now beseeching his insensitive bitch with a box of chocolates.

This soft-sell attitude coloured much of the album from which

'Crawling Back' and the even less profitable 'Breakin' Up Is Hard To Do' were lifted. Co-author with Dees of most of *The Orbison Way*, Roy's increased creative input: intimated a more cheerful frame of mind. There were only three subjects, in Orbison's sweeping estimation, worth writing about: "boy-girl relationships, fellow man and a relationship with God. All the rest anyone writes about means nothing."[13] *The Orbison Way* concentrated exclusively on the first, apart from Dees' 'This Is My Land' which probed beyond lovey-dovey tribulations to a lost Texas on which an oil well had yet to be dug. A lesser utopia, 'Time Changed Everything' had a traveller returning to one still constant. Elsewhere there were more complex explorations. With expansive flamenco strings, 'The Loner' tackles a girl's illicit meetings with a town ne'er-do-well while a minute shift of scansion in its bridge fractures the emotive intent of Barry Booth's deliberative 'It Wasn't Very Long Ago'.

As its sleeve notes spell out, nothing on *The Orbison Way* was alien to "emotions any listener has experienced and can understand" but fans would still decipher lyrics like 'Breakin' Up Is Hard To Do' and the sardonic 'It Ain't No Big Thing' as a commentary on their idol's private life – which was still unsettled. Like most divorced fathers, his access to the children brought him in contact with their mother. No matter how much Roy may have feigned aloofness to retain composure, he stayed in the picture about Claudette's welfare. Covertly he noted how she had lost her vivacity as, on the verge of tears, she would postpone the last moment of each farewell. Come the New Year, he'd be back in Europe, so he told her – but he'd write.

After a trip to Scandinavia, he'd be engulfed in another UK tour by spring. Because of his reduced chart circumstances, there was again a danger of his being eclipsed by a support act. Omnipresent in Britain then were The Walker Brothers: three unrelated Americans who had become pin-ups in girls' magazines, filling the spaces left by The Byrds, another US act of like fascination. Booked for the Orbison tour, "Brother" John Maus's, assertion that "being on a bill with him has brought fantastic luck to other artists"[14] was acknowledged when, mid-tour, his group's fifth single, 'The Sun Ain't Gonna Shine Anymore', started a four-week reign at Number

One. Moreover, Maus's fellow long-haired heart-throb, Scott Engel, had the range, projection and impeccable control of a coltish Sinatra – and an Orbison too for that matter. Not only was he another proverbial "pop singer who can really sing" but his also was an aura – real or imagined – of one who has known sadness.

On opening night at Finsbury Park Astoria on 25 March, the battle of the billing seemed a foregone conclusion as, smothered in screaming hysteria, the Brothers' energetic gyrations were impeded when manhandling fans broke the barricade of shirt-sleeved security manning the front of stage. After this display, Roy risked a dismissal as archaic – particularly with his latest record nowhere near the Top Twenty. Collected and professional, this elder statesman of pop went the distance with his old favourites exacting their habitual sweet surrender to justify his closing the show.

It would be "a tour I remember more than any other".[15] At the Walthamstow Granada on Easter Monday, the curtains would divide on a seated Orbison with his left foot in plaster. No more lumbered with a worried wife to deter him, he'd been competing in celebrity motor-cycle scrambles since the previous autumn. Surprise gave way to delight, therefore, when to his Westbury Hotel suite was delivered an invitation to a meet at Hawkstone Park near Shrewsbury.

Three hours before the first race, a loophole in Roy's £250,000 insurance policy was brought to his attention. It stipulated that he wasn't to take part in any scramble if it was windy. With a gale lashing the racecourse, Orbison in belted overcoat resigned himself to glumly flagging in the winners. By mid-afternoon, however, the droning excitement overcame him and he begged champion rider Dave Bickers to lend him his 250cc Czechoslovakian machine for a lap of honour. To be identified more easily beneath the peaked helmet, the foolhardy pop singer did not remove his otherwise unnecessary sunglasses. Two hundred yards after kick-starting, the bike skidded off the track, throwing him onto the grimy grass. In front of 15,000 pop-eyed spectators, Roy gamely remounted. Back in the paddock, a mob clamoured for autographs. Among them were leather-clad Rockers whose greasy steeds roared with fiercer menace than the hated Mods' phutting Lambrettas. A precursor to 'Born To Be Wild', Roy's 'Ride Away' was a fixture on juke boxes in cafes frequented by Rocker gangs.

Escorted from the Hawkstone Park maidan by a cavalcade of mounted Rockers, nothing seemed amiss until Roy's Rolls Royce glided into East London as street lamps flickered. In Thorpe Coombe General Hospital near the Granada, a duty doctor in casualty treated the broken ankle. In Orbison's hearing an hour later, a theatre lighting technician muttered, "He doesn't have to sing with his foot, does he?" A stool was provided and, at showtime, a wincing Roy with knuckles whitened round the neck of his Gibson began a 'Running Scared' that pain honed to razor-sharp poignancy.

Of course, the more trivial tabloids latched onto the "irony" of his current single being titled 'Twinkle Toes', but this unlooked-for publicity wasn't sufficient to elongate its chart life of one month. A discotheque floor-filler with manufactured "party" ambience and trendy fuzz-toned 'Satisfaction' guitar as its irritant factors, feverish 'Twinkle Toes' was "about a dancing girl pretending to be happy and gay but I think she's lonely and covering up".[16] The notion first came to him, apparently, while watching a line of choreographed chorus girls at the Palladium on the Sunday he announced his reluctant divorce.

Now a year past that strange day, news of his injury reached Claudette in Houston, seven hours behind Greenwich mean time. Before nightfall, she had boarded a flight to England. Knowing Roy to have performed with a streaming cold, she was concerned that his insistence that the show must go on would not let the bones heal, and irreversible complications would set in. He could be an obstinate so-and-so. With old affections flooding her heart, it had also crossed Claudette's distressed mind that she might win her husband back.

From Walthamstow, the host had descended on Chester for a recital in an 800-capacity cinema. That Tuesday, it was in a hotel on the city's outskirts that Claudette caught up with Roy. Muzzy with pain-killers, he rose laboriously on crutches to embrace a pretty little pet with travel-tousled hair and rings under her eyes "then we both suddenly realised we didn't want to be apart – and that was it. It was wonderful to see Claudette again."[10]

After the tour wound down, the cast re-assembled in Soho's La

Dolce Vita restaurant on St George's Day to witness Roy slicing a guitar-shaped thirtieth birthday cake. A further cause for celebration was that Claudette and Roy – too late to cancel the decree absolute – had resolved to re-marry as soon as it could be arranged. The ceremony back in America would be as discreet as the divorce: "It was all a hush-hush affair. Only the essential witnesses were there."[17]

The best man was Bill Dees who continued to work on songs for the film – now with the working title *The Fastest Guitar Alive* – while the lovebirds took themselves off on a second honeymoon in Florida. Though they'd lost the knack of writing smash hits, Bill and Roy were as prolific as the Orbison-Melson team had been. On the latest LP, *The Classic Roy Orbison*, the only non-original was a drum-heavy rendition of 'Never Love Again' by popped-up cajun brothers, Rusty and Doug Kershaw. A more pronounced emphasis on percussion further instanced a new lyrical aggression that hardened the general climate of the album. Yes, there was a quota of old style string-laden love ballads – 'Where Is Tomorrow', 'Losing You', 'Going Back To Gloria' – and 'Growing Up' had a pretty-but-nothing bounce. Nevertheless, some of the faithful may have been alienated by clangorous attempts to address contemporary issues – as in the rushing agitation of 'City Life' and, devoid of melody, 'Pantomime'. A cynical but hedonistic Orbison reared up, shedding "electric sunshine" on "concrete sidewalks". Away from urban revelry, he'd come on like Pat Boone in 'Growing Up' and 'You'll Never Be Sixteen Again' – both Dutch uncle paeons to adolescent insecurity. Because you weren't sure how you were meant to take it, more fascinating was the whimsical quasi-rockabilly of '(No) I'll Never Get Over You' which namechecked 'Mary Lou', 'Peggy Sue' and 'Suzie Q' in its ineligible seraglio. However, this paled alongside 'Just Another Name For Rock And Roll', a similar litany which ran a gauntlet of US-only phenomena like the 'Mashed Potato' and 'Ubangi Stomp' in the same breath as the 'Hippy Hippy Shake' and 'Twist And Shout'. Three years out of date, it was a sort of "Orbison Goes Merseybeat" outing.

They had their moments as composers but nobody expected Roy and Bill to be the next Lennon and McCartney. In its pooling of so many accessories of mid-sixties pop, the neatest conclusion would be that *The Classic Roy Orbison* wasn't so much "classic" as typical of prevalent cultural conditions. Yet, weighing its *faux pas* against some startling breaks with the past, this last album of 1966 revealed an artist in uncertain transition, and is worth a listen for that reason alone.

On the domestic front, however, much of the old routine had been re-established. As if nothing had happened, he'd make time to accompany Claudette to the ski club while she'd be hand-in-hand with him at the annual country festival in Nashville. As he'd done in the poor-but-happy era before 'Only The Lonely', he'd traipse behind her with the trolley in the supermarket. With a relief that he did not articulate, Roy had cut down on work – though, with Claudette as prompt, he was trying to memorise his lines for *The Fastest Guitar Alive*. During the few weeks left to them, the Orbisons were savouring just being together again.

After sorting out a sitter for the children, Claudette and Roy were both packing for a June weekend at the National Drag Races held near Bristol, a resort 200 miles away on the Virginia border. With another couple, they travelled as befitted the occasion – Roy on his gleaming 120-mph Harley Davidson; Claudette on a slower BMW. Thundering homewards on 7 June, dusk found the four riders slowing down to pass through Gallantin, a small town only a few miles north-east of Old Hickory. A thirty-year-old truck driver named Kenneth Herald – later charged with involuntary manslaughter – pulled out from a side turning. With a braking scream, Claudette Orbison on her BMW vanished beneath the articulated lorry's double wheels. Then she writhed in the main street dirt, her life puddling out of her as her husband's eyes bulged with helpless horror.

In the hospital an hour later, she was pronounced dead "and then it was left to me to tell our three boys. I explained to Roy Duane and he seemed to understand."[18] The eldest son would be permitted to attend the interment at Nashville's Woodlawn Cemetery.

So ended the first act of the tragedy. Myth would paint the cruel release of Claudette's spirit in the bright pre-Raphaelite sentiment of a "death disc": with his crash helmet on the tarmac beside him, a kneeling Roy in stage gear and thoughtful expression cannot prevent one crystal tear from falling on the unblemished face of Claudette cradled in his lap. She gazes up at him with calm quietude, as beautiful in death as she'd been in life.

CHAPTER SEVEN

Cry Softly, Lonely One

Nothing would ever be the same again – not even the past. Now so many of his old songs – 'Only The lonely', 'Leah', you name 'em – would imply portent for the most casual Orbison listener. In microcosm, this ghoulish search for profundities in lines like, from 'Borne On The Wind': "Between the sunset and the dawn/so tenderly/your memory/lingers with me all night long", anticipated the idolatry that was already elevating pop from ephemera to Holy Writ. Soon it would pass hastily through its classical period before what Roy Orbison would call "the crazy late sixties; not 1966-7 but after that when it got real weird – politics, music, fashion. Everything went crazy, sort of."[1] Crazy was the man whose obsessional analysis of Bob Dylan's lyrics was such that, in order to prove one pet theory, he placed a "wanted" advertisement in a New York underground magazine for a Dylan urine sample.

At the dawn of this Age of Aquarius, one of pop's eternal verities still held water. From Buddy Holly's Number One in 1959 to John Lennon's with 'Starting Over' in 1980, it was accepted that a death in pop tended to sell records. In the week following his wife's burial, Roy's latest single jumped from Thirty-Six to Eighteen in the British charts; his biggest hit for more than a year. That it was hoary old 'Lana', hauled from the vaults by Fred Foster, didn't matter. With all the publicity generated by the Orbison tragedy, it couldn't miss.

Within a fortnight, the widower faced the press. "That really is wonderful news – especially now," he replied to a London journalist's tidings about 'Lana'. Yes, he was keen to get to grips with *The Fastest Guitar Alive* next month. "In fact," he continued, "I aim to do a whole heap of work for the next few months. It'll help." Too polite to change the subject, he answered that, no, he hadn't been put off motorbikes because, "People have accidents in automobiles, in aeroplanes, just as much...at least, I'd like to feel this way about it. I don't know yet that I really do. My thinking just isn't connected at the moment. I think it's a bit early to say how I feel."[2]

Is that a cue for a song, Roy? Hot on the heels of Monument, you see, MGM had nipped in with a new forty-five infinitely more tear-jerking and profitable than 'Lana'. Leading off with Chopin-esque piano arpeggios and the sentence, "It's too soon to know if I can forget her", this despondent *lied* was a heaven-sent means whereby Orbison could be propelled into the public eye again after a perturbing chain of flops. The company had, after all, practically gone into hock to sign him.

While his handlers, past and present, derived what gain they could from the situation, the frailer human too grappled for sustenance. The black melancholy which now held him tight in its grip reduced to caricature that in which he had veiled most of his hits. It penetrated his worn-out slumber with shards of memory and disjointed thought: in dreams, I walk with you; in dreams, I talk to you...So often they were of trivialities – the canteen queue at college, a drizzling car park, dumb anguish in Houston, in her biker leathers at Bristol. Jerked from sleep, dawn seemed a year away when ghastly knowledge replaced the balm of ignorance: "Memories like falling leaves just fill the air."

Crowding in yet shrinking back when he tried to touch them, he'd snatch up the telephone before phantoms of his eddying imagination threatened to engulf him. Among sympathetic ears at his behest were those of Fred Foster whose childhood had ended with his father's sudden death, and, when home in Memphis, Jerry Lee Lewis whose son had drowned.

Next door to Roy lived another insomniac. Fresh from a failed marriage, Johnny Cash was a booker's risk with a police record for drug-related offences. The latest one was a thirty-day suspended sentence in January for possession. Once nearly a goner through overdosing, it hadn't been novel for Cash to come down from amphetamines in a cell, unable to recall fully the circumstances that had led him there.

Unalike temperamentally, Johnny of extreme behavioural strategy and mild-mannered Roy became intimates, as each confronted and mastered his own chaos. Johnny whose mouth had once marinated the air with swearing was now, through the love of a good woman, ripe for religion.

Already a practising Christian, Bill Dees – a pallbearer at the funeral – had been another on hand day or night when Roy in limbo needed to talk. Although his colleague did not attend church as regularly, Dees gathered from these and discussions in happier contexts that Orbison, true to his background, "Didn't just believe in God; he had a personal relationship with him." Though he would never demean himself with albums of musical Bible-bashing as Elvis did, many of Roy's songs – alone or with a co-writer – were as devotional in their boy-girl way as hymns.

In autumn 1966, however, as always happened in the dark hours of his life, nothing would come. Almost eagerly, he'd sit down to compose with Bill but, after strumming a while, all the bits of song would sound the same to him, just infantile vibrations dangling and fading away. Glazed languor would set in and he'd drift off to the lake, the television, the refrigerator, anywhere but to the job in hand. Bill said nothing. Roy would get over it. He always would.

Already written, the soundtrack album for *The Fastest Guitar Alive* would have to tie-in with its premiere. Therefore, to both satisfy MGM and provide occupational therapy, Orbison plunged into a project that, when suggested to Fred Foster, had been shrugged off as "an exercise in futility". MGM, thinking otherwise, were most enthusiastic about a twelve-track Orbison album of songs by Don Gibson. That any product at all could be levied from the bereaved star was enough.

As a taster, 'Too Soon To Know' had come within an ace of topping the UK chart – though only hovering round the middle of the Hot 100. Produced by Jim Vienneau, *Roy Orbison Sings Don Gibson* did not re-invent its raw material anywhere near as much as New York's Vanilla Fudge who would grab The Supremes' 'You Keep Me Hangin' On' by the scruff of the neck and wring the life out of it a few months later. Much of Roy's most public declaration of his artistic debt to Gibson adhered unambitiously to the original arrangements. Opening side one, for instance, 'I'd Be A Legend In My Time' was pleasant enough but listless against a Frank Ifield version, not to say Ray Charles' gravely overhaul also from 1963. Most of the LP's most inspired brush-strokes occurred when unusual instruments were brought into faster items such as the balalaika in 'What About Me' or when the bass part is assumed by a kazoo in 'Lonesome Number One'. In fairness, while *Roy Orbison Sings Don Gibson* is less than spectacular, it added up for Orbison – with his sojourn in the US charts all but spent – to give his still potent overseas markets songs by a composer of whom the majority had never heard. It was all new to them.

His moods had fluctuated but, as the Gibson sessions had progressed, so had Roy contributed more to their outcome rather than simply singing along to Vienneau's ideas. Day by day, he was coming to accept the loss: "Teach your heart to smile/and live a little while in memories." As happened so often in his life, the balance was redressed quickly: "I had reasoned it out that if you take all that is good in life, you must accept tragedy if it comes along."[3] He wasn't the only single parent in the world. His elderly but supportive parents had taken charge of the children splendidly, even uprooting from Texas to install themselves in a house in Hendersonville in order that their famous son could "get on with all the work I had to do. I wanted to be able to remove myself and look at what had happened objectively before I retired, before I quit, before I dropped out or became convinced that life was not worth living. I just turned away."[3]

Looming largest on the agenda was *The Fastest Guitar Alive* whose script had been re-written in a more light-hearted vein as specified by its producer, Sam Katzman. A Donald McGill among film-makers, Katzman had had no highbrow pretensions either about adapting legion Elvis Presley excursions, bearing out Roy Orbison's opinion that, "Once I started seeing his movies other than *King Creole* and *Jailhouse Rock*, I thought they were mistakes."[4] By the mid-sixties, Katzman could dash off an Elvis vehicle in less than a month; each one a quasi-musical of cheery unreality usually more vacuous and streamlined than the one before.

Shortly after the cameras rolled, Roy scented that *The Fastest Guitar Alive* wasn't a taut espionage drama any more. In lieu of their nervous leading man's economic acting ability, Katzman and his director, Michael Moore, had had the story re-modelled as a "rollicking western comedy-drama in which all kinds of hot and hilarious adventures ensue".[5] At MGM's insistence, a last minute cameo had been written for a Domingo Samudio who as "Sam the Sham" was picking the bones from 'Wooly Bully', a gloriously dim world-wide smash from 1965. MGM thought he needed the exposure. As Samudio was a Texan-Mexican, surely Katzman could fit him in somewhere.

Another hurdle jumped was that of Orbison's mousy countenance. Thanks to a daily cosmetic miracle, Roy would walk onto the set as Johnny Banner, Confederate officer. In contact lenses, processed hair and beautified almost beyond recognition by an hour of make-up, he was every inch if not a film idol, then a gigolo. As if auditioning for The Merseybeats or Los Paraguayos, he posed for a syndicated publicity shot in a bat-winged blouse like whipped cream. Seated, he held an acoustic guitar in mid-thrum.

This was no ordinary six-string – more a six-shooter. As a *boulevardier's* walking cane could convert conveniently into a duelling rapier, so Johnny Banner's guitar would, at high speed, become a rifle to fight off marauding Indians – a frequent obligation throughout the film. "Based on actual historical fact,"[5] Banner and his comic sidekick, Steve – played by Presley regular, Sammy Jackson – with the blessing of their superiors, rob the US mint in San Francisco to finance the beleaguered Rebel forces. Fleeing with the resulting wagonload of gold bullion – to the' tune of 'Heading South' – they learn halfway to army headquarters in El Paso of Robert E Lee's surrender at Appomattox courthouse in April 1865. Thereby downgraded from soldiers under orders to common crooks, the honourable Johnny and Steve elect to return this prize of war. To this end, they are hampered by bandits, pistoleros and other dastards casting covetous eyes on the loot. However, it would have been an odd Katzman pot-boiler if Banner and his Tonto hadn't cleared their good names in the nick of time.

If apparently capable of "rattling strings like a Gatling gun", Banner ignites no nimble fretwork fireworks but instead integrates his picking supinely to the general good of the film's musical interludes. The essentially rigid strictures of the plot would bring forth a soundtrack album that was seen as either an aberration or a refreshing change from a stylistic diet unbroken since 1960. From a time when he could smile, Roy seemed to have had fun recording it. Traces of earlier Orbisonia in some pieces – most markedly 'Borne On The Wind' in 'Whirlwind' – left a peculiar aftertaste and, as expected, its cover portrait of a gunslinger mowing down a pursuing horde of whooping savages was an accurate guide to content. It encompassed tunes generous1y elongated and lyrics pertinent to imagined visual scenarios as epitomised by 'Good Time Party' with its gambolling clavichord and bandstand brass, and the home-spun philosophising of 'Best friend': "a diamond is a diamond, a stone is a stone but a man's not all good or all bad." In one number, from merely adopting a slight lisp, Roy actually breaks into Spanish for a couple of verses prior to a pistolero's incarceration "six feet underground".

The title song, according to the actor-composer was "supposed to describe my way of life but I had a problem living up to that" while 'Rollin' On' was written "because I had to tell these girls we had to leave with the gold, and I guessed the only way to get out was to sing a song."[6] From the cantering of 'Pistolero' to the shivering strings of 'Whirlwind' to the lazy saddle-tramp trot of 'River', it was almost the sound at any given. moment that mattered rather than separate pieces. Like any semi-incidental music, little was designed to divert attention from the action. Nonetheless, the enduring influence of *The Fastest Guitar Alive* was most keenly felt by England's Dave Dee, Dozy, Beaky, Mick And Tich who seemed to have borrowed from it for 'The Legend Of Xanadu' – all bullwhips and ruined haciendas – which, in 1968, became their only UK Number One.

Citizen Kane it wasn't but critics were kind to Roy when the film went on general release. Their quills blunted in sympathy perhaps, the general verdict was that, as a thespian, Orbison had coped quite well with, admittedly, an undemanding role. If not a natural actor like Presley, he'd put up a better show than Ricky Nelson, Dave Clark and other pop stars who, over the years, had fancied themselves as cinema attractions. Obviously Roy's aeons at the drive-in gawping at Hollywood hadn't been wasted.

It was noted by some that Johnny Banner's clinches with his female lead, Maggie Pierce, had been shot in non-committal shadow; Roy's ingrained Pat Boone prudity detracting him from lingering embraces with a married woman, no matter how above board the situation. Though one wasn't in evidence when he attended the film's New York premiere on 15 January, 1967, there were whispers of a lady friend. A few weeks later, the paparazzi named Francine Herack, a twenty-three-year old air hostess from Los Angeles as the "new pretty woman in Roy's lonely life". Even so, there was no inkling of any impropriety, other than whatever sleazy mileage was inherent in Orbison's forlorn hope that busy Miss Herack might visit him on tour: "But it looks as though it is impossible – so we're thinking of spending a holiday in Jamaica instead when we can really get to know more about one another."[7] After a moment's pause over the typewriter keys, some hacks then implied similarities between Francine and the late Mrs Orbison. This new bird, she's American – and a brunette too. Weird, eh?

Roy's romance with his TWA girl might not have been as serious as the more trivial tabloids made out but the root cause of its floundering – as it was with other of his "constant companions" – may have been the three boisterous young strangers in need of a mother: "A father isn't enough. I can only take them part of the way."[7] After that creepy 1966 Christmas, Orbison steeled himself to sift through over 2,000 written applications from all over the free world for the well-paid but exacting task of nannying Roy Duane and his brothers.

By April, he'd whittled these down to a matronly Englishwoman, Mrs Dorothy Cook who, like the less official Janet Martin before her, was advantaged by secretarial skills, having risen to head typist with a County Durham insurance firm. Sharing her apartment in the Orbison mansion would be thirty-year-old Mrs Cook's husband Bob who Mr Orbison had agreed to take on as occasional chauffeur and to maintain the fleet of vintage cars. For as long as they were able, the childless couple's ministrations *in loco parentis* would counterpoise those of the boys' grandparents while the *paterfamilias* embarked on a round of international commuting more hectic than any undertaken before.

Monument's "best of" compilation would always sell steadily, and there was enough life left in the old dog for unforeseen jackpots like the merry-go-round lilt of 'Penny Arcade' would be in Australia. However, an overall drop of Orbison record sales had necessitated this more intense focus on touring. Concentrating on the possible, much of the next few years Roy would spend largely ignoring the United States as its pop consumers were ignoring him: "I tended to fulfil commitments around the world and then come home to rest."[8]

On his own soil, he was, by 1967, something of a has-been, lost to an outer darkness of Midwest 3,000-seaters and thence to the supper clubs. As early as January 1966, Roy Orbison had played his first cabaret date. In that Atlanta night club, customers in obligatory ties purchased pricey liquor and guzzled starters, main courses and desserts while a sunken orchestra sight-read discreet muzak as showtime crept closer. Sickening him more was a return to engagements in the Nevada desert city where he'd once lost at roulette: "If you do well in Las Vegas, they cut the show short because they want to get the customers to the tables. Vegas is there for the gambling; it's no place for an artist despite the big money you can make."[4]

Other than side trips to New York, Los Angeles and back to Atlanta, Roy's North American stock-in-trade had boiled down to small town cinemas, civic halls and the larger social clubs – where he'd be subjected to a build-up by some buffoon of a compere who'd just regaled the audience with gags that would shock a drunken marine. On the same bill, there might be a fallen Bobby pandering blatantly to assumed desires with an irreconcilable mixture of olde tyme rock 'n' roll and a less well-received *vita nuova* as a third-rate Sinatra. He'd also chuck in his one or two self-generated hits as old as the hills.

Yet even in these desperate backwaters with their dubious preludes, Roy Orbison – like fettered Samson, eyeless in Gaza – invariably brought the house down. Within minutes, the most disinterested became involved as this master of his field rode 'em on down to be dragged back after The Candy Men's playout for an encore. Running through his best-loved songs for the people who loved them – and him – best of all in a back-of-beyond palais in Missouri or Nebraska wasn't such a bad place for anyone to be in 1966. Considering the wretched fates of Gene Vincent, Frankie Lymon and others trapped in a vocation founded on short-lived novelty, Orbison's greater chart grandeur would guarantee work for good money for as long as he could stand: "I'm making more money now than I did before; I play to more people than I did before, and

I sell relatively as many records."[9] On such a plateau, a hit record can be only a sideshow. Perhaps the Roy Orbison story should have ended there.

Of Orbison merchandise arranged in the foyers of these oases of entertainment, you could bank on *The Very Best Of Roy Orbison* selling briskest of all. As he didn't bother with much beyond the hits, it hardly seemed worthwhile displaying *Cry Softly, Lonely One* – his later album – or the *Fastest Guitar Alive* soundtrack, issued within weeks of each other to the detriment of both.

Cry Softly Lonely One paralleled *There Is Only One Roy Orbison* which had likewise masked the non-productive trough of its maker's private worries. Discounting the Don Gibson tangent, this was the first post-Claudette collection. Like the "divorce" album, it showcased but five Orbison-Dees compositions out of twelve selections. Otherwise, there was the heavy-hearted 'Just One Time', left over from the Gibson masters, plus another half-dozen from the bowels of Acuff-Rose. These included 'Here Comes The Rain' – a slow waltz from Mickey Newbury, first of a new breed of southern writers – and, from the old firm, Joe Melson's title track. Though he'd composed this with Jim Gant who would produce the *avant-garde* 'Southbound Jericho Parkway' for Roy in 1968, Melson couldn't resist inserting some antiquated nonsense syllables – "chung-chung-chung-bee-dooby-chung-chung" – *à la* 'Only The Lonely' and 'Blue Angel'.

Onto this reconstruction, the alien technology and virtuosity of the later sixties impinged as much as anywhere else on the LP. Detailed by varying degrees of acoustic overspill and minor intricacies such as the reptilian piano glissando in 'Memories', Orbison's voice floats effortlessly over layers of treated sound. Gadgetry and constant retakes intruded upon grit and the non-retractable margin of error that had put teeth into the records on which Roy had had to sing at the same time as a full orchestra.

Rolling like treacle over 'Girl Like Mine' was a Hammond organ whose purr was to the sixties what the polysynthesiser's snotty grate would be to a less innocent pop generation. Cropping up too were fragments of jive talk – "groovy", "a gas" – peculiar to the age. The sequence of moods on 'Cry Softly, Lonely One', however, belonged only to Orbison. He censures himself for flirting in 'That's A No No' while finding his home empty without her in 'Time To Cry' where Floyd Cramer's commiserating note-crushing is echoed by the strings. In this track, plus 'She' and – hidden away in the of side two – 'Memories' Claudette's spectre effuses from the speakers.

Simultaneously personal and universal, 'Memories', especially, avoided laying it on with a trowel. However, had it – rather than 'Too Soon To Know' been extant in summer 1966, 'Memories' might have been too mawkish for release by even the most obtuse MGM programmer: "Even in the darkest night when dreams fade away/when your love has gone, you'll never be alone with memories." Accompanied only by piano, bass and drums, Roy's elegant resignation was as loaded as his sonorous wails had been amidst the massing high tide of 'It's Over'. Probably Orbison and Dees' most fetching libretto too, 'Memories' satisfied every qualification required of a "standard" like 'September Song' or 'Yesterday'. Amazingly, it was consigned to a B-side while lesser songs like 'She', 'Cry Softly, Lonely One' and the hard-talking 'Communication Breakdown' were lifted from the album as top sides. All, it must be said, sold like hot cakes in Australasia and the Far East if nowhere else.

In the British Top Twenty, he had signed off with 'There Won't Be Many Coming Home' which, unhappily, had sloped off the charts when he commenced a tour there in March 1967 with The Small Faces. Luckily for Roy, this Cockney quartet's current single, 'I Can't Make It', lived up to its title.

With 'Best Friend', 'There Won't Be Many Coming Home' had been composed when *The Fastest Guitar Alive*, first of all, was meant to be a serious film. "It really refers to the American Civil War but it could also apply equally to the Third World War. People could take it as applying to the Vietnam fighting if they wanted to."[10] They did. Despite – or because of – Orbison's clean, conservative image, 'There Won't Be Many Coming Home' earned him – albeit briefly – the approbation of the blossoming hippie subculture. Though not as multi-purpose a protest as, from that same year, 'Eve Of Destruction' by Barry McGuire or Hedgehoppers Anonymous' 'It's Good News Week', Roy's slow march donation to the anti-war effort was seen as a rebuttal of RCA's fastest selling disc of 1966, the jingoistic 'Ballad Of The Green Berets' by fellow Texan, Sergeant Barry Sadler.

Orbison's lyrics might have been less perfunctorily boy-meets-girl but they did not coincide with the accelerating musical complexity after another sergeant's syncretic and expensive Lonely Hearts Club Band intensified the notion of pop as an egghead activity rather than simple and harmless entertainment. The Beatles, Rolling Stones and other humble beat groups were now pseudo mystics, dictating shifts in musical – and social – consciousness that had even penetrated below the Mason-Dixon line. As far down as Texas, there were psychedelic combos whose very names – Infinite Staircase, ? And The Mysterions, Mechanical Switch, Thirteenth Floor Elevators – intimated more abstract leanings than those of The Wink Westerners and The Teen Kings. While sitars whined, tapes looped and Frank Zappa inquired, "Who are the Brain Police?" old Roy "didn't hear a lot I could relate to so I kind of stood there like a tree where the winds blow and the seasons change, and you're still there and you bloom again."

For most of 1967, it was, indeed, business as usual. After the Small Faces stint, it was Down Under again. Greeting him backstage at the first engagement were the familiar faces of The Walker Brothers. Like Roy, their predominantly slowish, ballad style had rendered them archaic to the younger hip audience in the Summer of Love. Worse still, they were too young and longhaired to cut much ice with admirers of 1967's paradoxical prize chart exhibit – stardust-and-roses crooner, Engelbert Humperdinck, whose syrupy 'Release Me' had kept The Beatles' *meisterwerk*, 'Strawberry Fields Forever', from Number One in Britain. This and other counter-revolutions of schmaltz during that watershed year were applauded by Tin Pan Alley and Nashville's equivalent in Sixteenth Avenue.

Cause for a milder celebration had been the fall from grace of another act supporting Orbison in Australia. Innovative though it was, The Yardbirds' highbrow single, 'Happenings Ten Years Time Ago', had recently put the tin lid on their chart career. Some considered it an aural nightmare while others shared one pundit's claim that it was "possibly the greatest forty-five ever released".[12] Shaking baffled heads in the wings, Orbison and his Candy Men inclined towards the former view – while Yardbirds drummer Jim McCarty's concentration wandered as the star turn "seemed to be doing all his old hits in chronological order".

Neither faction appeared to be aware of underlying similarities. Whereas Orbison had superimposed Ravel, flamenco and a balalaika onto his musical grid, so The Yardbirds had investigated Gregorian chant, Indian raga and other eruditions. Each had made use of symphonic tempo changes and dynamics. In two years' time, Roy would record the surreal 'Southbound Jericho Parkway', aswarm with jarring vignettes of music spliced together to coalesce his sung narrative. In retrospect, the chasm between 'In Dreams' and 'Shapes Of Things' is not unbreachable but, in 1967, The Yardbirds played "rock" – which only the finest minds could grasp – while Roy Orbison was seen by *Rolling Stone*, *International Times* and similarly "groovy" journals as an outmoded perpetrator of vulgar "pop".

The Yardbirds and Roy, nevertheless, parted cordially with the headliner presenting one of the quintet's guitarists, Jimmy Page, with some Fender accessories from Nashville. However, the coast-to-coast package tour had had its day. Because they'd ceased to perform on stage shortly before pop left its turbulent adolescence, The Beatles were spared having to be "real" musicians. These days, "bands" – not groups – that carried any weight were demanding public attention for lengthy concept albums, rock operas and other epics that couldn't be crammed into a ten-minute spot between The Terry Young Six and Erkey Grant. Co-related with this transfer of emphasis was a greater respect for instrumental proficiency as outlines dissolved between rock and jazz. Instead of swooning hysteria, there was knotted-brow "appreciation" of guitar heroes like Jeff Beck, Alvin Lee – the "fastest guitar alive" – and Eric "God" Clapton whose high decibel trio, Cream, were known to extrapolate a three-verse blues for nigh on twenty po-faced minutes to snowblinded applause. This was as much a case of the King's New Clothes as screaming at The Fourmost or Freddie Garrity had been, but the divide between rock and pop had become such that mismatched pairings like Roy Orbison and The Yardbirds were no longer mutually beneficial.

If there was room for another act on the same bill as Cream, The Jimi Hendrix Experience or, now, The Rolling Stones, it wouldn't be filled by anybody who just stood up and sang fiddly two-minute singles without embellishment. Not only was it uncool for collegiate youth to own up to liking him, but hitting Roy harder was the realisation that he couldn't get an American pop hit to save his life. Foreseeable already were dwindling returns everywhere else. So depressing were the prospects that Orbison no longer studied the charts.

Physically, he was none too hale either. Noticeably tubbier, he'd also had to cancel several engagements in autumn 1967 owing to a severe throat infection. Moreover, by the New Year, he'd twice be under the scalpel for the removal of a kidney stone. Other than these and like forced-rest periods, he hadn't taken a holiday since 1959.

Why not pack it in? Wise investments had ensured that he could live quite comfortably into his old age if he retired at thirty-two. Nonetheless, although he would tell reporters that he was "really doing it for the people who made me a millionaire",[13] he could not articulate – even to himself – that he enjoyed the life of a travelling celebrity. How would he have felt if he hadn't been recognised during his surprise appearance in the 1966 London to Brighton historic commercial vehicle run? There he was in green-tinted specs and fingers festooned in diamond rings, behind the wheel of a bright maroon 1920 Maxwell charabanc with its roof peeled back for all to see. More uncomfortably conspicuous beside him was a blonde in an Edwardian picture hat.

He called the bluff of another American star who'd been "complaining to me that he couldn't get away from his fans. I felt like telling him to go home to the States if he wanted to go unrecognised."[14] However awkward the time or place when autograph books were thrust his way, Roy would still sign and smile. Like deified Caesar in Gaul, he'd offend none by refusing votive-offerings like the piece of fabric from Baron von Richthoven's Fokker Triplane received from his New Zealand fan club. Then there were the birds awaiting his collection from Britain's Budgerigar Information Bureau during the 1968 tour. He'd intended them to be a coming-home present for the boys. Instead, they'd go to the fan club in London.

One of the cheapest and yet intrinsically most valuable gifts was the demo tape of 'Penny Arcade'. With deceptive casualness, this musical prècis of an idle hour was pushed onto Orbison's table in a Beefeater grill in Leeds by its composer, Sammy King. "It's the only time this sort of thing has happened to me," Roy would recall a couple of years later, "and it turned out a winner."[15]

'Penny Arcade' would almost but not quite do the trick. Unfashionable as he was, Roy Orbison was quite prepared to stick it out, in the firm belief that another big record would surface, because, "When I hear a favourite artist of mine who is not getting hit product, I can still hear what I love about the artist in there. There comes a saturation point where people like to move on to newer things, not necessarily better. It's the way it should be – then if you're into something new, you can look back and say, 'Was this really as good as I thought it was?' And in many cases, it is, and in a lot of cases you say, 'That's better than I remember it being and it's still part of my life,' so it could be that people move on temporarily."[16]

With good reason, Orbison would rate much of his output from this lean interval at least equal to his earlier smashes. 'Walk On' was a 'Running Scared'-type crescendo ballad with a state-of-the-art production that corresponded with the multi-track ethos of the later sixties. More "poetically" in 'Yesterday's Child' recurred the themes explored in 'Growing up' and 'You'll Never Be Sixteen Again', while – running out of steam perhaps – 'Sugar Man' was a re-write of – you guessed it – 'Candy Man'. 'So Good' might not have been up to scratch either but the male backing counterpoint of 'Heartache' was every bit as breathtaking as some of The Beach Boys' choral convolutions. So disappointed was Roy in its dismal reception by the public that he would try again with a slicker re-make of 'Heartache' six years later. On a more adult tack, 'My Friend' predated country-and-western's relocation to the middle classes in its twist-in-the-tale delineation of a harrowing domestic dilemma.

This creative peak was motivated perversely by unresolvable vocational ructions between Dees and Orbison. For the past two years, Bill had been up there on stage to the far left of Roy, harmonising on lines and choruses he'd sung on the records. However, the concert was never the high point of the day for Dees. Back at the hotel after Roy had wound down, or in transit the next morning, the co-writer might be buttonholed long enough for Bill to demonstrate outlines that could evolve into songs.

Orbison didn't seem to have many ideas of his own anymore. Mind you, he hadn't had much encouragement of late. From the instant criticism traceable in audience reaction, Roy had detected less enthusiasm whenever he launched into his latest single – as opposed to another batch of fervently remembered oldies. When they heard him do 'Blue Angel', for just short of three minutes, Mr and Mrs Average were teenagers, lovestruck and irresponsible, back at high school. Was the sole purpose of Roy Orbison only to remind them of the good old days? In this large scale re-run of that post-'Ooby Dooby' slump a decade earlier, he was living on past glories.

A consolation was that, freed from the constraints of sustaining a run of hits, he was able to indulge himself in a patchwork of different musical styles on vinyl. Wilfully uncommercial, the unprecedented 'Southbound Jericho Parkway' lacked a discernible melody line as it darted from section to dissoluble section, utilising all instrumental elements available bar the proverbial kitchen sink. A production rather than a song, this psychedelic soap opera of a divorced father's suicide and its ramifications was a revelation for those who unearthed it on the B-side of 'My Friend'.

He was not the composer of 'Southbound Jericho Parkway' but, by thus dipping his toe into the oblique, Roy was vouchsafed sufficient temporary trendiness to be approached by arty Italian film director, Antonioni, to contribute a number to the soundtrack of *Zabriskie Point*. A hip *Catch Us If You Can*, this fantasy of wonderful young people running away from over-civilised old squares would also feature items by the likes of The Pink Floyd, The Rolling Stones and The Grateful Dead. Talk of a second film starring Orbison had fizzled out as had his attempt to form a London-based movie company with Peter Walsh. Responding gladly to Antonioni's tangible incentive, Roy's 'So Young', though necessarily referential to the film, was a self-written ballad in which youth was celebrated from the perspective of manhood. Portraying the distance he had travelled from the twixt-twelve-and-twenty agony uncle of 'Growing Up' in 1966, 'So Young' did not, however, signal a prolonged return to form.

Now very much in the easy-listening bracket in the States, his *Roy Orbison's Many Moods* album was not thought worth releasing elsewhere. Nevertheless, it gave many listeners genuine vicarious pleasure through beautifully-sung readings of snug chestnuts like 'Unchained Melody', 'Try To Remember' and, with period shimmering mandolins, 'More'. From the early sixties, a bolder standard, 'What

Now My Love', hung on a familiar bolero rhythm. These nestled among a mere three Orbison-Dees originals plus a handful more from the Acuff-Rose hold. Two of them – 'Amy' and Mickey Newbury's 'Good Morning Dear' – discharged the same wracked, drawn-curtain menace as that wrought in the fiercely emotional work of Belgian composer, Jacques Brel and, since the sundering of The Walker Brothers, his foremost interpreter, Scott Engel. By contrast, 'I Recommend Her' smacked of Motown.

This track was written by Mark Mathis, mainstay of The Newbeats, who was Bill Dees' new songwriting partner. Like Joe Melson before him, Bill had tired of his role as Orbison's Sancho Panza. "Writing needs to come from the heart not the pocket," was his muttered maxim whenever Roy summoned his assistance to knock out a new single for MGM. As well as drawn-out absences from his wife and four children, there'd also been a falling out with Orbison when Bob Montgomery – then riding high as producer of Bobby Goldsboro's *magnum opus*, 'Honey' – offered Dees an opportunity to cut a single. With Roy's creative malaise quashing misplaced loyalty, Bill Dees quit the road to retreat back to Tennessee. Signed to a label of no great merit, he recommenced a recording career held in abeyance since The Whirlwinds. Shamelessly, he'd plug his own version of 'Oh! Pretty Woman' on stage at the local venues from whence he came.

Though his work spectrum was on an international rather than parochial scale, Orbison's records as much as those of his former colleague had become incidental to a livelihood centred more and more on personal appearances on the supper club circuit. The hard-bought screaming had all but stopped. Nowadays, he appealed to those who, having satiated their appetites for novelty, had been turned-off by all this marijuana-smoking crap, didn't know about 'Southbound Jericho Parkway' and yearned for a bit of "decent" music. Not the most rampant pop consumers, Roy's new audience contained aging Teddy Boys, parents with teenage children, and young marrieds. There were incorrigible old Rockers too who didn't mind mothballing their leathers and jeans to squeeze into the Sunday clothes or smart casuals that were the frequent norm at Wigan Casino, Caesar's palace in Luton and other citadels of "quality" entertainment – above Bingo but a long way from Glyndebourne. In these places, there were rarely less than capacity crowds even if Roy Orbison's presence didn't turn a town on its head any longer.

His own head had been turned when, after finishing a show in Batley, Roy was persuaded to string along with a party off to a discotheque in nearby Leeds. This time, the city turned up trumps of a more personal joy than the 'Penny Arcade' tape. Worth more than a second glance was a girl with waist length black hair whose lithe exertions on the dance floor were at odds with her disinterest in the artistic worth of the noise pounding from the huge speakers. Never had eighteen-year-old German, Barbara Wellnoener-Jakobs, been crazy about pop singers. Other cavorters may have found Roy Orbison's descent into their midst impressively disturbing but not Barbara whose knowledge of him then began and ended with 'Oh! Pretty Woman'.

When he introduced himself, Barbara's daunting Teutonic directness put him on his mettle: "I was wearing a denim jacket at the time, and the first thing she said was what a terrible jacket it was. I told her it didn't belong to me, that I'd just borrowed it to stop catching cold. But I said that if she turned up at the show the next night, I would show her my best suit."[17]

Sartorially, he was spoilt for choice. A few days prior to the start of this particular British tour, he'd ventured from the Westbury Hotel "to get me some suits – around forty or so – and to see a little Scots fellow who makes my shirts. I need a few of them too – like around fifty or so. You have better workmanship in England – better materials too."[18]

These leisurely preliminaries typified Orbison's revised attitude to work. On doctor's orders, he could no more dismiss 1,000 miles between engagements as a few inches on a map. Hanging over him were mopping-up operations in hitherto unvisited minor territories like Crete and Taiwan, but to reduce the self-imposed strain of twice-nightly performances and battling with adverse acoustics in different auditoriums, "It seemed easier to sit in one place for a week and do the show than to hop, skip and jump."[19] After eight years forever on the move, he could sell out a month's residency at the prestigious Talk Of The Town – only walking distance from the Westbury. Arguably the highest paid cabaret artist in Britain, he sang his songs to faces and cleavages tanned on the ski slopes, bow-tied tuxedos, pearly adornments and drinks like melted crayons.

Much as operatic tenor Enrico Caruso had before the Great War, each classic would hush worshippers as a mass bell in Madrid while Roy Orbison waded through his demanding recitals. Puccini praised Signor Caruso's rapturous warbling as god-like; a London critic's more measured consideration of Orbison was that his "secret seems to be understatement...his programming is exquisite...a hypnotic attraction."[20]

Though he acquitted himself admirably before metropolitan swells, Roy wasn't above the scrupulous promotion of current singles on the radio. It made as much sense to amble down Memory Lane as well. In July 1968 on almost the final edition of the BBC Light Programme's pop showcase, *Saturday Club*, 'Walk On' – in the charts by a whisker – was cushioned between not tracks from any new album but 'Oh! Pretty Woman' and, for Gawd's sake, 'Only The Lonely'.

Recording the transmission in Birmingham, he'd been backed by the vocal trio and small orchestra from the Talk Of The Town. Under the baton of Barry Booth, the girls had been requested to "simmer a bit more. Camp it up a bit." For all his jocularity, the gifted Barry was dispirited by overwork. Between his Orbison obligations, demand for his services from London theatres was drawing him irreversibly back to England permanently. Dissatisfied with his own pressured efforts during the Talk Of The Town season, he named a deliberately unrealistic figure for future work; an ultimatum that he knew would provoke Acuff-Rose into paying him off.

For Roy to take Barry and the orchestra on the road was impractical anyway. As well as the logistics of shunting such an operation from A to B, economically it would be so close to break even point that there'd be hardly any profit margin. Besides, would there be room for everyone on the stages of Wakefield Theatre or the Double Diamond Club in Caerphilly? By exercising thrift, you could still put on an acceptable show. Partly through restrictions imposed by the British Musicians Union and partly because he'd an option on a cheaper alternative, Orbison had dispensed with The Candy Men; four of whom were then absorbed into the ranks of studio session band, The Atlanta Rhythm Section while the sharp-eyed might have spied others sweating it out with The McCoys and Buffalo Springfield. No matter how far he'd wandered into showbusiness proper, thus was affirmed the respect still held in rock circles for former Orbison cohorts.

For the next few years, Roy would be backed mostly by The Art Movement, an English sextet recommended by Acuff-Rose's New Bond Street office. Modelling themselves vocally on The Beach Boys and Four Seasons, and instrumentally on the politer exactitudes of Blood, Sweat And Tears, their Decca single, 'Loving Touch', had been bland enough for a spell on the playlists of the BBC's two new national pop radio stations whose cautious programming was rendering the UK Top Thirty shallower and less subversive in content. Harmless purveyors of popular song in outsized bow-ties and dung-coloured stage costumes, the grinning Art Movement were granted their own spot before the Big O's Grand Entrance.

After the gruff taciturnity of The Candy Men, Roy was refreshed by The Art Movement's easier professionalism and blither dedication to their craft. Indeed, with drummer Paul Munday as main protagonist, he was even amenable to their advocating changes in his time-honoured set. Gradually, outlines merged between the ensemble's warm-up and their tractable employer's act. As once he'd broken up the ballads with common-to-all ravers like 'Mean Woman Blues' and 'What'd I Say', Orbison was inserting Art Movement mainstays between his hits. As well as down-to-death set pieces from the beat boom such as 'Money' and 'Land Of 1,000 Dances', some onlookers were nonplussed when Roy also slipped in 'Help Me Rhonda' and even the drippy 'Loving Touch'.

The zenith of this willing appeasement was the appearance of an album, *Big O*, recorded in London. As their photo with freshly shampooed hair on its cheap beige sleeve testified this product was as much The Art Movement's as it was the Big O's. Tedious listening it made too. The unmistakable lead voice apart, there was the discomfiting suspicion that had *Big O* been offered anonymously to record companies, it might have courted rejection. This appeared to be corroborated by its non-release in the States. Shrill and neatly dovetailed accompaniment, was not a recipe for excitement. As well as the new up-tempo numbers, there were flaccid renderings of 'Only You' from The Platters and Harry Belafonte's 'Scarlet Ribbons'. For good measure, some Acuff-Rose bagatelles were thrown in such as

John D Loudermilk's overvocalised 'Break My Mind', issued as a single. *Big O* was supplemented further by 'Penny Arcade' in which the Nashville session players' smooth handling of its tricky switches of tempo put the pointless frenzy of other tracks in a bad light.

Roy Orbison was thus plodding a well-beaten path from maturity to dreary repetition, making the most of every chance that came his way. On this, his most public journeying, he "was just basically working. I didn't know where it was leading." By 1969, he didn't care much either. The scapegoat for his broken fortunes was MGM who "in the first five years of the contract, there were six different presidents, and then someone bought the company and then sold the real estate, so they were not in the record business, so I don't know what I could have done had they been really solid."[16]

For their part, the powers at MGM blamed Orbison's decline on a further family trauma drying up his output. Moreover, though it had made headlines, it hadn't procured a big hit as his wife's motorbike crash had done. When he returned to public life, however, thousands of latecomers had had to be turned away from one Ipswich ballroom where he was appearing. Of these, a good few were morbidly inquisitive with only the vaguest notion about the entertainer they were trying to see. Inside, they looked at him and wondered. Onstage was not a common-or-garden pop star but a man from hell.

On the morning of 16 September, 1968, road manager Bob Blackburn had phoned The Art Movement at their digs in the Midlands to inform them that the Bournemouth Pavilion show that night – the last of a six-week tour – had been cancelled. As he spoke, Roy was halfway across the Atlantic, remembering another death, another day when lightning had struck from a blue sky. Fuzzy with an injected sedative though he was, the thousands of miles from Middlesex to New York to Nashville provided him with an opportunity for continuous thought.

From the backstage disarray in Birmingham, he'd missed the news by minutes. Learning that he and Blackburn had decided to drive through the night to Bournemouth's Royal Spa Hotel, the London office had even left messages in motorway service stations *en route* but, with a full tank, the limousine didn't stop once during the two-hour journey to the seaside.

Leaning back into the deep upholstery with an arm spread along the back seat, speeding along the open road made Roy feel relatively pleased with life. That German girl had showed up the second night at Batley. Away from the disco's flashing lights and deafening row, their eyes had met and something had clicked. Before she'd left afterwards for her friend's university residence up in Leeds, Barbara and Roy had exchanged addresses and promised to keep in touch.

Business-wise, things were a bit slack right now but people were still paying to see him, regardless of passing trends. When MGM's time was up, he'd get back on course. Hadn't 'So Young' proved he could still do it? He couldn't wait to see the film. For all anyone knew, a chance to Hit The Big Time again was lurking just round the next bend.

Nearer the coast, it started to rain heavily. He hit the sack as milk floats wafted along the promenade. At around five am, Bob Blackburn was roused. There was someone on the line. When Bob panted into the foyer moments later, the night porter looked up from a newspaper that didn't know. Blackburn asked for a doctor. What's up? You look a bit off-colour, mate. For Mr Orbison, is it? Are you sure? He seemed perfectly okay when you checked in an hour ago. Ten to one he's sleeping like the dead.

With the drowsy MD at his elbow, Bob shook Roy and came straight to the point: "I can remember it word for word still. Bob said, 'Your house has burnt down. Roy and Tony are gone.'"[22]

Devoid of will, he was steered downstairs, dressed and with his cases packed before the town woke. Eyes bloodshot with fatigue, Blackburn hurtled through the downpour towards Heathrow with poor Roy Orbison: "I was totally shattered, probably because I was not close to them," said Roy. "I was here. They were there. I didn't know about my mother, my father or my youngest son until my [road] manager put me at ease about them an hour later."[22]

In the middle of the American night, the limpid waters of Old Hickory were still alive with the brightness of the blaze that the wooden structure and air-conditioning had accelerated. Shivering despite the heat, the grandfather was absolving himself as a policeman jotted down facts. On the Cooks' night off, Orbie Lee had been the only adult in charge. Early that evening after Wesley had nodded off at last, the other two boys had been messing about in the basement where petrol was stored for the antique cars. Alerted by the first of a series of explosions down there, Orbie Lee – while clasping the now bawling baby – had managed to shepherd Roy Duane and Tony up the steps as fire hastened thirstily after the life-giving fluid. Only a few yards from the front door, there came the loudest bang of all. Glancing back like Orpheus at Eurydice, the hapless old man froze in shock as his grandsons were snatched from him forever, disappearing "in a wall of flame".[23]

Brushing past a pitiless *woomph* of flashbulbs, the father crossed the tarmac of Kennedy airport. In the VIP lounge, he waited knowing that the internal flight to Tennessee would be the final sanctuary before he'd no longer be able to stifle the images of those that the horror had swallowed so mercilessly.

By the time he arrived, the rubble and the blackened shells of his automobile collection were still belching smoke but most of the fire engines had gone. At first, he was a detached spectator with no interest or stake in the disaster. Then the truth that he had refused to avow inflicted itself upon him. He could no longer not believe it.

CHAPTER EIGHT

I Wanna Live

After the funeral in Hendersonville's Philip Robinson Chapel, theirs would be the last funeral he'd ever bring himself to attend. One day he'd be able to assimilate what good had come from there being two white Cadillacs this time. He'd accept this second tragedy and thoughts of his own – self-administered – end would vanish into the sky. With extraordinary resilience, he'd conquer desolation by anchoring himself to the notion that he would live. He'd cry his tears, then would come catharsis and a dull ache. It couldn't be now though – nor for a while yet.

Wesley and the grandparents had left for the recently-purchased home-away-from-home, high in the hills overlooking Malibu beach in California. In a Nashville hotel room, Roy Orbison was shrouded in darkness and squalor as he waited for the madness to subside. With no glad welcome guaranteed, anxious friends would brave the depressing fug to check on him. In the midst of food leftovers, crumpled bedclothes and overflowing ashtrays, some would quote the Scriptures but, "If you weren't religious before," Roy philosophised, "then I think it would be hypocritical to start praying."[1] That would come much later.

Just a gesture or word would set him off: "Someone will use a particular phrase and I'll recall that Roy Junior used to say that too."[2] From Bielefeld, her family home in the Rhineland, the most vital source of solace during these care-worn hours was Barbara

Wellnoener-Jacobs, the discotheque *fraulein* who'd criticised his scruffy jacket. At the end of the line as Roy bared his soul, "Perhaps the most important thing she has done for me is to help me talk about Claudette and the boys instead of it all being bottled up inside me,"[3] he admitted.

Gradually, his rising from half-death became perceptible. One of his session musicians, Harold Bradley, was summoned to that gloomy suite to discuss the merits of a new make of guitar. The wheels cranked further into motion as tour and recording dates were pencilled in. The flame-ravaged site of the catastrophe was sold to Johnny Cash who grew an orchard there. Cash's lead guitarist, Luther Perkins, had also perished in a Nashville house fire.

A few hundred yards along the peninsula, building commenced on a Bavarian-style chalet for Roy and his surviving son: "I know it is close to where my old home used to be," he explained, "but your own life can't stop. You can only go on doing the things you did before and learn to live with memories."[4] As well as a view of the lake from each window, the new house would be secured with alarms hooked up directly to the appropriate station. Roy also gave the go-ahead for work to begin on "US Recording", his own studio.

He'd coped before by burying himself in his career but, when the music was over for the day, he'd lay with eyes open and temples throbbing as sorrow flooded his already overloaded mind. He'd long to be at rest but fingers of despair would reach in and sleep wouldn't come for all the potions and droughts he'd been prescribed. Down the motel corridor were those who understood that what was a tour for them was occupational therapy for Roy. In the months prior to their respective resignations, Bill Dees and Barry Booth were parties closest to Orbison's emotional convalescence. Barry's recollection of their part in the healing is worth reiterating at length: "He wasn't exactly a Bible-basher or even a practising church-goer but he had as many questions crossing his mind as any thinking person. He could do no more than voice those that presented themselves – such as why anyone should have so much bad luck in one go, and what were the implications? How do you relate to that? How do you come out of it? What was the driving force, the personality, the spirit, the soul, whatever you call it? What is the reaction meant to be? What is the best thing to learn? It is an experience, after all, that is denied most people: certainly very unpleasant. It was the old 'what is the meaning of life?' I couldn't say that either Bill or myself would be preaching but I think that the three of us would find ourselves in long discussions, asking questions and offering possible answers. Roy did intimate as such that it was a great help at the time to talk through rather than having to bear that amount of grief in solitude. I also found it better from my point of view – that we could talk about it rather than just keep a respectful silence. I would be one to ask, 'What are you thinking? What are you feeling about it? What's it doing? Let's be open. Let's use our intelligence rather than keep separate on it.' After a period of self-examination, he came through all right. The point is: he kept on working."

Bill Dees may have commented on Roy's troubles in 'If Only For A While'. Tactfully, Barry Booth decided not to submit the second song he'd written with Orbison in mind, the premonitory 'The Last Time I Saw You Was Tomorrow'. The gentlemen of the press, however, had no such inhibitions about quizzing Roy at virtually every interview about his dead wife and children, just as they'd been there to take their macabre pictures as he'd hurried across Kennedy aerodrome. That'd made a marvellous leading article, hadn't it? Yet, patiently and without yielding any of his self-esteem, he'd always give unblinking copy when probed on the subject: "It was a long, long time ago, but I'm trying to reach back and really give you what went on as opposed to what I would like to have had happen," he said later. "It was a devastating blow but not debilitating. I wasn't totally incapacitated by events – and I think that's stood me in good stead. You don't come out unscathed, but you don't come out murdered, you know?"[5]

In the hungover morning after the Swinging 'Sixties, this topic was the case closed on Roy Orbison. In common with other pop stars past their sell-by date, he'd answer perfunctory and unnoted enquiries about whatever current record the reporter would or wouldn't ever hear. Then he'd have to retell the old, old story of his distinguished past for the trillionth time. These days, so he'd heard, even the Sun material that he'd only listen to under sufferance, never mind sing, was prized by the increasing multitudes scouring bargain bins, junk shops and jumble sales for overlooked artefacts from earlier musical eras. Attempts were being made by some to arrange and perform the outmoded sounds. Reacting against the distancing of the humble pop group from its essentially teenage audience, "street level" acclaim was afforded British Teddy Boy revivalists like Crazy Cavan and Shakin' Stevens. Conversely, managed by vintage record shop proprietor Malcolm McLaren, The Sex Pistols' exploratory rehearsals in 1974 would hinge on forgotten Mod classics. Across the Atlantic, fifties rock 'n' roll specialists such as Sha Na Na and Flash Cadillac were paving the way for a resurgence of rockabilly in the late seventies spearheaded by The Cramps – "psychobilly" – and The Stray Cats whose concert set would include 'Ooby Dooby'.

Along with retrospectives in pop journals and the snowballing of more erudite "fanzines", these haphazard cells of archivist-performers appealed to Roy's well-developed sense of historical perspective: "We didn't play our Sun records onstage for a long time – until about 1970, I think, when it became instant history, you know?" he said. "All the information coalesced to the point where everybody thought that was a beginning – and so I took it more seriously myself because I had had a few years to reflect – and Presley started singing 'That's All Right' and I started singing 'Ooby Dooby.'"[5]

Though he was no more unproud of his Sun discs, Orbison was rated at a lowly twenty-seven – below even such doubtful inclusions as Adam Faith and Brenda Lee – in a British fanzine poll devoted to classic rock.[6] His was a unique stalemate. At home, he'd already set his face against overtures to appear on nostalgia revues with the likes of Bill Haley and Little Richard – but no doubt he'd have seized the advantage had he been a spent force everywhere else as well. As there were plenty of Monument re-issues behind the counters, neither had he yet succumbed to re-recording any of his big hits as had, say, Gene Vincent with 'Be-Bop-A-Lula '69' or Carole King's reworking in 1971 of 'Will You Still Love Me Tomorrow' – which, as a Brill Building tunesmith, she had written for The Shirelles eleven years before.

This song had been a highlight of Carole's *Tapestry* album, a less self-obsessed example of the early seventies school of singing songwriters – "self rock" – that infested both college bedsits and the hit parade. The drab uniformity of most of its practitioners was but one symptom of the post-sixties doldrums. With all the charisma of a tin of beans, solemn James Taylor, the twee Melanie or someone like them would whinge "beautiful" cheesecloth-and-denim inanities on television specials, outdoor festivals and sold-out stadiums. They'd caught the general tenor of the bland "Woodstock Generation" – a re-run of 1967 without colour, daring or humour – whose anthem was Simon and Garfunkel's piteous 'Bridge Over Troubled Waters'; who flocked to see *Zabriskie Point*, who adored the high-pitched quavering of Neil Young, a self-rock colossus.

What had been merely implied by Roy Orbison, Young carried to absurd lengths of morosity as demonstrated by his mopish rehash of Don Gibson's 'Oh Lonesome Me'. Nonetheless, given Neil Young's known admiration, 'So Young' in *Zabriskie Point* and the downbeat musical mood, the hour may have come for Roy Orbison – a precursor of singing songwriters if not self-rock – to regain a toehold in the States as an album artist on the university circuit. Heaven knows he could outsing any precious self-rocker. Onstage, you didn't have to do anything except sing to your guitar and beam a small, sad smile every now and then. They especially liked it if you sat on a stool.

Because some hip names had been printed on one of his LP jackets, it was even cool to dig an easy-listening Mister Wonderful like Andy Williams. If, like Williams, he'd adapted just enough of this trend to not turn off older fans, Roy might have had a walkover had he had enough new songs of his own to sing then. As always, however, personal upsets had severely curtailed that aspect of creativity – hence the Art Movement hotch-potch and, for US ears only, *Hank Williams, The Roy Orbison Way*.

Tributes to Hank Williams over an entire album had been rendered previously by others – the most reverential being that of rockabilly balladeer Jack Scott from Ontario who, in 1960, sang "the tunes as though he'd inhaled the Nashville air for months on end".[7] Both a Nashville resident for years not months, and a Southerner to boot, Orbison with his advisers felt entitled in 1971 to take more liberties with the original arrangements – such as grafting the undulating riff of Johnny Ray's 'Such A Night' onto 'Jambalaya', and jarring accent shifts on 'Cold Cold Heart' and 'I'm So Lonesome I Could Cry'. Elsewhere, there were mid-song key changes, lavish orchestration and insertion of modern guitar distortion devices – most prominent on 'You Win Again' and 'Cold Cold Heart'. The most innovative updatings occur on the opening tracks. Riven with a stomping rhythm section, *Big Country* strings and tough guitar-harmonica interaction, Orbison's 'Kaw-liga' was arguably the most impressive Hank Williams cover ever recorded, while 'Jambalaya' rode roughshod over The Carpenters' hit single version of 1974. Most of the other selections, however, were merely passable and, like 'Jambalaya', blemished by jaunty big band brass and slushy cinematic strings effusing nonchalant complacency. Knowing the songs backwards, Roy was, nevertheless, in excellent voice throughout.

For issue in Britain ten years later – as *Big O Country* – three old Don Gibson interpretations were added to make up the short needle time. To the chagrin of the most fanatical overseas enthusiasts, two other Orbison albums would be confined to North America too. Sales there were enough to make such projects a practical proposition but elsewhere new records became more and more a mere adjunct to Roy's roaming the earth in cabaret. These days, "Mr 1960" as one reviewer dubbed him,[8] had no incentive for foisting on ticket holders anything but the contents of the wall-to-wall hits compilations that still topped album charts – as K-Tel's "as seen on TV" *Best Of Roy Orbison* would in Australasia, Britain and Canada in 1976. Though one of the more popular curios from the recent past, Orbison's market killing exacerbated a shortage of new original talent. This was reinforced by similar triumphs of repackaging by the likes of The Beach Boys, Glen Campbell, The Dave Clark Five and even Perry Como. There were also attempts at seventies rebirth by The Byrds, Animals, Spencer Davis Group and Small Faces.

With nostalgia as his calling card, Roy Orbison had become an archetype – and only serious practitioner of his particular pop niche. Therefore, it made more sense to plug the seemingly timeless sixties chartbusters, while left to fend for itself was what was now the annual new single – recorded almost for form's sake. You never know your luck but no-one was interested in the latest by Little Richard, Bill Haley or, for that matter, The Beach Boys either.

Turning his back on the contemporary stage, Roy submerged himself in a world where current chart status had no meaning. As sure as the sunrise were the yearly world tours. He'd pride himself on knowing an oft-visited country's geography better than most of its inhabitants. Back at the same venues time and time again, he had at least the opportunity to form genuine friendships rather than play backstage host to a residue of stargazers: "Whether I'm in London, Sydney or Hong Kong, it makes no difference," he insisted. "There is always someone who knows me...I must be one of the unloneliest people in the world."[3]

In this less hectic phase of his stardom, he would take up conversations started the previous year with night spot managers, catering staff and patrons who now realised how privately ordinary – even boring – was the icon they'd once worshipped from afar. Reserving a little of his Southern charm for everyone in this orbit, he'd ask after their families, notice whether they'd lost weight or grown a beard, and bring them up to date with the new car collection or Wesley's reading. Yet, for all this hail-fellow-well-met familiarity, he was quite used to them suddenly falling silent in the manner that every old star comes to identify – an awestricken sense of *déjà vu* mingled with a touch of scepticism as though you aren't quite real.

To the most snowblinded members of his fan clubs, it was as if time had stopped in 1966. No matter how mundane he appeared to others, how long he'd been hitless, how unrecognised he was in restaurants, "to say he looked incredible would be almost an understatement", ran *Texan Star*, one club magazine. "Tanned, slimmer than for ages, smiling from behind his dark glasses, with his black hair completing the picture as he stood there, unmoving himself but moving every emotion in every member of the audience, resplendent in his gold studded black regalia. This was...this is...Roy Orbison 1975!"[9]

Nobody was getting any younger and, though he could still belt out the old magic, he was actually weighing in at an unhealthy fifteen stone. More often nowadays, he'd wake feeling groggy and out-of-sorts. Nevertheless, he'd salvaged contentment from the shambles of recent years since plighting his troth in March 1969 to his long-distance comforter, Barbara. As besotted as a man in middle life could be with a shapely, beautiful girlfriend fourteen years his junior, Roy would swing from hangdog gloom to a breezy vitality, amazing those who found it hard to believe he'd ever been a rock 'n' rolling Teen King: "She has helped me make a new Roy Orbison – and, when this happens, you find very quickly that you don't want to be your old self,"[9] he said. At Barbara's suggestion, he began brushing his hair forward like a teenager's.

Actively looking for a mother for Wesley, he'd flown to Germany for the dual purpose of meeting the Wellnoener-Jacobs and inviting their daughter to his homeland to see if she'd fit in there. As well as a spell as Honorary Consul for Panama, Barbara's aristocratic father also owned Bielefeld's dress factory. The success of each of Baron Wellnoener-Jacobs' occupations depended on maintaining appearances and creating good impressions. Was it so strange, therefore, that after a girlhood in such surroundings, Barbara should elect to make her way in the world of fashion upon finishing school? A career of catwalks and cloth had still been on the cards the night she met her husband-to-be.

However odd a choice this American pop singer may have seemed on first encounter, *Vater* and *Mutter* raised no objections when, on returning to the Fatherland, Barbara announced that she wanted to marry the boy. A month after the wedding, Roy presented his brand-new wife at a Westbury Hotel press conference to publicise three weeks of English cabaret dates.

These were down to a fine art: one week up north, the next in the Midlands and the last down south. On one visit, his band played the Star Trek theme as overture – as Presley's orchestra in Las Vegas did 'Also Sprach Zarathustra' from *2001*. However, starting with 'Only The Lonely', it was often the same set in the same order as the previous outing – but this didn't affect the takings and he'd be rebooked for next season before he left the building. If unqualified to appear on BBC's *Top Of The Pops*, there was still an occasional showcase like 1974's *Roy Orbison Sings Roy Orbison* – and he was more than welcome to guest on *Sez Lez*, *Saturday Night At The Mill* and other light entertainment programmes that flashed the beery joviality of a working man's club into your living room. The stand-up comic around whose personality the series was built would complete the sort of facetious introduction that a disinterested Roy was hearing over and over again these days: "Without further ado, ladies and gentlemen, I'd like to bring on a *grrrrrreat* entertainer I know you're all going to enjoy – well, my late grandmother was quite fond of him..."

A raffle ticket might win you a dining table at Wigan on Roy Orbison night. You don't get many laughs but he ain't half professional. He always sings just like his records – slurring the first line, second verse of 'Running Scared', growling just before the middle bit in 'Oh! Pretty Woman'. You know where you are with that bloke. When required to fill only thirty minutes, he'd even swallow the pill of a medley so that nobody could complain that he hadn't sung their favourite. Taking this and other lines of least resistance, in playing 125 concerts in 105 consecutive days in 1974, the road really did seem endless. "In the seventies, I got to the point where I just didn't want to go on," he admitted. "You'd begin another tour; you'd get a bit ill and a bit confused and, finally, you can't see the point in either touring or not touring. It was only around 1975, after I'd called a halt to the whole thing and reassessed the point of it all, that it started getting to be fun again."[10]

Closing the show for casts of vile comedians and dodgy variety acts, he'd become the epitome of Adam Faith's assertion that, "The worst thing in the world is to be an ex-pop singer doing the clubs." Yet Roy Orbison played them all from England's heavily industrial Black Country to outback towns in Western Australia. On one such evening in Batley, Barry Booth was saddened to see his old boss cutting corners with only a guitar-bass-drums backing group: "I don't want to sound disparaging but the band was a bit lacklustre after the kind of entourage he'd been used to when you'd get a small orchestra on stage."

He'd become rather commonplace. Like a London bus, if you missed one performance, another would come along if you waited. Orbison was a "forthcoming attraction", spoken of in the same breath as Les Dawson (of *Sez Lez*), Freddie And The Dreamers or pianist Mrs Mills – all thoroughly diverting entertainers in their fields but hardly Sadler's Wells, hardly 'It's Over'. Around a thousand pounds a time would buy Roy Orbison – more than he'd ever realised as a chart contender. If he wasn't available, how about Del Shannon?

Every passing year was a little shabbier, a little less respectful. "House full" signs would still go up but small paragraphs in evening newspapers would mention the verdicts of High Court writs that Orbison or Acuff-Rose had served on club owners and agents for breach of contract. Roy had suffered "substantial loss of reputation"[11] for example, when the Sands in Brighton cancelled at short notice a widely-advertised four-night run in 1972. Damages were awarded that same year because army manoeuvres had wiped out a ten-day tour of US military bases in Germany.

In similar circumstances was another vocal aesthete, Scott Engel. As well as working the clubs; the former Walker Brother had lapsed from Brel translations and his own stream-of-consciousness creations to middle-of-the-road budget long-players of film songs and standards, both mainstream and country-and-western. Roy Orbison would never arrive at this pass but there was, nevertheless, a feeling of his marking time musically in the three collections that saw out his MGM commitments. The overall hue of each album might vary from the three-in-the-morning *Roy Orbison Sings* to the more buoyant *Memphis* and *Milestones* but musical direction was governed by the engulfment by the "silent majority" of a genre known as "country-pop".

Traditionalists like Charlie Pride, Hank Snow and Roy Acuff kept the faith there still but Nashville had, by the seventies, embraced more generalised pop – albeit of a kind not uninfluenced by C&W's lyrical preoccupations and melodic appeal. A particular preference of Orbison's was Lynn Anderson's 'Rose Garden', written by the outspoken country-rocker Joe South whose reply to his own rhetorical question, 'Do They Love Country Music In The South?', was, "They sit around in the studios cutting hot licks to assure each other, 'Man, I don't play this country stuff. I just do it for a living.' Then when the tape comes up, they go real country-and-western. They all hate it. There are no country pickers left. They all died and passed away. How can anyone be a real country picker who was born and raised in the middle of a city?"[12]

Country-and-western may have died of old age but it wouldn't lie down. The *Grand Ole Opry* was now broadcast from a purpose-built concert hall while tourists could stay at the kitsch Opryland hotel with its stadium-sized atrium of palms and cascading rivers. They could also touch Presley's gold Cadillac in the Country Music Hall of Fame, and torture their eyes in Conway's "Twitty City" with its "million coloured lights at Christmas".

Twitty's *magnum opus*, 'It's Only Make Believe', had been revived in 1970 by Glen Campbell who'd been among the first to profit from the commercial viability of countrified pop. He followed this, incidentally, with a retread of 'Dream Baby'. On the same bandwagon, one of Roy's Sun stable mates, Charlie Rich, despite his silver hairs, was in for an unlooked-for chart bonanza come 1974. Jerry Lee Lewis too had risen anew as a country star. In 1972, Del Shannon was recording a country-pop album in Nashville. Elvis also had got wise with 'Kentucky Rain', Tony Joe White's 'Polk Salad Annie', Neil Diamond's 'Sweet Caroline' *et al* – either hit singles or highlights of his Caesar's Palace pageants. The last most people would ever see of him would be in the white garb of a rhinestone cowboy *sans* stetson.

Taking their cue from both Nashville's spellbinding gaudiness and its revamped music, licensed premises throughout the world transformed themselves during the seventies into parodies of either Wild West saloons or truckers' roadhouses. Barging through the swinging half-doors of a Canberra bar or Oxfordshire pub, you'd bump into Calamity Jane lookalikes, dundreary coves in bandanas, Vegas Presleys and buckskinned quaffers of Southern Comfort. Belying daytime guises as clerks or teachers, their conversations would be peppered with Deep South slang – "mess of grits" for "plate of food" – picked up from Merle Haggard albums and forty-fives like CB McCall's citizen's band monologue, 'Convoy', from the film of the same name starring Burt Reynolds. In *Roadie*, four years later, Roy Orbison and Hank Williams Junior as singers in a bar band would hush a brawl with 'The Eyes Of Texas Are Upon You' but more likely inclusions in such a group's repertoire would be 'Sunday Morning Coming Down', 'Okie From Muskogee', 'I'm The Man On

Susie's Mind', 'Crystal Chandelier' and Kris Kristofferson's 'Help Me Make It Through The Night'. Even if these hadn't made the Top Ten, they were as well-known as many that had.

'I'm The Man On Susie's Mind' had been co-written by Joe Melson with whom Roy had resumed his songwriting partnership. With Don Gant, Joe had also been the brains behind 'Run Baby Run' which had restored Mark Mathis' Newbeats to the hit parade after a long absence. Roy duplicated both this and 'I'm The Man On Susie's Mind' on *Memphis* which he and Melson produced at US Recording as they had four tracks from *Roy Orbison Sings*.

Like *There Is Only One Roy Orbison* and *Many Moods*, this album had been another of Orbison's mixed bags, released to keep investors sweet while he found his bearings. From the same session as 'So Young' came 'It Takes All Kinds Of People' while Wesley Rose and Don Gant joined the movable feast of producers for the remaining selections. So not to short-change British buyers, 'Yesterday's Child' from *Many Moods* was tacked onto the end of side two. Despite Roy's explanation that, "I've never really had the time to devote to albums like I wanted to and they usually wind up being twelve singles,"[13] there was little discernible difference in quality throughout *Orbison Sings...*, *Memphis* and *Milestones*.

Elvis had beaten him to 'Sweet Caroline' but Roy was first to 'Danny Boy' – from the Gaelic ballad, 'Acushla Mine' – a sentimental cabaret diehard. Moreover, the title track of *Memphis* stole a march on the King's rediscovery of Chuck Berry in 1975 whereby, in 'Promised Land', he sounded curiously like Orbison. While Roy's 'Memphis' quotes the 'Candy Man' ostinato, as outrageous is the 'Auld Lang Syne' intro to his re-recording of 'I Can't Stop Loving You'.

The rendering of 'The Three Bells', however, sticks as close to the Browns' 1959 hit as Brian Poole's version had in 1965. Apart from the phased drumming, the outlaw lope of 'I Fought The Law' – written by Sonny Curtis for El Paso's Bobby Fuller Four in 1966 – likewise emerged intact from the Orbison studio. Nevertheless, this song, 'Memphis' and 'Run Baby Run' were light relief against the mature country ballads that were the backbone of this final MGM trilogy. What Roy had merely alluded to in 'My Friend' came out into the open in Gene Thomas' 'Ring Of Gold' – her adultery – and Roy and

Joe's own 'Help Me'. Sex rears its head again in the spicy 'Cheyenne' – sung straight from the nostril – though it's laced with love in another Orbison-Melson original, 'Harlem Woman', about a mother forced by poverty into prostitution.

In a friskier vein is Eddy Raven's 'Plain Jane Country (Come To Town)' – a Beverly hillbilly without the money. More country-rock than country-pop is Jerry McBee's 'Run The Engines Up High' with its over-amplified fretboard scrawl. Roy also taped McBee's 'Why A Woman Cries' and 'Take Good Care Of Your Woman', both of which vaguely confirmed Roy's views about a woman's role: "I think equal pay for equal work is fine but I think the majority of women would like to be treated like a woman, and I don't think it can be any other way. I think they are entitled to more fairness but I wouldn't go along with some of these radical Women's Libbers who think that they can lift the same amount that a man can – which is impossible – or that they can control their emotions under certain situations. Certain women could but not women in general."[14]

What would Germaine Greer think of that not exceptional standpoint of a Southern male? For those who traced Roy's fortunes and feelings in the grooves, it appeared – if 'God Love You' and 'I Wanna Live' are to be believed – that he'd not only come through his trials sane and philosophical but also his new life with Barbara was joyful. Like 'Claudette', an eponymous song he'd written for her was given away to a duo – not Don and Phil but Don (Gant) and Joe (Melson). However, on *Roy Orbison Sings*, his interpretation of Mickey Newbury's 'Remember The Good' – as had 'Memories' in 1968 – put Claudette in perspective: "Heaven knows I've learnt to live without her...for all she meant to me, I'll remember the good."

No hit singles stuck out from the three albums but, unlike *Big O*, Roy was no more a listless passenger, a pliant executor of another's ideas. Nevertheless, assuming that most listeners would have a glimmer of its maker's personal history, the juxtaposing of 'The Three Bells' before the 'Danny Boy' finale was most insensitive. However much you tell yourself that they're just LP tracks by a highly-paid pop singer; that 'The Three Bells' is only a re-write of the nursery rhyme about Solomon Grundy; that Workington's answer to

Tom Jones crucified 'Danny Boy' one beer-sodden evening in the Red Lion the other week, who could prevent a knotted stomach, a lump in the throat, even tears when, after the third bell ushers in the line "one rainy morning dark and grey/a soul winged its way to heaven/little Jimmy Brown had passed away", another graveside ballad now from a father to his son – follows. Otherwise, all you can do is get the giggles in the teeth of its oppressive mawkishness. 'Danny Boy' was among Roy Orbison's most magnificent performances on record but his domestic tragedies and the tragedy yet to come have bequeathed it a piquancy as unbearable as that in John Lennon's 'Beautiful Boy' after the ex-Beatle's pavement assassination in 1980.

That Roy found the emotional detachment to tackle songs so close to the bone was testament to his relaxed equilibrium: "I have the balance in my life to see what the bad is, what the good is and where the in-between lies."[15] There had been another death – brother Grady of a coronary in 1973 – but, against all the odds, "My outlook is optimistic. I always look on the brighter side of life. If I were describing myself, I would say that I am a man who has to wear several hats; an artist, sometimes a songwriter, a business man." He was also the father of two more sons: Roy Kelton Junior born in October 1970, and Alexander who arrived four years later. Though more removed from public gaze than Claudette's children had been, the two well-favoured, blond boys could not help but become aware of Daddy's celebrity, but Mummy assured them, "It is a job just like other dads have...like doctors, lawyers, train drivers or anything else. If they think their father is something special, something different, too soon in life, it can destroy their sense of values."[16]

"She has done many things for me," remarked Orbison of his wife, "and she has not failed me in any one of them."[11] As well as her maternal virtues, he was fortunate in having in Barbara one with an instinct for the commercial and economic machinations of the music industry. Negotiations with showbusiness accountants, attorneys, managers and agents were not mysterious for long to the daughter of an important government official. With an icy ruthlessness formidable to those accustomed to Roy's glib bonhomie, Barbara came to take charge of the day-to-day running of the family's business enterprises.

Of these, the studio complex was proving a worthwhile investment. By the mid-seventies, it was attracting a few famous names such as Jerry Lee Lewis, Floyd Cramer and Tom T Hall – who, like the Killer, was signed to Mercury. Hoping to repeat the same success they'd had with Jerry Lee's immersion in country, this same company took on Roy Orbison in 1974 for a one-shot LP when, at long last, he was extricated from the clutches of MGM.

Unavailable outside America, the resulting *I'm Still In Love With You* painted a rosy picture in its liner notes, promising that the three singles derived from it were all surefire hits. Yet, for all this and the flashiness of its front portrait, the music of this first and only Mercury album was something of a false dawn. Mostly, his singing was strained or unimpassioned as he went through the motions once more. With one of his former guitarists, Jerry Kennedy, assigned as producer, and arrangements by an even older colleague, Bill Justis, Roy cranked out the Don Gibson cover, the token ballad, the 'Heartache' re-make, the re-modelled C&W oldie – 'Crying Time' with flutes and robotic drumming – and a couple of *nouveau* country outings – Bud Reneau's 'All I Need Is Time' and Larry Gatlin's 'Circles', the record's strongest song. While this begins like The Troggs' placatory 'Anyway That You Want Me', Orbison and Melson's makeweight 'It's Lonely' – one of the singles – recalls The Searchers minus the smooth Scouse harmonies. The other three new compositions have more substance – though the holiday romance, 'Spanish Nights', with its stock castanets, flamenco twiddling and Costa del Nashville strings was a pastiche that Joe and Roy could have written in their sleep.

This B-sided 'Hung Up On You' on which was imposed a half-hearted "funky" rhythm of four-to-the-bar snare and a defiantly sparse bass line. It was intended as a concession to disco fever, then sashaying towards its John Travolta zenith. If you'd decided to sit that one out, there was the third forty-five, 'Sweet Mamma Blue', a slow waltz about a fictional New Orleans club pianist who, after hours, functioned as a sort of musical agony aunt. Rounding off Roy Orbison's weakest album, was a tepid 'Pledging My Love' – a posthumous hit for Johnny Ace in 1955 that The Teen Kings used to play. Nearly twenty years on, their leader was nearly overwhelmed by the spirited backing "shoop-dooby-ooo-wah-ooos". In 1977, Elvis would make a better job of it on what no-one knew would be his valedictory album.

For Roy Orbison, however, "The best is certainly yet to come." Thus spake the cover notes again as Mercury neglected to pick up an option on a second album. Why had he gone so stale? Since their reunion, he and Melson had been unduly worried about surpassing their previous standards. Back in the suffocating emptiness of Odessa in the fifties, they'd often shed ideas non-stop. Now hours would trudge by without a ghost of a tune or lyric. Such songs that did get underway all hovered round the age-honoured formula melodies and buzz-words: "If I try to write for Roy Orbison, it doesn't work," the singer explained. "It takes forever and is no good anyway."[17] Like the alchemists, they'd explore the same worn-out themes over and over again from new angles in the wrong-headed expectation of finding gold. Now and then, they'd stray far enough from habit to accommodate the humoresque caprice that breathed life into 'Changes' off *Roy Orbison Sings*. That the underlying – and rather puerile – concept of 'Sweet Mamma Blue' should be extrapolated for over four minutes was a sure sign of creative bankruptcy. With the scanty critiques of the Mercury album lukewarm at most, neither Joe nor Roy could convince the other that they'd ever equal or better 'Running Scared', 'Blue Angel' and all the rest of them.

He confessed as much to Fred Foster with whom he'd been in touch again regarding a query over the back-catalogue. During a Canadian tour in 1975, Roy had been badgered by K-Tel, a conglomerate specialising in re-issues, who wanted him to re-record all his hits for world-wide release on its Arcade subsidiary. On the verge of consenting, he checked first with the keeper of the original masters. Quick on the uptake, Fred Foster knew that there'd be no need. Though Monument compilations of Orbisonia had been pressed in largish quantities since 1966, Fred saw greater fiscal opportunities in leasing the ancient tracks to K-Tel whose budget would stretch to the saturation television advertising that would perk up sales from tens of thousands to close on a quarter of a million a year.

Since parting with Roy, Fred's company had diversified from pop into country and black music – although several of its signings crossed over into the Hot 100 as did soul singer Robert Knight with 'Everlasting Love' in 1968. Among whites who also managed this were Kris Kristofferson and Tony Joe White, Southern singer-songwriters considerably less mannered and artistically self-centred than the Melanies and Neil Youngs of the North. From Elvis downwards, their compositions attracted numerous cover versions. Broadly speaking, the *modus operandi* of these two individuals could be described as "country-soul".

Fred Foster realised that Roy Orbison – divested of all the schmaltz he'd recorded lately – could fit that category too. With old affections flooding his heart, it abruptly made sense for Roy, now a free agent, to return to the fold. That he was fresh out of new numbers didn't bother Monument. Fred was certain that a well-produced album of other writers' material would restore Orbison's confidence – and that's when his own songs would materialise. They could go on the next one.

To symbolise both this intended renaissance and the prodigal's homecoming, the first project would bear the title *Regeneration*. White and Kristofferson were each delighted to pen a song for Roy – as were two lesser lights on Foster's file, Bob Morrison and the many-sided Dennis Linde. As well as the cream of Nashville session players, imported from Alabama would be the crack in-house horn section from trendy Muscles Shoals studios. Their beefy riffing had serviced many a soul smash. Just you leave everything to Uncle Fred. All you have to do for now is sing.

In deferring to Foster, Roy became a challenger again. With punk's distant thunder out of earshot, the American pop scene was glutted with Woodstock Nation idols still. Even if there was no immediate sales animation, *Regeneration* was, therefore, "contemporary" enough to suggest that the reinstatement of Orbison in the charts was not improbable.

The hero of *Regeneration* had been Dennis Linde, provider of nearly half its songs – including the first promotional forty-five,

'Belinda'. His was mainly a country-rock bag but, with clipped guitar *chukka-wukka*, his 'Under Suspicion' soul stew was as implausible a setting for Orbison as 'Southbound Jericho Parkway' had been. Nonetheless, on a piece better suited to "Godfather of Soul" James Brown, Roy coped admirably. As always since 1959, whatever he sang sounded like Roy Orbison. Without affectation, he was also convincingly out of character as the wine-drinkin', skinny-dippin' hedonist "makin' love in the pale moonlight" in Tony Joe White's steamy '(I'm A) Southern Man'. More typical fare included Morrison's stately 'Born To Love Me' and Kristofferson's 'Something They Can't Take Away' – which dwelt in the vicinity of 'Memories'. Though there wasn't much love lost between Foster and Wesley Rose – with whom Roy was becoming estranged too – a smouldering work-out of Fred Rose's 'Blues In My Mind' led off side two. All on tape within a few days, every item on *Regeneration* was enacted with more guts and conviction from both artist and musicians than any on the watery Mercury effort.

Admittedly, Roy had been almost a cipher on his own album but *Regeneration* was of harder metal than the soporific country-rock wafting from the West Coast. Then in vogue were the ilk of Loggins and Messina, the sugary John Denver, Linda Ronstadt – a singer-songwriter type except she didn't write many songs – and The Eagles[18] whose *Greatest Hits* collection would be ensconced in the US album chart for most of 1976. Also popular that year – and in succeeding years – was New Jersey's Bruce Springsteen with his Yogi Bear vibrato and an energetic vitality that put him a cut above James Taylor. Prudently, Mercury had quoted a line from 'Thunder Road' – about Roy Orbison singing "for the lonely" from Springsteen's latest "Orbison-soaked album"[19] in the press-release for 'I'm Still In Love With You'.

Subtler traces of mid-period Orbison had infiltrated the classical-rock fusions of best-selling British bands such as Queen and the Electric Light Orchestra. Bryan Ferry, *führer* of the arty Roxy Music, was also a big Orbison fan – while the ghoulish Alice Cooper's 'Only Women Bleed' relied structurally on a Big O crescendo, as did 'Don't Cry For Me Argentina', *the* hit song of 1976.

Around this period, 'Love Hurts' by, respectively, Nazareth and

Jim Capaldi, had clambered up the North American and British Top Tens. The following year, 'Blue Bayou' would shift ten million – nine million more than the original – for Linda Ronstadt; its composing royalty giving Roy's bank balance a welcome shot in the arm. Catapulted to international prominence with the allegorical 'American Pie', Don McLean's version of 'Cryin'' was, at this time, rejected by his record company as "too slow".

However, issued later following laudatory viewer reaction after he'd sung it on Dutch television, McLean's 'Cryin'' – backed by The Jordanaires – was, in many countries, even more successful than 'American Pie'. A British Number One, it also clambered into the US Top Five.

Suddenly, Roy Orbison's was a name to drop in hip circles, prompting favourable critical notices for *Regeneration*. Though this album hadn't been as tidy as he'd have liked, there was talk of him performing a couple of its titles when he hit the road again. In from the cold, he could now tour the States on grounds other than nostalgia. Dignifying one audience at an exploratory engagement in California were members of The Eagles, The Steve Miller Band, current chart-toppers Jefferson Starship and faddish comedy band, The Tubes. Some of these worthies could not restrain themselves from joining the Big O on stage for the encore segment – a snippet noted in the glowing report of the show in the *Los Angeles Times*.

Returning to Tennessee, he was introduced by Fred Foster to another big name of the later seventies, Emmylou Harris whose band comprised many revered country-rock figures, some of whom had been hired in the past by Elvis. However, though her records sold well, Emmylou's harmony vocals were so admired that she became as renowned for her many duets with other artists. These included John Sebastian, ubiquitous Linda Ronstadt, Johnny Hallyday and, a singular honour, Bob Dylan. Possibilities of another such liaison may have crossed Emmylou's mind when she invited Roy to "one of those picking parties that happens sometimes. Everybody was passing the guitar and he sang. I remember commenting that I'd probably never sell that house because Roy Orbison had sung in it."[5]

No time was better for Orbison's comeback but the moment was lost when, in January 1978, he went under the scalpel for a triple-bypass heart operation.

Chest pains during the *Regeneration* sessions had been, concluded his doctor, no cause for alarm. Watching a football game in the company of the Presley clan in Memphis a few weeks later, the agony gripped again after a dash up several flights of the stadium's stairs for refreshments. Reeling to a pay phone, he explained the now abating symptoms to a local GP who prescribed an immediate return home for another check-up. Further tests – involving camera insertion – revealed extensive arterial blockage. "But that didn't bother me too much, thank goodness," the star said. "The doctor said, 'Roy, we're going to have to have open heart surgery,' and I said, 'Well, be sure to leave a nice scar because I wear open-necked shirts.'"[20]

This flippancy pre-empted post-operation medical advice to avoid stress in future. Roy was less enamoured with cutting down on cigarettes, and the recommended diet to reduce both poundage and blood pressure. Nevertheless, the freeing of his arteries and consequent increase of brain oxygen spurred a renewal of professional activity as, by April, a livelier Orbison was back on stage.

It was now a false economy to employ cheapskate pick-up groups who couldn't or wouldn't reproduce the original arrangements. He could afford to pick and choose nowadays. His eye had alighted on Skwydro Heegie, an Oklahoman sextet who'd worked at US Recording. The name a spoonerism of a water pump component, five of Skwydro Heegie were brothers called Price. The eldest, forty-one-year-old Ron, had been a member of The Velvets who, missing only one of Orbison's footsteps, had recorded at Norman Petty's in Clovis and been signed to Monument. They'd even twice cast their shadow in the Hot 100 in 1961. Moreover, a third Velvets single contained 'Lana' – and 'Laugh', one of the better Orbison-Melson compositions not appropriated by Roy himself.

Like The Art Movement before them, Skwydro Heegie's liking for The Beach Boys would be evident whenever they were required to precede the Big O with their own spot. They did not presume, however, to interpose their own unsolicited ideas and corporate personality onto the established status quo. Skwydro Heegie knew their place: "We followed his career and we never dreamed we'd be playing with him one day. We took his *Greatest Hits* album and played the songs exactly like the records."[22]

The group were not alone in finding Mrs Orbison rather intimidating too. Since Wesley Rose's retirement after, apparently, selling his company to the owners of Opryland, Barbara had become, by the late seventies, very much the power behind the throne. When in London, the family would now be staying at the Mayfair Hotel rather than the Westbury because she had taken offence over an incident involving Roy Kelton Junior and a harassed chambermaid. A more absolute alienation would take place in 1982 when the Orbisons, claiming lost income from royalties, sued a shocked Wesley Rose for thirty million pounds: "Barbara and I felt we had to put everything in order in my career," Roy explained. "We never had the right management, the right agency, the right record company all at once."[5]

On the last count, the outcome of this re-evaluation was a two-year vinyl silence after *Regeneration*. During Roy's recuperation following the heart operation, he informed Fred Foster that, "He didn't want to do any more records for a while so would I release him from his contract? This I did." In relinquishing this and other commitments, Roy came as close as he'd ever been to a pain-free existence: a lovely and supportive wife, three adorable children and so rich – a sterling millionaire – that work was a diversion not a necessity. Could anyone begrudge Roy his bliss?

Never a miserly fellow, his new home matched his money. Its six bathrooms and three kitchens alone occupied thousands of square feet. The rosewood from which expensive guitars are made lined the master bedrooms. Carpets underfoot were *objets d'art*, never mind the one on the wall: "Yes, I suppose I have a feeling for the aristocratic way of life – and to have been in Berlin and Paris in the twenties would have been my cup of tea,"[16] he surmised. Between the wars, however, no monocled grandee's eerie would have known the embarrassment of labour-saving devices such as the electronic speaker system in Roy's leather-padded writing room whereby he could communicate with any part of the house. At the push of a bedside button, a meal would be automatically delivered for the couple to devour while watching the fitted large-screen television.

With no obligation to rise from his silk sheets, what did Orbison do all day? Well, there was the swimming pool, the guitar-shaped radio, the workshop where he constructed his model aircraft. Sharing this child-like enthusiasm, guitarist Benny Birchfield – later Roy's tour manager – would spend jolly open-air afternoons with Roy sending their radio-controlled toys soaring into the endless blue.

Orbison took more impersonal pride in his replenished treasury of vintage vehicles. As before, he was contemplating their storage in a museum open to the public. He'd accumulated so many old cars now that he'd had to sell some to make space for more valuable purchases such as a 1937 Jaguar and a Mercedes ten years older. After acquiring the latter's chassis in 1969, the task of rebuilding its bodywork was entrusted to an English mechanic, Peter Gray, whose Worthing garage had serviced other such antiquities for Orbison since 1965. Roy had been dismayed, so he said, that procrastination had allowed another collector, former Yardbird Jimmy Page, to outbid him for an American Cord rarity.

As with Claudette, Roy had inducted Barbara into the thrills of motorbiking – as he also would the teenage Wesley. Like his late elder brothers, Wesley had inherited musical skills, and was showing promise as a songwriter. Alexander was a bit of an enigma as yet but, to Roy, the other two were "a reflection of me. They both like what I like and are very, very busy right now, having a lot of fun."[14]

On the surface, therefore, Roy Orbison seemed much the same as he'd always been: "You should not give up the things to which you are accustomed. If you keep late hours, for instance, you should continue. If you have a hobby, you should continue – or, at least, try to continue your interests and career and let time take care of everything else. If you get off the track and give up this and that, you will never find yourself again."[15]

The most profound change over the decade was his drift back to the Church. He'd begun with what he knew. Soberly attired, the family attended matins at the Church of Christ in nearby Madison for several years before rededicating themselves to Hendersonville's Baptist ministry. As other famous worshippers there included Kris Kristofferson, Johnny Cash and Skeeter Davis, a sign would appear at the lychgate warning "Absolutely No Autographs Or Pictures Taken Inside This Sanctuary".

Even at the extremities of despair and elation, Roy had never lost that simple Christianity of his childhood – the "religion" he'd figured out at the age of six; regular affirmation of which had been impractical during his global wanderings. His recording of the hymn, 'I Belong To Him', with Waylon Jennings and Jessie Coulter would be, however, Orbison's most public declaration of faith. He would never be as vigorously evangelical as Johnny Cash or prone to loud bouts of piety like Jerry Lee Lewis. Instead, his moderate personality dictated reticence on the subject unless specifically asked: "I don't have a pure statement but I believe in Jesus Christ and try to live by the rules of morality and conduct and a certain faithfulness in all things. That helps a great deal – so does common sense. It's very important to me. Your mind is created by a higher power and common sense will often tell you what to do."[15]

Coping less well had been a more illustrious contemporary: "I know Elvis had a strong faith but it was just that there was no-one close enough to him, that loved him enough, to tell him what he was doing to himself."[23] Prey to obesity, hypochondria and paranoia, the self-destructive King's reign had been drawing to its close – and there would be no replacement. However, if – as some of his chroniclers would allege – he was as nutty as a fruitcake behind closed doors, nothing had seemed amiss when, in December 1976, the mutual admiration society of Orbison and Presley met for the last time. From the audience, Roy had taken a bow when, up on stage at Caesar's Palace, Elvis introduced him as "quite simply, the greatest singer in the world". This opinion, unaltered since 1959, may have been pleasing but the Big O suffered for the compliment when mobbed for 2,000 autographs after the lights went up at the finish of the first house. Laughing it off, he filtered backstage to pay homage: "We hadn't seen each other in years. He hugged me. We talked about everything: Jerry Lee Lewis, touring...he was a little overweight but looked really good."[23]

So impressed was Orbison with Presley's appearance that, back in Britain the following March, he appeared on stage in an iconoclastic *white* leather fringed jump suit, rather like the one into which the ailing Elvis had stuffed his podgy bulk in Vegas. No more slogging round tatty clubs, Roy – no stick insect either – was filling many of the theatres he'd first packed out in the mid-sixties. Some nights, there were even a few screams. Plainly, the lay-off had been worth it.

Augmenting Skwydro Heegie were string and horn sections in black evening dress to contrast with the star's sartorial volte-face. The hour-long performance was nothing if not vulgar. A line of choreographed cavorters, for example, was more prominent than Roy himself during 'Land Of 1,000 Dances'. Nonetheless, the already-converted acknowledged that he was taking more trouble this trip.

Needless to say, Orbison was despised by those journalists whose living seemed to depend on their toadying to someone called "Johnny Rotten", chief show-off with The Sex Pistols. In Britain – and, to a lesser extent, in the States – the punk rock storm had broken. It was a fierce time and no mistake. The musical content of 'Anarchy In The UK', 'Sheena Is A Punk Rocker' by The Ramones, Generation X's 'Wild Youth' and other two-minute bursts of self-conscious racket was irrelevant. What counted was that, more so than skiffle or rockabilly, anyone could do it – even if most punk outfits looked and sounded just like The Sex Pistols: ripped clothes, short hair, safety-pin earrings plus three chords thrashed at speed to machine-gun drumming behind shouted denigration of the old, the wealthy and the established. In August 1977, news of Elvis Presley's bathroom death reached a basement club frequented by London punks, some of whom raised a gleeful cheer.

As you can gather, 1977 was a bad year for Grand Old Men like Roy Orbison. "We're another generation," scowled Joey of The Ramones. "They're rich and living in another world altogether...to them, it's just another way of making money."[24] Buried in the fawning coverage afforded this new wave in the music press, a review of the Orbison show at the Bristol Hippodrome corroborated Joey Ramone's jaded appraisal: "There can be few businessmen around building themselves such a large pension fund with such ease."[25]

Benignly, Roy refused to bitch back, seeing only "a bunch of fresh, new people trying to do their thing like we did in 1954...disgraceful we were, degenerated because we played that kind of music and everything. So that's exactly what they are, what we were then."[26]

As with rockabilly, the grubbing showbusiness industry stole punk's most viable ideas and persuaded the more palatable new wave entertainers to ease up, grow their hair maybe, talk correct and prepare to take the States for every cent they could get. The aptly-named Billy Idol of Generation X, for instance, was groomed as an updated Ricky Nelson. With one of his songs absorbed into – it's that woman again – Linda Ronstadt's canon, one of the first British new wave ambassadors to clean up over the Atlantic was a weedy young man in glasses who'd been given the *nom de guerre* "Elvis Costello". Not content with this affinity to the King, Costello also borrowed Roy Orbison's uncommunicative stage persona.

Crucially, the genuine article's voice was still a thing of wonder. A running joke with Skwydro Heegie was his poker-faced "Cover me for any notes I don't hit" just before showtime. Orbison's vocal resonance was now closer to its natural baritone but the hits were still played in their original keys. Sometimes he'd need to muddle through the 'Only The Lonely' opener to switch into gear. In a televised performance of 'Running Scared' during his "white period", he appeared to be struggling a little too.

It wasn't that he'd become a bad singer – just an old one. Tiredness, if not discernible in a rapt auditorium, made a marked difference when, in 1978, he was cajoled by the fashionable Elektra-Asylum – The Eagles' label – into cutting another album: "When I was cutting my older records, I had more control over my vibrato," he explained. "Now, if I don't want to have the vibrato in the studio, I have to do a session earlier in the day because, by the evening, it'll be there whether I want it or not."[5]

Roy's "miraculously singular voice" and the final track, 'Hound Dog Man', were deemed by *Rolling Stone* to be the only salvageable aspects of the new LP which was otherwise "an embarrassing travesty...maybe the most soul-less album ever recorded at Muscles Shoals."[27] Other criticisms of *Laminar Flow* – after an aeronautics term – were as harsh and Orbison himself felt it "was like a half-finished project to me".[6]

It was, indeed, easy to pull to pieces. Hardly any of the songs would have stood up had their orchestration been pruned down to just voice and piano. There was a velvet-smooth helping of the moderato soul style – more feathery than Stax or early Motown – that had emanated from trend-setting Philadelphia from the likes of The Stylistics and Jerry Butler. At its worst, 'Philly Soul' would have limpid sweetening of strings, vibraphone and woodwinds plastered over a muted but jittery rhythm. This would be crowned by vocal burbling of lovey-dovey mush to a gambolling flute or saxophone obligato. As Roy had processed 'Under Suspicion' on *Regeneration*, so he made the best of Terry Woodford and Clayton Ivey's productions of 'I Care', 'We're Into Something Good' and 'Tears'. No doubt these exhaled from many a late evening stereo, facilitating the winning of maidenly hearts by smitten young executives in penthouse apartments the world over.

From Philadelphia too had come David Bowie's "plastic soul" album, *Young Americans*, from which, in 1975, was taken his first US Number One, 'Fame'. A laughable theft of the riff central to 'Fame' cropped up in the tedious funk exercise 'Lay It Down', while plunging Orbison further into disco were 'Warm Spot Hot' and 'Easy Way Out' – though this began with an unsettlingly funereal string passage.

More foreign to Roy was Chris Price's libretto to 'Movin''. Though this put some realism into the overworked myth of the rock 'n' roll lifestyle, it was somehow disappointing to hear that nice Roy Orbison drooling over "those front row women" and – albeit *sotto voce* – twice interjecting an oath you'd never have imagined him using. It wouldn't have mattered so much had not Ivey and Woodford's session crew been so gutlessly precise. Perhaps the rowdier edge of Skwydro Heegie might have saved the day.

Almost as deplorable was when Roy sang in 'Friday Night' of picking up a female hitch-hiker who "put her little hand on my knee" to encourage nature to take its course – and him a God-fearing, happily married man and all. You wouldn't read about it – except that, for the first time on an Orbison disc, the words were printed on the inner sleeve.

Meaning did not take precedent over phonetics in 'Warm Spot Hot' and 'Lay It Down' but 'Love Is A Cold Wind' and the vengeful 'Poor Baby' – tracks closest to the Orbison of the sixties – betray some lyrical flair, though neither overdid the insight. Possibly because it didn't have a weather eye on passing trends, the stand-out *Laminar Flow* song was the Elvis eulogy, 'Hound Dog Man', from an idea of Barbara's in 1974. After cash-ins such as Danny Mirror's 'I Remember Elvis Presley' and the ghastly 'The Greatest Star Of All' by Skip Jackson, it "was long enough after all the exploitation. It's on an album for sale but it wouldn't bother me if no-one heard the song. I really did it from me to him. Also, I've got the credentials to sing it."[27]

Coming after all the sequencers, synth-drums and other treated clutter, the no-frills arrangement and unvarnished narrative of 'Hound Dog Man' only compounded the artistic mismatch and loss of direction that was *Laminar Flow*. Apart from Barbara's third of 'Hound Dog Man', composing credits were split roughly between the Muscles Shoals house musicians and, at Roy's request, the Price brothers. Though he'd only contributed a few melody lines to this album, Roy had "decided that if I did record new things, I would have a hand in the writing of them – because it makes me feel responsible. If I wrote them and they weren't successful, that's okay It was my responsibility."[28]

During the year of Don McLean's 'Cryin'', Roy's role in *Roadie* went some of the way towards overcoming his writer's block. On a varied soundtrack – which also included donations by Jerry Lee Lewis and Alice Cooper among others – he joined the synergetic Emmylou Harris in his own 'That "Lovin' You" Feelin' Again'. Originally on the B-side of the spin-off single, it picked up more airplay on C&W radio than its coupling, Craig Hundley's 'Lola'. By autumn 1980, it had come not only to top the country chart but had also earned the pair a Grammy award – a pop music Oscar – for best-country-performance-by-a-duo-or-group.

Partly on the strength of this, Orbison found himself touring California with The Eagles. Winning over largely adolescent following, it was almost a throwback to days when he'd had the onerous duty of preceding The Beatles or Stones onstage, "But it was a modern day thing and a lot of fun,"[26] he insisted. There wasn't much time left but he wasn't wasting it: "Things are moving at a very good pace. I got this feeling around 1954; I got this feeling around 1959, and I get this feeling now that what I want to do is going to happen."[28]

CHAPTER NINE

Not Alone Anymore

The Grammy – his first – had been an unexpected but deserved accolade. A resurgence of desire for an old flame, 'That "Lovin' You" Feelin' Again' had been a well-integrated duet with sure-footed harmonies. Of course, its success owed much to cinema exposure, and, as the new decade of commodity over creativity progressed, more work of this kind would fall into Roy Orbison's lap. Between *Zabriskie Point* and *Roadie*, less deserving beneficiaries of Orbison's singing had included *The Moonshine War* – a curate's egg of a hillbilly melodrama – and the rather featureless *Zig-Zag* (*False Witness* in Britain) – dying man frames himself for unsolved murder so that wife gets reward.

Set for spring 1980 had been *The Living Legend*, Roy's authorised film biography: "I want to avoid people having a wrong account of my life."[1] Martin Sheen from *Apocalypse Now* had been wooed for the title role, and two soundtrack songs completed by Orbison with Chris Price. However, unhappy with the low budget and long delays, Roy withdrew from the project. This was considered regrettable but by no means disastrous by its backers. With hardly a break in schedule, *The Living Legend* was remodelled as a generalised fiction about a pop star more like Elvis than anyone else.

That Orbison could dismiss such an opportunity said much about his new standing as pop's history as much as its present was seized on as an avenue for selling records. Teenagers, you see, were no longer pop's most vital consumer group, having been outmanoeuvred by their Swinging Sixties parents. Even the mighty *The Wink Bulletin* now defined rock 'n' roll as "a type of music preferred by adults aged thirteen to sixty".[2] No matter how it was tarted up – twelve inch megamix on polkadot vinyl or whatever – the pop single had become a loss leader, an incentive for grown-ups to buy an album, hopefully on compact disc.

Britain in the mid eighties, for instance, would be sodden with nostalgia for the sixties. At one stage, every fourth record in the chart was either a re-issue or a revival of an old song. In the States, jumping out of albums as the sampler single would be an act's disposable revamp of an oldie – as exemplified by Cheap Trick's ham-fisted 'Don't Be Cruel' – also recorded by The Judds – and Michael Bolton's Top Forty cover of Otis Redding's 'Dock Of The Bay'. In 1982, heavy metallurgists Van Halen touched Number Twelve with 'Oh! Pretty Woman' – which the year before had resounded in the UK Top Ten as part of Tight Fit's 'Back To The Sixties' medley.

It was now not out of the question for stars no longer young to re-enter the hit parade with their latest releases too, holding their own amid post-punk me-generation entertainers. After The Kinks rematerialised in 1983, yonder loomed second comings for – amongst many others – Tom Jones, George Harrison, The Bee Gees (for the umpteenth time), Steve Winwood and, too late, Roy Orbison. More than ever, the words of John McNally of The Searchers rang true: "You don't have to be young to make good records."[3] For all their wrinkles, galloping alopecia and belts at the last hole, these exhumed suzerains fascinated the young and artistically bankrupt who were envious of their elders' unquiet past. "Looking back on both the Presley era and The Beatles and Stones era, those two bursts of energy were quite amazing," surmised Roy Orbison. "It was like people had something to say and they really loved saying it. I don't know whether there's been so much of that since then. The energy's still there in some ways but there either isn't so much of it or there are so many different kinds of artists now that the energy has been dissipated."[4]

Among myriad salutes by the young to a more vibrant past were ABC's 'When Smokey [Robinson] Sings' and 'Godstar' – about drowned Rolling Stone, Brian Jones – from Psychic TV. Many would try to buttress their positions with credible influences. Two singles by The Art Of Noise were collaborations with, respectively, Duane Eddy and Tom Jones while one of George Michael's biggest sellers was a duet with Aretha Franklin, a soul singer well into her forties – and subject of Scritti Politti's 'Wood Beez (Pray Like Aretha Franklin)'.

Although he'd rest on past laurels until the eleventh hour, Roy Orbison's name would come up too. On a par with Chuck Berry and Duane Eddy in a *Record Collector* popularity poll, he could look down on the likes of Johnny Cash, Del Shannon and Carl Perkins. In April 1982, he and Jerry Lee Lewis had been major attractions at London's Country Music Festival. This was the first time they'd appeared on the same bill for nearly thirty years – though there had been a close shave in the seventies when both had been booked for a televised *Johnny Cash Christmas Special*. However, Cash's objection to Jerry Lee referring to himself by name in the third person – "I'm dreaming of a white Christmas/just like the ones old Killer used to know" – caused the Lewis section of the show to be edited out.

There would be no hard feelings, however, when the three old campaigners convened with Carl Perkins to record an album together back at the now much-modernised Sun studio back in Memphis. The idea for this had been conceived four years earlier when Sun issued a jam session from 1956 allegedly involving the "Million Dollar Quartet" of Lewis, Cash, Perkins and Elvis Presley. Documentary rather than recreational for the listener, this thirty-minute sing-song, nonetheless, provoked sufficient interest for a premeditated eighties reconstruction for the "Class of 55" to be organised with Roy filling in for the departed Presley.

The consequent *Homecoming* – as it would be called – if short on spontaneity, was a likable enough sentimental journey, rife with tuneful reminiscences, slices of autobiography in song, a commemoration of Elvis – 'We Remember The King' – and three numbers with "rock 'n' roll" in the title. Cash and Orbison seemed the least active of the chicken-necked principals, submitting only one solo turn each against the others' two. The remaining four tracks were communal efforts with verses doled out more or less equally with everyone in raucous harmony on the choruses.

At opposite poles were the voices of Jerry Lee – darker and bereft of all ingenuity – and Roy forever sweet and innocent, especially on his own ballad-soliloquy, 'Coming Home'. Opening the second half, this led a separate life from the rest of the album. The first half of its melody was not unlike Nilsson's 'Without You' from 1972. But, free of the name-dropping and "Memphis beat" that seemed compulsory on other tracks, 'Coming Home' – if not a masterpiece of song – conveyed the required back-to-the-roots aura without olde tyme retrogression.

In the LP's eight-minute "party" number, 'Big Train (From Memphis)', the four legends and their backing musicians' guests spanned all ages of pop. In Sam Phillips and Jack Clement, there were the opinionated console sages whose musical conditioning process had primed four country boys for greener pastures. Ricky Nelson was there too as was noted songwriter Toni Wine and John Fogerty, composer of 'Big Train' and mainstay of Creedence Clearwater Revival. Another revivalist was Welsh guitarist Dave Edmunds whose adolescent imagination had also been captured by rockabilly and its off-shoots – whether Jerry Lee Lewis's hollered arrogance or the eldritch cry of Roy Orbison.

Lending a hand too were The Judds, a mother-and-daughter team from Kentucky who, for better or worse, had been calibrated as part of a late development in country-and-western, marketed as "New Tradition". More than the Glen Campbells and Lynn Andersons of the decade gone, the differing aptitudes of The Judds, kd lang, Randy Travis, Dwight Yoakam, The Sweethearts Of The Rodeo and others were rescuing country from its decline by forsaking much of its rhinestoned tackiness for a leaner more abandoned approach. In North America anyway, it found favour with a younger audience for whom C&W had been the corniest genre in pop.

Glancing at kd lang's spiky hair-do and artlessly laddered stockings, it is tempting to rationalise this movement as bearing roughly the same "new broom" parallel to country as punk had to mainstream pop. However, inherent in its very name was a respect for country's down-home maturity and veneration for its elder statesmen. As Jason Ringenberger, leader of Texan New Traditionists, The Scorchers, explained: "We're not trying to slaughter country or walk all over it. We feel that we have a lot in common with singers like Hank Williams – obviously not in sound but we're out there on a certain edge."[5] Putting action over debate, Dwight Yoakam collaborated on an album with Buck Owens. From the more recent past, Emmylou Harris attended likewise to The Judds while kd lang dusted off 'Rose Garden' on her *Angel With A Lariat* LP. For the film *Hiding Out*, and the passage of lang – formerly Kathy Dawn Lang from Canada – into the US pop chart was assisted by her formidable duet of 'Cryin'' with Roy Orbison.

Making up for lost time, perhaps, the homeland that had written him off as a has-been was now beating a path to Roy's door: "It seems as though America is saying, 'We loved you back in the sixties and we still love you today,'"[6] he reflected. With Elvis plucking a harp on a cloud, surely he was one of the next best things. With the right song, Orbison was ready to reap another vinyl harvest.

One recording that had all the qualities of a smash but none that actually grabbed the public was 1985's 'Wild Hearts', another film souvenir. The commission from the reputable Nicolas Roeg – *Performance*, *Don't Look Now*, *The Man Who Fell To Earth* – was an honour for Roy, still a lay expert on films. Pleasing too was the release of 'Wild Hearts' in various mixes and sizes by ZTT, then on a crest of a wave with Frankie Goes To Hollywood who – in Britain at least – were swamping the Top Ten. Teetering on the edge of the charts, 'Wild Hearts' may have been issued in the States by ZTT had the rather pretentious movie, *Insignificance* – "the story of life, death, sex and the universe" – done better at the box office. Instead, 'Wild Hearts' faded – as the film did – from general circulation.

Unfortunately, it was Roy's strongest single for years. For those who hadn't heard a lot of him since 1966, it was much how they may have expected him to sound in the eighties. Largely the product of polysynthesizers rather than flesh-and-blood orchestration, a lengthy prelude slides into a protracted *diminuendo* until you're caught off-guard by Orbison's headlong "wild hearts run out of time/when you're up against the night" – and he's away. With cold charm, the pre-recorded backing effortlessly keeps pace as Roy descends a lonely valley, scales its rim and takes a breather overlooking the next concourse. Then he set forth for the other purple-headed crag and a 'Running Scared' cadence. Though it was musical fell-walking rather than 'It's Over' mountaineering, it had been ages since he'd climbed this high.

Orbison's songwriting partner on 'Wild Hearts' – and others – was Will Jennings, a professional wordsmith. His lyrics also graced the music of The Crusaders – a revered jazz-rock outfit from his native Texas – and, lately relocated to Nashville, Steve Winwood whose *Arc Of A Diver* LP of 1980 had rescued a deflated career, thanks in part to Jennings. Rather than burden the listener with clumsy tracts about the wrongs of the world as Winwood's previous helpmate had done, Will approached tunes with detached efficiency and the reasonable argument that the words should blend with the music – and the singer's personality: "I look for an identity between myself and the person I'm working for."[7]

If his 'Coming Home' for Roy Orbison was repetitive, it nevertheless rolled off the tongue without pomp or affectation. As Winwood was Jennings' main concern – and source of revenue – his work for others, though competent, tended to pay his mortgage rather than sate him with pride. 'Wild Hearts', for example, repeated a key phrase – "in the sunshine of your mind" – first heard on Winwood's 'Help Me Angel' three years earlier. However, another Orbison job, 'Life Fades Away' for the soundtrack of *Less Than Zero* – from the Bret Easton Ellis novel – was a succinct intimation of mortality pertinent to the death scene in the script.

Though it upset Barbara when he smoked, it didn't occur to anyone then that Roy's own days might be numbered. Attention to his own well-being may have been diverted by his mother's hip operation but Orbie Lee's decline after heart surgery brought home to his son what fatal weakness he – and Grady – had surely inherited. The producer of 'Life Fades Away', Rick Rubin would recall that though the singer's favourite fizzy drink was frowned on by his doctor, "It was time to do the vocal and he was in the booth, and he made us get him a Coke – because he'd never made a record without having a Coke."[8] The chest scars had been discreetly airbrushed out and he was probably holding his stomach in, but the sleeve photographs of *Laminar Flow* – taken a year after treatment – were pictures of health. With the best of intentions, he tried to stick to his diet – "not meaning a restricted food intake but the proper food" – and exercise "from time to time".[8] Nevertheless, beneath the fringe that he still dyed, the face grew chubbier, the chin doubled, the waist thickened – though, in 1988, he became suddenly and noticeably thinner.

Whereas once the show might have gone on, minor afflictions now prostrated him. An attack of flu would write off a televised return visit to the London Palladium on 15 November, 1987. At another British concert a couple of years earlier, Michelle Booth "knew he was unwell because he had to be helped from the stage – but I didn't know how serious things were."

That was Michelle and Steve's farewell – and, on that same tour, Barry Booth's. At Croydon's Fairfield Hall, "I was very struck by the sense of continuity," he said. "The act was – apart from two recent additions – the same. It was really strange to be sitting there in a box, looking down and watching the performance with a synthesizer player doing the orchestral bits. I could not avoid making comparisons. I don't think it's merely memory distorting reality but some items certainly deserved a full complement of musicians. The economic considerations that dictate that the synthesizer player will actually take the place of a string section was a shame. It isn't as good. Although the show was wonderfully well-received – I found it most entertaining – that comparison that there was a time when he was touring with woodwinds, brass, strings, a full rhythm section and three girl singers still held – and that was what he deserved."

The "two recent additions" were the disinterred 'Ooby Dooby' and now its B-side, 'Go Go Go' alias 'Down The Line'. Otherwise, apart from these historical footnotes, Roy admitted, "I do all the more popular songs in my stage show. I get asked many times, 'Don't you get tired of singing those old songs?' and I say, 'Gracious, no, because I've worked a lifetime to do a show of just my own material.'"[9]

While 'Wild Hearts' and 'Life Fades Away' boomed in half-empty cinemas, a re-cut 'In Dreams' was mimed by actor Dean Stockwell during an eerie sequence in the more acclaimed *Blue Velvet*, directed by David Lynch who'd also been responsible for the interesting-but-boring cult movie, *Eraserhead*. So delighted with the new 'In Dreams' was Lynch that its sound would engulf the cast and crew of *Blue Velvet* at fixed intervals throughout the shooting. David Lynch would produce too re-makes of another eighteen Orbison relics for release by Virgin America, the company with whom Roy, after much wavering, came home to roost in 1985: "I decided on Virgin because of the personalities of the people behind it and their attitude and gusto."[10] Roy's enthusiasm had been shared by other negotiable names – among them Bryan Ferry, Scott

Engel and The Sex Pistols – all of whom had fallen under founder Richard Branson's hoodoo. After he'd been with Island for over twenty years, Steve Winwood had also defected to Virgin. Not prone to excessive thrift, the company's publicity department would not stop at simply mailing a pre-release copy of so-and-so's latest record to a *Rolling Stone* reviewer. Far better to make money work in half-page advertisements in national dailies, TV commercials and street hoardings.

Thus was *In Dreams: The Greatest Hits* laid before the populace. Impairing another re-issue of the Fred Foster masters had been legal problems following Monument's liquidation in 1981. Re-recordings of well-loved smashes can leave a peculiar aftertaste – particularly if the original had some emotional significance for the listener. Sometimes the reason is purely musical as exemplified by a synthesizer wreaking havoc on The Hollies' 'Just One Look' of the eighties or Dave Berry's thankfully unreleased rehash of 'The Crying Game'. However, as the retrodden 'In Dreams' – and a note-for-note 'Ooby Dooby' in *Insignificance* – had remained faithful to the old arrangements, so did 'Only The Lonely', 'Blue Angel' and all the rest. Some indefinable trace element might have been missing, "But God has a way of giving you the lyric and the melody and, if it stands up over the years, that adolescence, that innocence helps to keep its intentions pure. That innocence is the big ingredient that keeps my songs alive, that makes them stand tall."[11]

To hear him perform these songs of innocence in person, cramped and iron-bladdered devotees from all walks of life stood until the witching hour in Harlesden's Mean Fiddler auditorium the Tuesday prior to the cancelled Palladium spot. Because of the nation's obsession with the sixties, Roy with his usual modesty felt "a bit awkward about being in England at this time. It looks like a set-up to me."[12]

Drawn into the depths of the dark double-breasted suit that he'd still be wearing jet-lagged hours later on breakfast television, a feverish Roy Orbison walked onto a British stage for the last time. As the sound balance evened out, however, his voice shimmered like full moonlight on the midnight sea of bobbing heads. From the raving barrage of rapture that splintered the silence after the second number in – 'Leah' – there emerged a meshing of onlookers and singer as through 'Dream Baby' and the other uptempo items, the jigging crowd assumed the role of rhythm section, stamping and clapping on the off-beat. When required, Roy's guitar picking was a revelation as he attacked the strings with a raw intensity on chordal solos extended for that very purpose. Moreover, an interlude of hesitant duelling fretwork with his speedy lead guitarist sneaked unrecognisably into 'Ooby Dooby'.

During his previous visit, he'd cracked a jaw-dropping joke during the show in Ipswich. There's be no such wit in the Mean Fiddler but the mood would be as friendly. Though he didn't respond to a bawled request for 'Borne On The Wind', he was still quite chatty, bless him. "That was the first record I ever made," he announced after 'Ooby Dooby' – and then, "This is the first song I ever wrote," before the lengthy instrumental exordium to a 'Down The Line' embracing shades of Bill Haley. Later, he introduced the band by their forenames and thanked the audience for being wonderful.

He'd drooped slightly during 'It's Over', almost deluged by the backing vocalists, but he'd more than recovered for the 'Running Scared' big finish and its reprise. Over the play-out, Roy Orbison grinned, waved at the baying blackness and vanished into the wings. It was such an easy, unceremonial parting as he left forever the people who had never ceased adoring him.

'Running Scared' had given its name to a US cops-and-robbers film in 1986, as 'Pretty Woman' would to a movie starring Richard Gere and Julia Roberts, while in the BBC series *Tutti Frutti*, The Majestics –Glasgow's self-styled "Kings of Rock" – would include 'Only The Lonely' and 'Love Hurts' amongst their salaams to departed glory. Like hags at a jumble sale, younger striplings pounced upon the Orbison songbook too. As well as recording 'Cryin'', T'pau would plagiarise the title of 'Only The Lonely' for one of their own creations. In the States, Johnny Cougar awoke a tired 'Oh! Pretty Woman' while, back in Scotland, 'It's Over' from the golden throat of The Associates' Billy McKenzie may have caused Roy a nervous backward glance – and he'd have been enchanted by The Flying Pickets' *a cappella* 'Only The Lonely'. Delving deeper than the obvious were Australia's Mental As Anything with 'Working For The Man'.

Most sincerely garrulous in praising the Big O was Bruce Springsteen, now so grossly over-rated that he'd put himself forward as a second Elvis. Be that as it may, he might not have been falsely self-effacing when, in

January 1987, he had inducted Roy Orbison at the second Rock And Roll Hall Of Fame ceremony. On the podium in New York's upper-crust Waldorf-Astoria Hotel, Orbison recalled, "He was saying that I had been part of his life when he was in New Jersey in that little room. He said I could make it seem like it was any place in the world...and so many flattering things that I can't repeat them all."[13] Wilting at the side during this laudation before the cream of the American music business, Roy "felt I had been truly recognised, you know, justified. 'Validated' might be the word."[11] Dumbfounded when accepting his ovation and statuette, Roy afterwards requested a copy of Springsteen's speech which had finished with an explanation of the initial intentions of 'Thunder Road': "I wanted a record with words like Bob Dylan that sounded like Phil Spector – but, most of all, I wanted to sing like Roy Orbison. Now everybody knows that no-one sings like Roy Orbison."

Springsteen would demonstrate that he didn't when, months later, he made his presence felt on an Orbison television spectacular in California. He wasn't alone in this most public patronage of pop's methuselahs. Through the offices of Dave Edmunds, Carl Perkins had hit British screens in 1986 with a concert from a small London theatre. Among the devout guest musicians seated at his tapping feet for the finale were ex-Beatles, former Stray Cats, Eric Clapton and Rosanne Cash, daughter of Johnny. In a more back-slapping fashion, the sixtieth birthdays of Fats Domino and Chuck Berry were sanctified before the cameras with attendance by some of the famous who'd grown up to their music.

Roy's turn came On 30 September, 1987 in the Coconut Ballroom in Los Angeles' Ambassador Hotel. This glittering extravaganza was the brainchild of Barbara and its baggy-suited musical director, Joseph "T-bone" Burnett. An owlish Texan who had assisted David Lynch on Orbison's 'In Dreams' collection, Burnett's star-studded production kudos was indicative of his elevation to hip omnipresence after years of anonymous studio sessions.

Flying back from a more orthodox concert on the day of the reckoning, Roy had but the haziest notion of who would be accompanying him. At the afternoon rehearsal, as well as Springsteen, one of T-Bone's clients, Elvis Costello – looking more like the Orbison of 1960 than ever – had been roped in to further clutter the Coconut Grove stage that evening. Darting hither and thither too would be chin-bearded post-beatnik Tom Waits. Polarised round Presley's Las Vegas rhythm section, the mixture of West Coast showbusiness periphery getting in on the act and those with actual affinity to the main event would include a backing chorale of kd lang, musical archivist Ry Cooder, JD Souther – who had helped Roy and Will with 'Coming Home' – and Eagles' associate Jackson Browne plus two currently modish chanteuses Bonnie Raitt and Jennifer Warnes.

It could have been a self-congratulatory disaster with the glut of guitarists, the reliance of many on chord charts, dry ice and a string section in mickey-taking sunglasses. There was also the egos of some involved. Yet, though flawed, it was a triumph, partly because everyone wanted it to be. With Roy's vocal entry in the predictable 'Only The Lonely' starter, an almost palpable wave of goodwill washed towards him from an audience whose jewelled celebrity took him back to the Talk Of The Town. With heartfelt gratitude that his pipes were in firm fettle when he reached the sticky "yoooooou gotta take" bit, they loved him for wanting to please them. Not for nothing had he spent over thirty years perfecting his craft. For the remainder of his hour-long performance, they'd worry if he showed signs of strain, cheer when he rallied and glow when, ultimately, he went down well. As they would at the Mean Fiddler, hurrahs greeted the loud and clear G sharp of 'Running Scared', the mumble that began 'It's Over' and the Bob Hope "grrrrrr" in 'Oh! Pretty Woman'.

No-one in the rank-and-file could upstage him – not even the animated Springsteen whose little "hah" was heard in the two-second gap after the fake ending to 'Dream Baby'. The Man Who Would Be Elvis had shared Roy's microphone on that one and on 'Uptown'. Hovering in the background, he mouthed Roy's words, wrinkled his nose, clenched his teeth or smiled as if he had a mouthful of salts. Costello and Waits elbowed in with a minimalist organ solo each and the former's harmonica in 'Candy Man'.

Orbison's cohorts had done their worst but it was far from a death touch. At least they had the grace to keep out of the way on the ballads on which Roy sang his heart out with an ear focused on the tightly-arranged undergrowth beneath the posturing, appreciating the trouble that had been taken.

Joe Public might have preferred a more typical recital,

unencumbered by the famous friends who had given Roy Orbison another contemporary seal of approval. You could understand the commercial motives for their inclusion but harder to take was the topsy-turvy camerawork on Virgin's subsequent video in sixties monochrome. Despite this inducement of mild seasickness, *Roy Orbison And Friends: A Black-And-White Night* was seen by over fifty-thousand domestic viewers within weeks of its release in May 1988.

The expected re-run of the hits was fulfilled in part on film – though here were a few bewildering moments. Chief among these was the coda of 'Oh! Pretty Woman', prolonged to permit guitarists Orbison, James Burton and "The Boss" to exchange licks. There were also two items that could not be identified without squinting at the listing on the video casing. Neither Elvis Costello's 'The Comedians' nor '(All I Can Do Is) Dream You' – co-written by Billy Burnette, latter day guitarist with Fleetwood Mac – seemed out of place among the customary goods. Melodically unsurprising, the Burnette number was a resume of 'In Dreams' with its strummed preamble and sly lyrical references: "I close my eyes...I don't ever know why I let us drift away."

'The Comedians', however, ranked with the best of Orbison's eighties swansongs. Thrice spiralling from a rapping snare drum to a surging drench of strings, Roy conducted himself with shocked dignity in the teeth of a dirty trick at a funfair whereby he was left dangling all night at the top of a ferris wheel by its operator. The latter's donkey-jacketed virility had, apparently, bewitched Roy's grounded harpy: "not just that you're never coming back to me/it's just the bitter way that I was told."

Both these new songs would be T-Bone Burnett's production contributions to Roy Orbison's posthumous *Mystery Girl* LP that would be two years in the making. Its sleeve credits would read – in pop terms – as voluminously as the cast for *Ben Hur*. In the forefront was Jeff Lynne, studio boffin, former leader of the symphonic Electric Light Orchestra, and Orbison admirer from way back: "I finally got a tape with all his songs on and played it non-stop for, like, five years," he admitted. "It's still hard for me to believe that I got to work with him and have him trust me."[8]

Lynne was much in demand then after his co-production of George Harrison's *Cloud Nine* album had been instrumental in steering the former Beatle back into the spotlight after years of artistic quietude. Actually, Jeff had to postpone work on *Mystery Girl* in April 1988 to oversee one final and trifling detail of his prior commitment to Harrison – a bonus number for a European twelve-inch single. Tagging along while the two Englishmen discussed this matter over lunch in Los Angeles, that Roy was so well-versed in British comedy stunned George with whom he'd had only sporadic contact since the ravages of Beatlemania: "Roy knew every word to every Monty Python song and the dialogue to all the movies and the TV series," George recalled. "I mean, he was a gentle person but he had a good sense of humour."[8] George was elated when, over dessert, the jocular Orbison volunteered to sing with him on this extra track. Well, it might be a laugh. Fun is the one thing that money can't buy. Anyway, it was doubtful whether many would bother playing it anyway.

As it wasn't worth booking anywhere expensive, Harrison rang his pal Bob Dylan whose unsophisticated studio garage in Malibu was available the next day. Duly rolling up at the agreed hour, Roy shook hands with guitarist Tom Petty whose group, The Heartbreakers, had backed Dylan on his last world tour: "Well, George had to stop by Tom Petty's house to pick up his guitar and Tom said, 'Hey, I'm not doing anything. Can I come along?'"[14] Roy explained.

By the evening, flesh had been layered on the bones of a piece entitled 'Handle With Care', onto which had been added what Harrison called "a lonely bit" for Roy – while Dylan wheezed his trademark mouth-organ on the fade. Coalesced with an ascending five-note riff, 'Handle With Care' – about an idol's human frailty – could only have radiated from a cast long pampered and deprived within a dehumanising bubble of stardom.

At this juncture, the gathering was not meant as any permanent "supergroup", that most fascist and smug of all pop cliques. The world was not going to be troubled with one more Blind Faith – a 1969 compound of Cream and Steve Winwood's Traffic – or sedative Crosby, Stills, Nash And Young – a Byrd, two of Buffalo Springfield and a Holly. More like Roy's "Class of 55", it was the gods at play over a long afternoon. Orbison spoke for everyone: "We all enjoyed it so much. It was so relaxed. There was no ego involved and there was some sort of chemistry going on."[14] Apart from his and Dylan's distinctive voices, none would suppose that 'Handle With Care' was special.

The next day, Dylan continued preparing for his summer tour, Roy left for a one-nighter in Anaheim near Long Beach and Harrison tooled round to his record company with the new tape. There it was pronounced too potentially profitable to hide its light under a twelve-inch forty-five. In conference with Lynne afterwards, a quantity of Mexican lager worked its short-lived magic and George warmed to the idea of cutting an entire LP with the 'Handle With Care' line-up. When the pair skidded up to his house with the plan, Petty jumped at the chance while, over the phone, Dylan's affirmative was more brusque.

That evening, Tom, Jeff and George plus their wives drove down the coast to Anaheim to put it before the Big O. In the dressing room, Petty would remember, "He was so calm – 'Sure, sounds like a lot of fun' – then we went out and watched the show."[8] As Orbison went through his paces, it may have struck the party that, as a singer *per se* he outclassed all of them and Dylan too. So he wasn't a prolific songwriter but he could pitch notes way beyond their own central two octaves. Nonetheless, Bob and George at least were in an oligarchy of endearingly idiosyncratic vocalists who could warp an intrinsically limited range and technically wrong delivery to their own devices.

Safe in this knowledge, the album was completed over the summer. Most of the composing – with everybody on acoustic guitars – took place at the LA home of the hospitable Dave Stewart of The Eurythmics, then Dylan's producer. Sustained by a continuous running barbecue, this companionable atmosphere bred matey abuse, coded hilarity and mutual reminiscences about the old days. Jeff and Tom, for example, had, on different occasions, recorded with Del Shannon – as Bob had with Johnny Cash, and George with Duane Eddy. Roy and George shared acquaintance with Michael Palin, Barry Booth's lyricist and one of the Monty Python cabal whose *Life Of Brian* feature film had been floated on a loan procured by Harrison. The Beatles may have integrated the 'Oh! Pretty Woman' riff into their concert 'Daytripper' but would Bob bring up the demo of his 'Don't Think Twice It's All Right' that was sent to Roy in 1963: "I must have been thinking of something else at the time because I turned it down. Next thing 'Blowing In The Wind' was on the radio and then I knew I'd made a mistake."[4]

Early on, George and Jeff had made up "The Traveling Wilburys" (sic) referring to studio gremlins – as a name for the pretend group. "We wanted a lighthearted name as opposed to anything serious," Orbison would tell the *Boston Globe*. "We were thinking of The Beatles in *A Hard Day's Night* – something along those lines."[15] With his HandMade film company one of the pillars of British cinema, Harrison would later think aloud about a full-length movie based on the sleeve notes – attributed to Michael Palin – to the album. Masquerading as half-brothers born of the same lothario father – Charles Truscott Wilbury, Senior – the five would be name-checked on this cover under chosen pseudonyms; Roy's being "Lefty Wilbury" in recognition of Lefty Frizzell. Entering further into the spirit of this elaborate joke, the oldest Wilbury sibling would remark, "Some people said Daddy was a cad and a bounder but I remember him as a Baptist minister."[8]

As to the "group" going on the road, "We did sort of discuss it but really only got as far as discussing the order we'd go on stage – and there's no second album planned," Roy explained. "The 'Volume One' on the first record was just, well, in the spirit of the Wilburys. Anyway, we couldn't repeat the ploy on the record companies the second time round."[14] None of the labels involved had raised any fuss when *The Traveling Wilburys Volume One* was presented as a *fait accompli*. Nobody wanted to be unpopular. One executive simply muttered something about not standing in the way of history before hanging up on the Wilbury concerned.

Out of step with the march of hip-hop, acid house *et al*, the release of *Volume One* was like a Viking longship docking in a hovercraft terminal. After the songs had been written, only ten days could be set aside for the actual taping owing to Lucky Wilbury's forthcoming tour, but any lifting of this restriction may have detracted from the proceedings' rough-and-ready appeal. Though it was still the product of gentlemen who could afford to muck about, minor experiments such as hired drummer Jim Keltner whacking a refrigerator's wire grille with brushes reflected the LP's uncomputerised, do-it-yourself air. Closer in execution to skiffle or rockabilly than even *Homecoming* had been, Harrison went on about the Wilburys being "like the Green Party. You've got to battle against all these whales stuck in ice – namely the music industry – to release all these people from feeling guilty for not using a synthesizer and not being able to programme it" – which Lynne capped with, "Don't even bother learning – just play the bleeding piano."[16]

Swimming with the tide, Roy's heard contributions were more or less equal in amount to those made on *Class Of 55*. He'd been featured singer on 'Winged Serpent' – inspired by William Blake's 'The Sick Rose' – but this had been tossed aside to leave 'Not Alone Anymore' as Roy's sole lead vocal contribution while Dylan had four. Within the off-the-cuff climate of the situation, 'Not Alone Anymore' re-cast Orbison as the cuckolded boyfriend turning up when he wasn't wanted as he'd done in 1970's 'She Cheats On Me', an obscure US-only single. Rather than massed strings, he was just as effective with chugging guitars, Jeff's one-finger fairground organ crash-diving, some staccato "sha-la-las" and a Beatle-esque secondary riff of unison piano and guitar. As always, his singing made him a being apart as Lynne observed during Orbison's vocal takes: "Everybody just sat there going, 'Wow! It's Roy Orbison!'" In the booth with one hand steadying the headphones and the other with the inevitable Coca-cola, "Even though he's become your pal and you're hanging out and having a laugh and going to dinner, as soon as he gets behind that mike and he's doing ,his business, suddenly it's shudder time."[8]

Having dumped his load with 'Not Alone Anymore', Roy took a back seat for the other tracks – backing harmonies, the odd bridge, a verse or two. On 'Dirty World', he unfurled his *Son Of Paleface* growl like a conjuror reproducing a popular effect amuse children.

In tying the Wilbury loose end, Roy not only managed that long-threatened return to the charts but also brought much of the aura of a fresh sensation to those young enough not to have heard of him before. In a way, it was the same old scene. In Virgin's soft-focus publicity shots, teenagers saw not a portly dotard or even the-oldest-swinger-in-town. He was a mysterious but unthreatening man-of-the-world, a well-spring of kismet supercool. In other words, he was as he'd appeared to the Mods and Rockers of yore – apart from a few modern touch-ups like the mirrored wine-red spectacles and a lately-grown pigtail. With an old-young countenance drained of colour and unmarred by perceptible hair-loss, only Orbison's known maturity distanced him from many current hit parade incumbents.

Those who remembered felt vaguely re-assured that his cowboy-operatic larynx was still going strong. When 'You Got It', the first single from *Mystery Girl* reached the counters, some would try to will it to Number One as a verification of the lost value of someone singing a song as opposed to producing a production.

Roy Orbison's era as an outsider was, therefore, over. No more would he have to reaffirm his credibility as a contemporary artist by so gladly supporting an act like The Eagles. Who the hell were they anyway? Now he could fill stadiums on his own. Leaving them wanting more, he'd bound off-stage wreathed in smiles but some noticed that his eyes were full of tears: "I've been taken aback by the way things are going. It's very nice to be wanted again but I still can't quite believe it."[17]

During this most gratifying transition, musicians years junior to any Wilbury had been buzzing round him. The most staggering conversion was that of guitarist Steve Jones, formerly of The Sex Pistols, who as both a songwriting partner and person was, to Roy, "just a sweetheart real open and honest".[6] No Orbison-Jones opus would fit on *Mystery Girl* but 'She's A Mystery To Me', composed and produced by members of U2 – then even more the toast of America than The Eagles had been – would be its second hit single.

Backtracking from their punk beginnings, this Irish quartet had tumbled onto Orbison through the *Blue Velvet* soundtrack. Of 'In Dreams', vocalist Paul "Bono" Hewson enthused, "It breaks all the rules of pop music. I hadn't realised he was such an innovator – and I'd never heard a voice like it...there seemed to be all the dreams and nightmares in there, all mixed up."[8] In common with 'Dream You' and 'In The Real World' – a Will Jennings number in possible homage to Jacques Brel – 'She's A Mystery To Me' was another angle on Roy Orbison's fantasy world of sleep: that's all he ever sings about, isn't it? The U2 romantic utopia inhaled a breath of the Orient in Orbison and Bono's droning guitars beneath a vocal understatement of the poetic couplets – bleeding hearts, fallen angels crying out from hell and all that.

While in collusion with these newcomers, Roy did not renege on his past for into the *Mystery Girl* cauldron was decanted 'Windsurfer', a concoction with Bill Dees. Throughout the seventies, Roy had made a point of regularly recording songs Bill had written with other collaborators. From the lesson of Roy's irresolute reconciliation with Joe Melson, the reunited Orbison and Dees knew better than to block out new ideas by trying to supersede 'It's Over' and "Oh! Pretty Woman'. Though one new song, 'The Way Is Love', had to be discarded, 'Windsurfer' as an initial recorded sortie suggested at least half a chance of the old firm being back in business. With an appropriate Beach Boys tinge about the backing vocals and swooping Hawaiian guitar, an indifferent sportsman unlucky in love "practised in his dreams" – that again – until his loneliness carried him away on the tide to oblivion; his sail a smudge on the horizon.

With Bill back in Amarillo, further Orbison-Dees output might have been hampered by geography. As remote was Joe Melson who had returned to Odessa. In November 1988 had come a call for Joe from Roy in Malibu. It was just a chinwag. Roy, Barbara and the two youngest were off to Europe next week; Roy to collect a Wilbury video award in Holland while Barbara and the boys visited the in-laws. Wesley was staying at his grandmother's. At twenty-three, he was now old enough to start a career. He was going to be a songwriter but, though having a famous father opens doors, it also increases expectations. Ask Julian Lennon. Nevertheless, he was shaping up really well. Some might call it nepotism but Roy was considering one of Wesley's songs for inclusion on *Mystery Girl*.

With Steve Cropper on guitar and conducting the Memphis Horns, a master had already been recorded. George Harrison had played on another track. Actually, 'You Got It' had been mixed in George's private studio in Henley-on-Thames by Jeff Lynne. He and Tom Petty had helped Roy with some of the *Mystery Girl* originals. Maybe Joe and Roy ought to try once more.

Like riders on the old frontier, the two old comrades went their separate ways without formal goodbyes. In Midland's Chaparral Centre not far from Melson's, Roy Orbison had already settled his score with the land that bore him. On 25 April, 1987, he'd headlined an "Oil Aid" charity concert for those entangled in that industry's recession. Infinitely more than the Class of 55, this had been the real homecoming. However trying his Wink adolescence had been, Roy's earlier years had overflowed with happiness. For all his wanderings since High School, his regional loyalty and identity had often brought him back. In 1981, he'd sung during the festivities in Lubbock surrounding the unveiling of Buddy Holly's statue.

Well, here he was again – the Local Boy Made Good. In the throes of backstage lionising, he learnt from the editor of the *Wink Bulletin* that the town council had voted to rename Langley Way in his honour. Thrilled as he was, the Big O perversely chose to open the show with 'Cryin'' but, as the *Bulletin* newshound reported, "As anyone could guess, the loudest and longest cheers for 'Ooby Dooby' came from those of Wink and formerly of Wink."[18] Despite his good nature, the Wink High Old Boy on stage could not be blamed for relishing this metaphorical nose-thumbing at those who had once belittled and embittered him. Absent or not from the Chaparral Centre, they were still there, weren't they?

After an Elvis Presley Memorial Concert in Atlantic City two months on was a reminder of a later and better-disposed condescension. As they posed in a dressing room for a snapshot, Gordon Stoker whispered to Roy. He'd just remembered an instruction he'd been given by Chet Atkins in 1958 to sing along in ancillary unison behind a bag of nerves in his early twenties. It had been on a number called 'Seems To Me'. With the same orphaned smile of thirty years ago, Roy seemed quite overcome with rose-tinted sentiment; unusually so, thought Gordon, because "he didn't show his feelings too much".

A few mornings later at Nashville airport, who should Orbison bump into but Mr Guitar himself? Another of Claudette's pallbearer's, Chet Atkins had remained close to Roy in spite of the teacher-pupil gulf of the RCA sessions: "I feel lucky to have been associated with him in his early years," Chet said. "He is a truly great artist and just as great as a person. I am one of his greatest admirers." On equal ground now, Chet graciously accepted a Roy Orbison lapel badge during the usual cordial conversation with its giver.

During the last month of his life, more pricklingly intimate was Roy's dialogue back at Old Hickory with the custodian of what would forever stand as his best-remembered testaments. He couldn't help liking Fred Foster as the waspish old rascal confessed to liking 'That "Lovin' You" Feelin' Again'. That was praise indeed. "We made a lot of good music, didn't we?" reciprocated Roy with a look that would haunt Fred through his years.

To some who knew him less well, Orbison had also seemed strangely contemplative – even though this might be wisdom after the event. Several of those who'd later claim to have scooped The Last Interview would insist that he looked a bit peaky too. Shortly before he and Barbara flew to Europe, Roy apparently told Los Angeles record producer Tony Pastor that, "He thought the end of the road was near and he didn't really care that his life had been a series of ups and downs that didn't really make sense. His exact words were: 'If I go tomorrow, it don't make no difference to me.'" Perhaps it was merely that he was still apprehensive about air travel. There'd been quite a few accidents recently.

Landing in the Netherlands in one piece, he performed his Wilbury duty and returned to Nashville via London where he was photographed wearing a chic dancer's sombrero and geometrically-patterned *mangas* cloak. He was also buttonholed by journalists who were informed that he was "totally centred", meaning that he was at peace with himself at last. Although it was great to be back in the limelight, he was too long in the tooth to make predictions: "My life is a never-ending dream. I take one day at a time and never look too far into the future."[19]

He did, however, reckon that it was time for his autobiography. Like Chuck Berry, he'd write it himself. There'd be no ghosts. He'd already waited too long. One British publishing house, Sidgwick and Jackson, had been seeking the UK rights to the Roy Orbison saga since September 1986. "Why Roy Orbison?" a bemused London monthly had enquired then of Susan Hill, one of the firm's director's. "Because he's actually done something, and has something to say," she replied. "It always helps if someone's had a few experiences, gained a bit of wisdom, and is capable of telling a story with some drama."[20]

Roy also dared to foresee *Mystery Girl* upholding his present flush of aided success. "It's not like this is the only album I'll ever make,"[11] he continued, dropping the names of Dylan and Springsteen as certain donors of songs for the next album. Yes, he'd be adding about thirty minutes of *Mystery Girl* to his act when he rehearsed for the world tour starting in March. He was sorry for lately neglecting his faithful British fans but there was now "too much ground to cover".[14] Nevertheless, he'd be back in England nearer Christmas for the shooting of a video for the second Wilburys forty-five. One direct quote – "at the moment, it's like the Devil chasing me around"[21] – would provide a chilling headline for one British daily within a fortnight.

The first few days of December, however, were relatively quiet. As Barbara was yet to jet in from Germany, he stopped with his mother and Wesley – whose song had made it onto *Mystery Girl*. Simultaneously universal and personal, the lyrics of 'The Only One' were a cynical dissection of self-pity following an unspecified tragedy. The view expressed was one shared by their singer who, years before, had cogitated, "If you take a good look at life, it teaches you that you are one of billions in the world with problems."[22] The three generations of the family under the same roof that fateful week had had more than their fair share of those. Nonetheless, death had ceased pondering and was about to hound the ill-starred Orbisons yet-again.

On Tuesday the sixth, Benny Birchfield and Roy spent a hectic afternoon out of doors with their miniature aeroplanes. "They were having a hell of a good time,"[19] one observer – country singer Jean Shepherd – would remember the next day. Puffed out, Roy called a halt and wended back to Nadine's to eat. During the evening, he complained of a tightness and then shooting pains across his rib cage. Maybe they would pass as they had at the Liberty Bowl in Memphis. He'd obviously had too much fun today. Near eleven o'clock, his exhausted heart came to a standstill in a seizure of shuddering gasps and cold sweat.

Panic-stricken, his mother summoned an ambulance. In the bathroom where he'd collapsed, the paramedics applied cardiopulmonary resuscitation and other procedures for half-an-hour before rushing the unconscious patient to the hospital down in Hendersonville. In the emergency room, there was nothing the doctors could do. While the town slept, Roy Kelton Orbison, Senior was pronounced dead.

In Bielefeld where it was mid-morning, the distraught Barbara must have known something of the unbelieving helplessness that her husband had felt when once rain fell on Bournemouth. Closer to home, Bill Dees turned over in bed, having been wrenched from sleep at six am by the telephone. With phlegmatic detachment, he'd taken comfort in John V 24: "He that heareth my word, and believeth on Him that sent me, hath everlasting life, and shall not come into condemnation but is passed from death unto life."

Under the editorial lash later that Wednesday, pressured journalists were more inclined to lean on yellowed, dog-eared cuttings from the sixties than the Bible as they cobbled together the hastier obituaries and tributes. Most were aware that Roy Orbison had been big in the mid-sixties and had just made a comeback. What had he been up to in between? Old rumours and figments of imagination were distorted even more. 'Too Soon To Know' was about Claudette's motorcycle crash. He advertised for a second wife and arraigned the best-looking applicants at the Westbury Hotel. He wore a toupee. One misguided provincial hack even confused him with Gene Pitney.

Who were these Dees, Melson and Foster characters? What's George Harrison got to say about it? Mick Jagger must have met Orbison. Anyone know his ex-directory number? Any comment from Michael Jackson? U2? With luck, McCartney might put his foot in it like he did over Lennon. Nobody's got a bad word to say about Orbison. If you can dig out any indiscretions, save 'em for Sunday. The jokes'll be sick by then.

There might be some human interest in this Michelle Booth story. Let's get her reaction. The Reading *Evening Post* can help on that one. He died in his mother's house, didn't it? What about "she cradled him in her arms until the medical men arrived and then held his hand as they tried everything to save him"?[23] It's got a certain informed melancholy about it, don't you think? It takes you back to Elvis in 1977.

The Sun newspaper in Britain compiled a dial-a-tune megamix of six Orbison hits at thirty-eight pence a minute. Estate agents wondered who would be doing the probate assessment. Publishers liaised with biographers.

Despite Springsteen's warning at the Waldorf-Astoria, audiences were bombarded with Roy Orbison numbers by singers such as Steve Harley who had a go at 'Not Alone Anymore'. US outfit Little Feat tried to dispel the gloom in London's Town And Country that Wednesday night by dedicating their 'All That You Can Dream' to the Big O. The Art Movement decided to wait a decent interval before recording a tribute to their old boss. However, already Major Bill Smith was in his Fort Worth studio taping a monologue entitled 'Big O'.

That same morning, Virgin with uncalculated guile shipped out advance copies of *Mystery Girl* and commenced pressing 'You Got It' –

which was destined to be Roy's first UK Top Five entry since 1966. This was accompanied by a video showing him very much alive, adhering to a straightforward synchronisation to the record with its timpani and guitar run-down. In accordance with the widow's wishes, none of the scheduled release dates were altered.

Barbara had approved too of a celebration of Roy Orbison that took place in a Los Angeles theatre exactly a week after his passing. This was the music industry's equivalent of a wake. Among its highpoints were Stray Cat Brian Setzer's frenzied 'Ooby Dooby' and a touching speech by Joe Melson. Fresh from the funeral in Malibu – with all the surviving Wilburys carrying the coffin – Barbara also managed a few words as did Will Jennings. Not as moving was a prepared panegyric from Virgin-America.

In Nashville, Vernon and Wink, flags had waved at half-mast. Hendersonville's collective grief was partly exorcised in a memorial service the Sunday after in the Baptist Church. Neither Johnny Cash nor Waylon Jennings were able to make it as both were in intensive care in Nashville's Baptist Hospital with heart conditions. A proclamation was issued in Wink by Mayor Maxie Watts declaring that 9 December would be Roy Orbison Day. In February, the Chamber of Commerce would launch a subscription scheme for the erection of a statue of one – the only one – who had put the town on the world map. A possible site was the vacant lot on North Roy Orbison Avenue where the family bungalow had stood.

As he might have wished, Wink's most renowned son had died with a record in the charts – albeit as one of the knockabout Traveling Wilburys. It was to be expected that the morbid publicity would boost sales for both the slipping 'Handle With Care' and its LP – particularly in the States. Elsewhere, a more common Christmas gift was one of the sixties compilations that had reappeared all of a sudden. In Britain, *The Legendary Roy Orbison* would start the New Year heading the album list while the Top Forty singles would not see the back of Roy for the first half of 1989.

During that final round of press interviews in London, he'd trotted out his recurrent litany about his best records being yet to come. When the beyond-the-grave *Mystery Girl* came out in mid-February, many could see Roy's point – even if, as with 'Danny Boy', it wasn't easy to be entirely objective. Though it had been severely close-miked in places, his singing was as ageless and glorious as ever. It had all the virtues and some of the faults of a virtuoso performance but at least it was an artist doing something he was good at, even if he was too old to learn new tricks. There'd never have been another 'Southbound Jericho Parkway'.

Most of the material was affiliated to some aspect of the Orbison mythology. Sardonically, he'd speculated whether anyone would offer him a song entitled 'Blue Dream'. On *Mystery Girl*, as well as a surfeit of dream references, love is lost in 'A Love So Beautiful' and found in 'You Got It' while 'Careless Heart' has Roy attempting to make the same amends as in 'Falling'. Far apart geographically, both 'Blue Bayou' and 'California Blue' are, nonetheless, home thoughts from abroad.

The *Mystery Girl* songs are not in themselves devalued by these comparisons; 'You Got It' and the lush 'A Love So Beautiful' are two that might have made the charts *circa* 1962. Like all Orbison's greatest work, *Mystery Girl* is not so "modern" that it'll sound dated by the turn of the century. It's only that the embedded sixties hits are advantaged by a head start of up to thirty years of availability and airplay. They are associated with pop's most unpretentious and optimistic period. In those days, Roy Orbison could steal the show single-handedly.

EPILOGUE

Memories

Michelle Howe, née Booth, cried when the news came: "He played a major part in bringing me out of my coma and I will always remember him for that." Steve had been told after it had penetrated from a workmate's transistor. That evening, the Howes mourned not the star but a modest, easy-going fellow who'd spent the afternoon at Fawley Road just relaxing over a nice cup of tea. Afterwards had been the limousine gliding to a meal at the London Hilton and the VIP guided tour of Broadcasting House by Radio Two's bow-tied director. Next came the chat shows before which Roy assured an apprehensive Michelle with the sweet lie, "I don't feel all that comfortable on radio or TV after all these years."

As their words were transmitted across the nation, Steve looked on, seated between a stetsoned Sammy Orbison and Michelle's younger sister, Debbie. He'd been too starstruck to press his compositions on his idol as Sammy King had done with 'Penny Arcade'. It hadn't seemed the time or the place.

Plans were afoot in 1988 for Steve to record his songs with a view to their eventual release. Capsizing an evening of blacksmith's daughters, chunky knitwear and 'Streets Of London', his requiem to Roy had been a poignant 'Only The Lonely' in one of Reading's more turgid folk clubs. He even drew participatory "dum-dum-dum-dummy-doo-wahs" from smirking mouths too supercilious to admit they'd ever bothered with vulgar pop: "I just had the radio on. I was listening to it."

They joined in partly because of the glowing obituaries they'd read in the more liberal newspapers. Apparently, Orbison was cool nowadays. Illustrative of this had been one reaction in 1987 to Roy's arrival in England without a suitable guitar for that jettisoned Palladium spot. Unwilling to expose his treasured Gibson to the pitfalls of airline cargo, he had been appalled to learn that the only such identical guitar in the whole of London belonged to one who sensibly refused to let anyone *look* at such a rare instrument let alone play it. "Who's it for?" the owner asked the desperate telephone receiver. "Roy Orbison," pleaded the Virgin executive. "Well, in that case," came the reply after the briefest pause, "where do you want it delivered?"

The chicness that had been Roy's at his departure might have fallen away after a few months as such obsessions do. U2 had now cottoned on to blues sexagenarian BB King. While the veteran guitarist's blistering obligations tore at their latest single, perhaps Bono and his boys tacitly wondered what they'd ever seen in a cloying old balladeer like Roy Orbison.

Of course, the Big O's time would have come again as it always had – and the classic records will endure regardless, even the *Mystery Girl* postscript. Though he'd been a most unlikely-looking rock star, his image and approach – "Caruso in sunglasses and a leather jacket"[1] as Tom Waits put it – was both tangential and capable of full integration to any pop era. Forever, his voice on the radio will bring butterflies to the stomach. Forever, the image will eclipse the man. "I may be a living legend," agreed Roy Orbison in one of his final interviews, "but that sure don't help when I've got to change a flat tyre."[2]

NOTES

Chapter One

1. Top Pop Stars (Purnell, 1965)
2. Punch, 12 December, 1988
3. New Musical Express, 14 June, 1963
4. New Musical Express, 20 December, 1980
5. The Face, February 1989
6. Rolling Stone, 26 January, 1989
7. Evening News, 3 June, 1972
8. Melody Maker, 13 August, 1966
9. In the Deep South, by R Kerridge (Michael Joseph, 1989)
10. Veronica Television (Dutch)
11. On The Beat, Radio Merseyside
12. Rolling Stone, 12 June, 1969
13. New Musical Express, 23 March, 1963
14. Tribute To The Big O, Radio Two, 5 January, 1989
15. Women's Choice, 21 September, 1974
16. Record Mirror, June 1970
17. Melody Maker, 11 October, 1975
18. "Authentic cowboys and their western folksongs" (sleeve notes, RCA RD 7776)

Chapter Two

1. The Wildcat, 1954
2. Record Mirror, 9 June, 1962
3. Rolling Stone, 26 January, 1989
4. New Musical Express, 20 December, 1980
5. On The Beat, Radio Merseyside
6. The History Of Rock, Vol I, No 5 (Orbis)
7. The Face, February 1989
8. The Guardian, 8 December, 1980
9. Melody Maker, 11 October, 1975
10. Veronica Television (Dutch)
11. The History Of Rock, Vol II, No 21 (Orbis)

12. Tribute To The Big O, Radio Two, 5 January, 1989
13. London News, 19 May, 1987
14. Pat Boone to Rolling Stone, 22 September, 1977
15. For The Lonely (LP) Rhino RI 71493
16. 'Twixt Twelve And Twenty' by Pat Boone
17. Goldmine, May 1981
18. Illustrated History Of Rock, ed J Miller (Picador, 1981)
19. Melody Maker, 12 March, 1966
20. Melody Maker, 13 August, 1966
21. Melody Maker, September 1987
22. Country Music Round-up, February 1989

Chapter Three

1. Rock Quotes, compiled by J Green (Omnibus, 1972)
2. Veronica Television (Dutch)
3. New Musical Express, 20 February, 1965
4. The Face, February 1989
5. 'Songwriter's Lament' by Buck Owens
6. New Musical Express, 20 March, 1965
7. Top Pop Stars (Purnell, 1965)
8. Encyclopaedia Of Rock, edited by P Hardy and D Laing (Panther, 1975)
9. The Wit And Wisdom Of Rock And Roll, by M Jakubowski (Unwin, 1983)
10. Beat Instrumental, March 1973
11. Chet Atkins
12. Bryant's sleeve notes to Orbisongs (Monument SMO 5004)
13. Fred Foster
14. Quoted in sleeve notes to Roy Orbison: For The Lonely (Rhino PL2 20574)
15. Rolling Stone, 26 January, 1989
16. New Musical Express, 14 June, 1963
17. On The Beat, Radio Merseyside
18. Joe Melson

Chapter Four

1. New Musical Express, 20 February, 1966
2. Melody Maker, 24 October, 1964
3. New Musical Express, 30 April, 1964
4. Veronica Television (Dutch)
5. The Face, February 1989
6. Tribute To The Big O, Radio Two, 5 January, 1989
7. New Musical Express, 20 December, 1980
8. Q, February 1989
9. Hit Parade, July 1963
10. Record Collector, April 1988
11. New Musical Express, 22 March, 1963

12. Country Music Round-up, January 1989
13. New Musical Express, 12 April, 1963
14. New Musical Express, 12 March, 1966
15. New Musical Express, 30 April, 1964
16. Kaleidoscope, Radio Four, 30 November, 1988
17. Evening Post, 7 December, 1988
18. Barry Booth
19. To Spencer Leigh
20. Daily Express, 2 May, 1966
21. Buddy Holly, by J Goldrosen (Granada, 1979)
22. Special Pop (ORFT, 1968)
23. Melody Maker, 25 May, 1963
24. Daily Mail, 8 December, 1988
25. Melody Maker, 6 September, 1988
26. Melody Maker, 6 October, 1962

Chapter Five

1. Disc, 23 May, 1964
2. Melody Maker, 11 March, 1967
3. Press conference transcript, 2 June, 1962
4. Melody Maker, 25 August, 1968
5. To Spencer Leigh, Radio Merseyside
6. Barry Booth
7. Daily Mirror, 8 October, 1988
8. Melody Maker archives – rejected photo caption
9. Tribute To The Big O, Radio Two, 5 January, 1989
10. New Musical Express, 12 April, 1983
11. New Musical Express, 20 December, 1963
12. The Face, February 1989
13. Veronica Television (Dutch)
14. The Playboy Interviews (Playboy Press, 1981)
15. Roy Orbison to Spencer Leigh, Radio Merseyside
16. The Beatles, by H Davies (Heineman, 1968)
17. Melody Maker, 26 March, 1977
18. New Musical Express, 24 May, 1963
19. Melody Maker, 24 October, 1964
20. New Musical Express, 14 June, 1963
21. New Musical Express, 30 April, 1964

Chapter Six

1. Melody Maker, 23 May, 1963
2. New Musical Express, 18 September, 1964
3. Punch, 23 December, 1968

4. Melody Maker, 13 August, 1966
5. Melody Maker, 20 February, 1965
6. New Musical Express, 31 May, 1963
7. New Musical Express, 30 April, 1964
8. On The Beat, Radio Merseyside
9. Daily Mirror, 8 March, 1965
10. Daily Express, 30 March, 1966
11. Daily Express, 1 April, 1966
12. New Musical Express, 20 December, 1980
13. Concert programme 1979
14. Daily Sketch, 1 April, 1966
15. Disc, 25 June, 1966
16. Melody Maker, 26 March, 1966
17. Daily Sketch, 8 June, 1966
18. Daily Sketch, 27 April, 1970

Chapter Seven

1. Radio Two, 20 March, 1980
2. Disc, 25 June, 1966
3. Daily Sketch, 27 April, 1970
4. Melody Maker, September 1987
5. Sleeve notes to original soundtrack album (MGM 5HTJ8358)
6. Melody Maker, 13 August, 1966
7. Daily Mirror, 9 March, 1967
8. Clifford Elson Publicity Ltd, press release, 1979
9. Melody Maker, 7 January, 1967
10. Veronica Television (Dutch)/Melody Maker, 17 December, 1966
11. The Face, February 1989
12. Rare Records, by Tom Hibbert (Proteus, 1982)
13. Daily Star, 8 December, 1988
14. Melody Maker, 26 April, 1969
15. Melody Maker, 8 May, 1971
16. Daily Sketch, 28 April, 1970
17. Melody Maker, 24 August, 1974
18. Daily Sketch, 24 July, 1968
19. Melody Maker, 27 July, 1968
20. Greatest Hits Of Roy Orbison (songbook, Acuff-Rose, 1970)
21. Sunday Times, 21 June, 1987
22. Daily Sketch, 27 April, 1970
23. Daily Express, 16 September, 1968

Chapter Eight

1. Daily Sketch, 27 April, 1970
2. Daily Express, 8 December, 1989

3. Sunday Express, 3 September, 1972
4. Daily Mirror, 24 April, 1971
5. Rolling Stone, 26 January, 1989
6. New Rockpile No 5, May 1977
7. I Remember Hank Williams, by Jack Scott (Top Rank BUY 054)
8. Melody Maker, 24 July, 1974
9. Texan Star, 1975
10. Melody Maker, September 1982
11. Evening News, 7 October, 1972
12. Beat Instrumental, July 1969
13. Melody Maker, 26 April, 1969
14. Women's Choice, 21 September, 1974
15. Evening News, 5 June, 1972
16. Daily Sketch, 28 April, 1970
17. Melody Maker, 26 March, 1977
18. Not the band who recorded 'Tryin' To Get To You' or the British group whose rocked-up adaptation of the Cornish Floral Dance was released in 1963
19. Greg Mitchell's sleeve notes to 'I'm Still In Love With You'
20. Tribute To The Big O, Radio Two, 5 January, 1989
21. Ron Price to Spencer Leigh on On The Beat, Radio Merseyside
22. Sunday Times, 21 June, 1987
23. Melody Maker, 27 August, 1977
24. Rock Quotes, ed by J Green (Omnibus, 1977)
25. Sounds, 26 March, 1977
26. New Musical Express, 20 December, 1980
27. Rolling Stone, 23 August, 1979
28. Veronica Television (Dutch)

Chapter Nine

1. Evening Standard, 8 April, 1982
2. Wink Bulletin, 8 December, 1988
3. Zabadak No 7, December 1988
4. Melody Maker, September 1987
5. Format, April 1988
6. Evening Standard, 12 November, 1987
7. February 1989
8. Rolling Stone, 26 January, 1989
9. Radio Two, 20 March, 1980
10. Today, 8 December, 1988
11. The Face, February 1989
12. Sunday Times, 21 November, 1987
13. Veronica Television (Dutch)
14. Time Out, December 1988
15. Melody Maker, 11 March, 1967

16. *Kaleidoscope, Radio Four, 30 November, 1987*
17. *Daily Mirror, 8 October, 1988*
18. *Wink Bulletin, 30 April, 1987*
19. *Daily Mail, 8 December, 1988*
20. *Q, December 1988*
21. *Today, 8 December, 1988*
22. *Daily Sketch, 27 April, 1970*
23. *News Of The World, 19 February, 1989*

Epilogue

1. *Rolling Stone, 26 January, 1989*
2. *Daily Express, 8 December, 1988*

DISCOGRAPHY

Singles

	UK		US
1956	Unissued	'Ooby Dooby'/'Tryin' To Get To You'	Je-Wel JE 101
May 1956	Unissued	'Ooby Dooby'/'Go! Go! Go!'	Sun 242
Sep 1956	Unissued	'Rockhouse'/'You're My Baby'	Sun 251
Mar 1957	Unissued	'Sweet And Easy To Love'/'Devil Doll'	Sun 265
Dec 1957	Unissued	'Chicken-Hearted'/'I Like Love'	Sun 284
Sep 1958	Unissued	'Seems To Me'/'Sweet And Innocent'	RCA 47-7381
Dec 1958	Unissued	'Almost Eighteen'/'Jolie'	RCA 47-7447
1959	Unissued	'Paper Boy'/'With The Bug'	Monument 409
1960	Unissued	'Uptown'/'Pretty One'	Monument 412
Jun 1960	London HLU 9149	'Only The Lonely'/'Here Comes That Song Again'	Monument 421
Sep 1960	Unissued	'Sweet And Easy To Love'*/'Devil Doll'	Sun 353
Oct 1960	London HLU 9207	'Blue Angel'/'Today's Teardrops'	Monument 425
Mar 1961	London HLU 9307	'I'm Hurtin''/'I Can't Stop Loving You'	Monument 433
May 1961	London HLU 9342	'Running Scared'/'Love Hurts'	Monument 438
Sep 1961	London HLU 9405	'Cryin''/'Candy Man'	Monument 447
Feb 1962	London HLU 9511	'Dream Baby'/'The Actress'	Monument 456

Jun 1962	London HLU 9561	'The Crowd'/'Mama'	Monument 461
Oct 1962	London HLU 9607	'Working For The Man'/'Leah'	Monument 467
Feb 1963	London HLU 9676	'In Dreams'/'Shahooroba'	Monument 806
May 1963	London HLU 9727	'Falling'/'Distant Drums'	Monument 815
Sep 1963	London HLU 9777	'Blue Bayou'/'Mean Woman Blues'	Monument 824
Nov 1963	Unissued	'Pretty Paper'/'Beautiful Dreamer'	Monument 830
Feb 1964	London HLU 9845	'Borne On The Wind'/'What'd I Say'	Unissued
Apr 1964	London HLU 9882	'It's Over'/'Indian Wedding'	Monument 837
Jun 1964	Ember EMB 5197	'You're My Baby'*/'Rockhouse'*	Unissued
Sep 1964	London HLU 9919	'Oh! Pretty Woman'/'Yo Te Amo Maria'	Monument 851
Sep 1964	Ember EMB 5200	'This Kind Of Love'/'I Never Knew'	Unissued
Nov 1964	London HLU 9930	'Pretty Paper'/'Summersong'	Unissued
Feb 1965	London HLU 9951	'Goodnight'/'Only With You'	Monument 873
Mar 1965	Ember EMB 5209	'Sweet And Easy To Love'/'You're Gonna Cry'	Unissued
Jul 1965	London HLU 9978	'(Say) You're My Girl'/'Sleepy Hollow'	Monument 891
Aug 1965	London HLU 9986	'Ride away'/'Wondering'	MGM 13386
Oct 1965	London	'Crawling Back'/'If You Can't Say'	MGM 13410
Jan 1966	London	'Breakin' Up Is Breakin' My Heart'/'Wait'	MGM 13446
Feb 66	Unissued	'Let The Good Times Roll'/'Distant Drums'	Monument 906
Mar 1966	London HLU 10034	'Twinkle Toes'/'Where Is Tomorrow'	MGM13498
Jun 1966	Unissued	'Lana'/'Summersong'	Monument 939
Jun 1966	London	'Lana'/'House Without Windows'	Unissued

	HLU 10051		
Aug 1966	London HLU 10067	'Too Soon To Know'/'You'll Never Be Sixteen Again'	MGM 13549
Sep 1966	Unissued	'Communication Breakdown'/'Going Back To Gloria'	MGM 13634
Sep 1966	London HLU 10096	'There Won't Be Many Coming Home'/ 'Going Back To Gloria'	Unissued
Feb 1967	London HLU 10113	'So Good'/'Memories'	MGM 13685
Jun 1967	London HLU 10143	'Cry Softly Lonely One'/'Pistolero'	MGM 13764
Oct 1967	London HLU 10159	'She'/'Here Comes The Rain Baby'	MGM 13817
Jan 1968	London HLU 10176	'Born To Be Loved By You'/'Shy Away'	MGM 13889
Jul 1968	London HLU 10206	'Walk On'/'Flowers'	MGM 13950
Sep 1968	London HLU 10222	'Heartache'/'Sugar Man'	MGM 13991
Apr 1969	London 10261	'My Friend'/'Southbound Jericho Parkway'	MGM 14039
Aug 1969	London HLU 10265	'Penny Arcade'/'Tennessee Owns My Soul'	MGM 14079
Oct 1969	London HLU 10294	'Break My Mind'/'How Do You Start Over'	Unissued
Jan 1970	Unissued	'She Cheats On Me'/'How Do You Start Over'	MGM 14105
Apr 1970	London HLU 10310	'So Young'/'If I Had A Woman Like You'	MGM 14121
Aug 1971	London HLU 10339	'Last Night'/'Close Again'	MGM 14293
Sep 1971	Sun 6094001	'Ooby Dooby'/'Devil Doll'	Unissued
Feb 1972	London HLU 10358	'God Love You'/'Changes'	MGM 14358
Apr 1972	Unissued	'Remember The Good '/'Harlem Woman'	MGM 14413
May 1972	Unissued	'Remember The Good'/'If Only For A While'	MGM 14413
Sep 1972	London HLU 10388	'Memphis Tennessee'/'I Can Read Between The Lines'	MGM 14441

Feb 1973	Unissued	'Blue Rain'/'Sooner Or Later'	MGM 14552
Sep 1973	Unissued	'I Wanna Live'/'You Lay So Easy On My Mind'	MGM
Sep 1974	Mercury 6167014	'Sweet Mama Blue'/'Heartache'	Mercury 73610
Apr 1975	Mercury 6167067	'Hung Up On You'/'Spanish Nights'	Mercury 73652
June 1975	Unissued	'It's Lonely'/'Still'	Mercury 73705 J
July 1965	Monument SMNT 1054	'Oh! Pretty Woman'/'It's Over'	Unissued
Feb 1976	Monument	'Only The Lonely'/'It's Over'	Unissued
May 1976	Monument 8690	'Belinda'/'No Chains At All'	Monument 258
Sep 1976	Monument SMNT 4797	'(I'm A) Southern Man'/'Born To Love Me'	Monument 45-200
Apr 1977	Monument SMNT 5151	'Drifting Away'/'Under Suspicion'	Monument 45-215
Jun 1977	Monument SMNT 5265	'Dream Baby'/'Blue Angel'	Unissued
Feb 1978	Monument SMNT 5971	'Oh! Pretty Woman'/'It's Over'	Unissued
Mar 1978	Monument SMNT 5972	'Only The Lonely'/'Dream Baby'	Unissued
Mar 1978	Charly CYS 0143	'Ooby Dooby'/Curtis Lee track	Unissued
June 1979	Asylum	'Tears'/'Easy Way Out'	Asylum F46048
Sep 1979	Asylum	'Warm Spot Hot'/'Lay It Down'	Unissued
Sep 1979	Unissued	'Poor Baby'/'Lay It Down'	Asylum E46541
Jul 1980	Warner Bros K17649	'That "Lovin' You" Feelin' Again' (with Emmylou Harris)/Craig Hundley track	Warner Bros WBS 49262
May1982	Monument	'Running Scared'/'In Dreams' SMNT 7076	Unissued
Jun 1985	ZTT ZTAS9	'Wild Hearts'/Instrumental	Unissued
Aug 1985	ZTT ZTAS9	'Ooby Dooby'/'Cryin''	Unissued
Aug1985	ZTT I2ZTAS9	'Wild Hearts'/Instrumental/'Ooby Dooby'/'Wild Hearts'	Unissued

Aug1987	Virgin ROY I	'In Dreams'/'Leah'	Virgin 7-99388
Jun 1988	Unissued	'Cryin'' (with kd lang)/'Falling'	Virgin 7-99434
Nov 1988	Virgin VS 1166	'You Got It'/'The Only One'	Virgin
Jan1989	Virgin VST 1166	'You Got It'/'The Only One'/ 'Cryin'' (with kd lang)	Virgin
Feb 1989	Virgin VST 1173	'She's A Mystery To Me'/'Cryin'' (with kd lang)	Virgin

Albums

	UK		US
1961	London HAU 2342	LONELY AND BLUE: 'Only The Lonely'/'Bye Bye Love'/'Cry'/'Blue Avenue'/'I Can't Stop Loving You'/'Come Back To Me (My Love)'/'Blue Angel'/ 'Raindrops'/'(I'd Be) A Legend In My Time'/'I'm Hurtin''/'Twenty-Two Days'/'I'll Say It's My Fault'	Monument M4007 / SM 14002
1962	London / HAU 2437 SAHU 6229	CRYING: 'Cryin''/'The Great Pretender'/'Love Hurts'/'She Wears My Ring'/'Wedding Day'/ 'Summersong'/'Dance'/'Lana'/'Loneliness'/ 'Let's Make A Memory'/'Nightlife'/'Running Scared'	Monument M4007 / SM14007
1964	London HAU 8108 /SHU 8108	IN DREAMS: 'In Dreams'/'Lonely Wine'/ 'Shahdaroba'/'No-One Will Ever Know'/'Sunset'/ 'House Without Windows'/'Dream'/'Blue Bayou' '(They Call You) Gigolette'/'All I Have To Do Is Dream'/'Beautiful Dreamer'/'My Prayer'	Monument MLP 8003 / SLP 18003
1964	Ember NR 5013 (reissued in 1980 on Charly CRM 2007)	THE EXCITING SOUNDS OF ROY ORBISON (UK)/ROY ORBISON AT THE ROCKHOUSE (US): 'This Kind Of Love'/'Devil Doll'/'You're My Baby'/'Rockhouse'/'You're Gonna Cry'/'I Never Knew'/'Sweet And Easy To Love'/'Mean Little Mama'/'Ooby Dooby'/'Problem Child'	Sun LP 1260 (reissued in 1969 as THE ORIGINAL SOUND OF ROY ORBISON

			on Sun 6467 005)
1964	London HAU 8207	OH! PRETTY WOMAN: 'Oh! Pretty Woman'/ 'Yo Te Amo Maria'/'It's Over'/'Indian Wedding'/ 'Borne On The Wind'/'Mean Woman Blues'/'Candy Man'/'Falling'/'Mama'/'The Crowd'/'Distant Drums'/ 'Dream Baby'	Unissued
1965	London HAU /SHU 8252	THERE IS ONLY ONE ROY ORBISON: 'Ride Away'/'You Fool You'/'Two Of A Kind'/ 'This Is Your Song'/'I'm In A Blue Blue Mood'/'If You Can't Say Something Nice'/'Claudette'/'Afraid To Dream'/'Sugar And Honey'/'Summer Love'/'Big As I Can Dream'/'Wondering'	MGM E/SE 4308
1966	London HAU /SHU 8279	THE ORBISON WAY: 'Crawling Back'/'It Ain't No Big Thing'/'Time Changed Everything'/ 'This Is My Land'/'The Loner'/'Maybe'/'Breakin' Up Is Breakin' My Heart'/'Go Away'/'A New Star'/ 'Never'/'It Wasn't very Long Ago'/'Why Hurt The One Who Loves You'	MGM E/SE 4322
1966	Monument LMO 5004 / SMO 5004	ORBISONGS: 'Oh! Pretty Woman'/'Dance'* '(Say) You're My Girl'/'Goodnight'/'Nightlife'* 'Let The Good Times Roll'/'Yo Te Amo Maria'/ 'Wedding Day'/'Sleepy Hollow'/'Twenty-Two Days'/ '(I'd Be) A Legend In My Time'	Monument MLP 8035 / SLP 18035
1966	London HAU /SHU 8318	THE CLASSIC ROY ORBISON: 'You'll Never Be Sixteen Again'/'Pantomime'/'Twinkle Toes'/'Losing You'/'City Life'/'Wait'/'Growing Up'/ 'Where Is Tomorrow'/'(No) I'll Never Get Over You'/ 'Going Back To Gloria'/'Just Another Name For Rock 'N' Roll'/'Never Love Again'	MGM E/SE 4424
1967	Monument	ROY ORBISON'S GREATEST HITS:	Monument MLP

	SMO 5007 (reissue MNT 64663)	'The Crowd'/'Love Star'/'Cryin''/'Evergreen'/'Running Scared'/'Mama'/'Candy Man'/'Only The Lonely'/'Dream Baby'/'Blue Angel'/'Uptown'/'I'm Hurtin''	4009/ SLP 14009 (reissue MLP 8000/SLP 18000)
1967	London HAU/ SHU 8318	ROY ORBISON SINGS DON GIBSON: '(I'd Be) A Legend In My Time'*/'(Yes) I'm Hurtin''/'The Same Street'/'Far far Away'/'Big Hearted Me'/'Sweet Dreams'/'Oh Such A Stranger'/'Blue Blue Day'/'What About Me'/'Give Myself A Party'/'Too Soon To Know'	MGM E/SE 442
1968	London HAU /SHU 8357	CRY SOFTLY LONELY ONE: 'She'/'Communication Breakdown'/'Cry Softly Lonely One'/'It Takes One To Know One'/'Girl Like Mine'/'Just Let Me Make Believe'/'Here Comes The Rain Baby'/'That's A No No'/'Memories'/'Time To Cry'/'Just One Time' ('Just One Time' not on MGM album)	MGM E/SE 451
1968	Unissued	THE VERY BEST OF ROY ORBISON: 'Only The Lonely'/'Cryin''/'Running Scared'/'It's Over'/'Candy Man'/'Oh! Pretty Woman'/'Blue Angel'/'In Dreams'/'Dream Baby'/'Mean Woman Blues'	Monument MLP 8045 / SLP 18045
1968	London HAU /SHU 8358	THE FASTEST GUITAR ALIVE: 'Whirlwind'/'Medicine Man'/'The River'/'The Fastest Guitar Alive'/'Rollin' On'/'Pistolero'/'Good Time Party'/'Heading South'/'Best Friend'/'There Won't Be Many Coming Home'	MGM E/SE 4
1968	Monument LMO/SMO 5013	EARLY ORBISON: 'The Great Pretender'/'Cry'/'I Can't Stop Loving You'/'I'll Say It's My Fault'/'She Wears My Ring'/'Love Hurts'/'Bye Bye Love'/'Blue Avenue'/'Raindrops'/'Come Back To Me (My Love)'/'Summersong'/'Pretty One'	Monument MLP 8023 /SLP 18023

1969	Monument LMO/SMO 5014	MORE OF ROY ORBISON'S GREATEST HITS: 'It's Over'/'Blue Bayou'/'Indian Wedding'/'Falling'/'Working For The Man'/ 'Pretty Paper'/'Mean Woman Blues'/'Lana'/ 'In Dreams'/'Leah'/'Borne On The Wind'/ 'What'd I Say'	Monument MLP 8024 /SLP 18023
1969	Unissued	ROY ORBISON'S MANY MOODS: 'Truly Truly True'/'Unchained Melody'/'I Recommend Her'/'More'/'Heartache'/'Amy'/ 'Good Morning Dear'/'What Now My Love'/'Walk On'/'Yesterday's Child'/'Try To Remember'	MGM
1970	London HAU /SHU 8406	THE BIG O: 'Break My Mind'/'Help Me Rhonda'/'Only You'/'Down The Line' (ie 'Go! Go! Go!'*)/'Honey'/'When I Stop Dreaming'/ 'Loving Touch'/'Land Of 1,000 Dances'/ 'Scarlet Ribbons'/'She Won't Hang Her Love Out (On The Line)'/'Casting My Spell'/'Penny Arcade'	Unissued
1970	Unissued	THE GREAT SONGS OF ROY ORBISON: 'Breakin' Up Is Breakin' My Heart'/'Cry Softly Lonely One'/'Penny Arcade'/'Ride Away'/ 'Southbound Jericho Parkway'/'Crawling Back'/ 'Heartache'/'Too Soon To Know'/'My Friend'/ 'Here Comes The Rain Baby'	MGM SE 4659
1971	Unissued	HANK WILLIAMS: THE ROY ORBISON WAY: 'Kaw-liga'/'Hey Good Lookin''/ 'Jambalaya'/'I Heard You Crying In Your Sleep'/ 'Cold Cold Heart'/'Mansion On The Hill'/'I Can't Help It'/'There'll Be No Teardrops Tonight'/'I'm So Lonesome I Could Cry'	MGM SE 4683
1972	London SHU 8435	ROY ORBISON SINGS: 'God Love You'/ 'Beaujolais'/'If Only for A While'/'Rings Of	MGM SE 4835

		Gold'/'Help Me'/'Plain Jane Country (Come To Town)'/'Harlem Woman'/'Cheyenne'/'Changes'/ 'It Takes All Kinds Of People'/'Remember The Good'/ 'Yesterday's Child' ('Yesterday's Child' not on MGM album)	
1973	London SHU 8445	MEMPHIS: 'Memphis Tennessee'/'Why A Woman Cries'/'Run Baby Run'/'Take Care Of Your Woman'/'I'm The Man On Susie's Mind'/'I Can't Stop Loving You'*/'Run The Engines Up High'/'It Ain't No Big Thing' (not the same song as that of the same title on THE ORBISON WAY)/'I Fought The Law'/ 'The Three Bells'/'Danny Boy'	MGM SE 4867
1973	Monument MNT 45159160 (import)	THE GREAT ROY ORBISON: 'Only The Lonely'/'Leah'/'In Dreams'/'Uptown'/'It's Over'/'Cryin''/'Dream Baby'/'Blue Angel'/ Working For The Man'/'Candy Man'/'Running Scared'/'Falling'/'Claudette'/'Ooby Dooby'/ 'I'm Hurtin''/'Mean Woman Blues'/'Lana'/ 'Blue Bayou'/'Oh! Pretty Woman' (double album)	Silver Eagle SE 1046
1974	Unissued	MILESTONES: 'I Wanna Live'/'You Don't Know Me'/'California Sunshine Girl'/ 'Words'/'Blue Rain'/'Drift Away'/'You Lay So Easy On My Mind'/'The World You Live In'/ 'Sweet Caroline'/'I've Been Loving You Too Long'/'The Morning After'	MGM SE 4934
1975	Monument MNT 69147	THE MONUMENTAL ROY ORBISON: 'Oh! Pretty Woman'/'All I Have To Do Is Dream'/ 'Yo Te Amo Maria'/'Dance'/'(They Call You) Gigolette'/'I Can't Stop Loving You'/'Paper Boy'/ 'Borne On The Wind'/'Today's Teardrops'/'Distant Drums'/'Loneliness'/'Here Comes That Song Again'/ 'Blue Avenue'/'Let's Make A Memory'/'With	Unissued

		The Bug'/'The Actress'	
1975	Monument MNT 69188	THE MONUMENTAL ROY ORBISON VOLUME TWO: 'Sunset'/'Dream'/'My Prayer'/'Pretty One'/'No-One Will Ever Know'/ '(Say) You're My Girl'/'Indian Wedding'/'Let The Good Times Roll'/'Lana'/'House Without Windows'/'Bye Bye Love'/'Cry'/'Sleepy Hollow'/ 'Nightlife'/'Wedding Day'/'What'd I Say'	Unissued
1976	Unissued	I'M STILL IN LOVE WITH YOU: 'Pledging My Love'/'Spanish Nights'/'Rainbow Love'/'It's Lonely'/'Heartache'/'Crying Time'/ 'Still'/'Hung Up On You'/'Circle'/'Sweet Mama Blue'/'All I Need Is Time'	Mercury SRM 1-1045
1976	Arcade ADEP 19 (K-Tel)	THE BEST OF ROY ORBISON: 'Oh! Pretty Woman'/'Borne On The Wind'/'Today's Teardrops'/'The Crowd'/'Cryin''/'Evergreen'/ 'Candy Man'/'Blue Angel'/'Uptown'/'Only The Lonely'/'It's Over'/'Lana'/'Leah'/'In Dreams'/ 'Pretty Paper'/'Blue Bayou'/'Running Scared'/ 'Falling'/'Goodnight'/'Dream Baby'	Unissued
1977	Monument MNT 81808	REGENERATION: '(I'm A) Southern Man'/ 'No Chain At All'/'Old Love Song'/'Can't Wait'/ 'Born To Love Me'/'Blues In My Mind'/'Something They Can't Take Away'/'Under Suspicion'/'I Really Don't Want You'/'Belinda'	Monument MG 7600
1979	Asylum K 53092	LAMINAR FLOW: 'Easy Way Out'/'Love Is A Cold Wind'/'Lay It Down'/'I Care'/'We're Into Something Good'/'Movin''/'Poor Baby'/ 'Warm Spot Hot'/'Tears'/'Friday Night'/'Hound Dog Man'	Asylum 6E 198
1980	Sun CDX 4	THE SUN YEARS: 'Ooby Dooby'*/'Tryin'	Unissued

		To Get To You'/'Ooby Dooby'/'Go! Go! Go!'/'You're My Baby'/'Rockhouse'/'Domino'/'Sweet And Easy To Love'/'Devil Doll'/'The Cause Of It All'/'Fool's Hall Of Fame'/'A True Love Goodbye'/'Chicken Hearted'/'I Love You'/'Mean Little Mama'/ 'Problem Child'/'I Was A Fool' (with Ken Cook)/ 'Tryin' To Get To You'*/'This Kind Of Love'/'It's Too Late'/'I Never Knew'/'You're Gonna Cry'/ 'Mean Little Mama'*/'You Tell Me'/'I Give Up'/ 'One More Time'/'Lovestruck'/'The Clown'/ 'Claudette'*/'Jenny' (with Ken Cook)/'Find My Baby For Me' (with Sonny Burgess)/'Ooby Dooby'* (double album)	
	Monument	GOLDEN DAYS:' 'Oh! Pretty Woman'/'Running Scared'/'Falling'/'Love Hurts'/'Mean Woman Blues'/ 'I Can't Stop Loving You'/'The Crowd'/'Blue Bayou'/ 'Borne On The Wind'/'Lana'/'Only The Lonely'/ 'It's Only'/'Cryin''/'Pretty Paper'/'All I Have To Do Is Dream'/'Dream Baby'/'Blue Angle'/'Working For The Man'/'In Dreams'	Unissued
1983	Decca TAB72	BIG O COUNTRY: Identical tracks to HANK WILLIAMS THE ROY ORBISON WAY (see 1971) with three extra tracks: 'Too Soon To Know,' 'I Can't Stop Loving You' and '(I'd Be) A Legend In My Time'	Unissued
1984	ZU ZAZZ A2006	'Problem Child'*/'This Kind Of Love'*/ 'I Never Knew'*/'You're Gonna Cry'*/ 'It's Too Late'*/'Chicken Hearted'* (instrumental) /'Tryin' To Get To You'*/'Problem Child'*/ 'Mean Little Mama'*/'This Kind Of Love'*/'Claudette'*	Unissued
1987	Virgin FGD 3514	IN DREAMS: THE GREATEST HITS: 'Only The Lonely'*/'Leah'*/'In Dreams'*/'Uptown'*/ 'It's Over'*/'Cryin''/ 'Dream Baby'*/'Blue Angel'*/	Virgin 90604-1

		'Working For The Man'*/'Candy Man'*/'Running Scared'*/'Falling'*/'I'm Hurtin''*/'Claudette'*/ 'Oh! Pretty Woman'/'Mean Woman Blues'*/'Ooby Dooby'*/'Lana'*/'Blue Bayou'*	
1988	Unissued	FOR THE LONELY: 'Ooby Dooby'/'Go! Go! Go!'/ 'Rockhouse'/'Devil Doll'/'Uptown'/'I'm Hurtin' /'Only The Lonely'/'Blue Angel'/'Cryin''/'Candy Man' /'The Crowd'/'Dream Baby'/'Running Scared'/'Leah' /'Working For The Man'/'In Dreams'/'Falling'/ 'Mean Woman Blues'/'Oh! Pretty Woman'/ 'Blue Bayou'/'Pretty Paper'/'It's Over' (Say) You're My Girl'/'Goodnight'	Rhino R1 71493
1988	Telstar STAAC 2330	THE GREATEST HITS: 'Oh! Pretty Woman'/ 'Only The Lonely'/'Love Hurts'/'Lana'/'My Prayer'/ 'Goodnight'/'Falling'/'Blue Angel'/ 'All I Have To Do Is Dream'/'The Great Pretender'/'Running Scared'/'Borne On The Wind'/ 'Mean Woman Blues'/'Pretty Paper/'The Crowd'/ 'It's Over'	Unissued
1989	Virgin V2576	MYSTERY GIRL: 'You Got It'/'In The Real World'/ (All I Can Do Is) Dream You'/'A Love So Beautiful'/ 'California Blue'/'She's A Mystery To Me/ 'The Comedians'/'The Only One'/'Windsurfer'/ 'Careless Heart'	

Class Of 55

Singles

	UK		US
1985	Unissued	'Birth Of Rock 'N' Roll'/'Rock 'N' Roll (Fais Do-do)'	Smash 884 760-7

1985	Unissued	'Class Of 55'/'We Remember The King'	Smash 888 142-7
1985	Unissued	'Sixteen Candles'/'Rock 'N' Roll (Fais Do-Do)'	Smash 830 934-7

Albums

1985	Smash 002	CLASS OF 55: 'Birth Of Rock 'N' Roll 'Sixteen Candles'/'Class Of 55'/ 'Waymore's Blues'/'We Remember The King'/ 'Coming Home'/'Rock 'N' Roll (Fais Do-Do)', 'Keep My Motor Running'/'I Will Rock And Roll With You'/ 'Big Train From Memphis'	Smash AR-LP-830 1001
1985	Unissued	Interview album: includes interview with Roy Orbison (mail order only)	Smash AR-LP-1001

The Traveling Wilburys

Singles

Sep 1988	WEA	'Handle With Care'/'Margarita'	WEA 927 732-78
Sep 1988	WEA 921081-2	'Handle With Care'/ 'Handle With Care'/'Margarita' (compact disc)	WEA

Albums

Sep	WEA	THE TRAVELING WILBURYS VOLUME	WEA

1998	925 796-1	ONE: 'Handle With Care'/'Dirty World'/ 'Rattled'/'Last Night'/'Not Alone Anymore'/ 'Congratulations'/'Heading For The Light'/ 'Margarita'/'Tweeter And The Monkey Man'/ 'End Of The Line'

All recordings have been listed in order of release rather than the order in which they were recorded. An asterisk (*) indicates an alternative version to that first released. On record labels and sleeves, there are variations in the spellings and renderings of titles. For example, 'Only The Lonely' is often followed by '(Know How I Feel)', while 'Cryin'' has more often been printed as 'Crying' since its original release. Some of the singles up to 1960 were first available at seventy-eight rpm.

There are many "various artists" albums containing Roy Orbison tracks first issued on either Sun or RCA. Among the most common of these are *Roy Orbison Sings* (Allegro ALL 778, 1964), *Roy Orbison And Others* (Ember Famous Artistes FA 2005, 1965), *Special Delivery* (RCA Camden CDN 5118, 1969), *Little Richard And Roy Orbison* (RCA CA Camden CDS 1077, 1970), *The Exciting Roy Orbison* (Hallmark SHM 824, 1974). Some of these have been reissued several times. Rarer is a cassette – *Younger Days* (Charly ZCSUN 18057, 1979) – which includes the Je-Wel version of 'Ooby Dooby'.

Of the film soundtrack albums issued, the US only *Zig-Zag* (MGM ISE-21-ST) contains one Orbison track ('Zig-Zag') while *Less Than Zero* (UK – DEF JAM 460449; US DEF JAM C44042) contains 'Life Fades Away'.

Other important album compilations include *Focus On Roy Orbison* (London FQSU 15/16 – double, 1976) which concentrates on the later MGM material and the TV advertised *The Roy Orbison Collection* (Monument NNT 10041). A free EP – the aptly-titled *Rarities* – was an extra gift with this collection. This contained the previously-unissued 'Darkness', 'How Are Things In Paradise', 'Yes' and 'Party Heart'.

A number of other extended play discs had already been issued in Britain. However, these were strictly either album chasers or hits collections – with the exception of *Hillbilly Rock* (London RES 1089, September 1957) which was the first time any of Roy's Sun recordings were released in the country – and two Ember offerings of 1964, including *Sweet And Easy To Love* (EP4563), which also bought previously unissued Sun items to the UK. The other EPs were *Only The Lonely* (London REU 1274), September 1957), *Roy Orbison* (London REU 1354, March 1963), *In Dreams* (London REU 1373 June 1963), *It's Over* (London REU 1435, August 1964), *Oh! Pretty Woman* (London REU 1437, December 1964), *Roy Orbison's Stage Show Hits* (London REU 1439, February 1965), *Devil Doll* – from *The Exciting Sounds Of Roy*

Orbison – (Ember EP 4570, 1965) and *Love Hurts* (London REU 1440, June 1965). In December 1976, another EP – also entitled *Roy Orbison* – was released by Charly (CEP 111). This contained items from the Sun catalogue.

The German record company, Bear Family, have also put out some interesting Roy Orbison material – such as *The RCA Sessions*. This compact disc album – which also includes tracks by Sonny James – contains not only both the 1958-9 singles but also the rejected 'Paper Boy' plus 'With The Bug' (alternate take) and 'I'll Never Tell'. *Double* however, remains in the vaults.

A more recent Bear Family release – *The Sun Years*, 1956-8 (BCD 15461) – has unearthed a different take of 'The Clown'.

Lest we forget, there was, in 1962, a German language single by Roy Orbison of 'Mama'/'San Fernando' (London DL P0 726) as well as a different mix of 'Memphis Tennessee' (London MSC 8474) which turned up in Europe around 1972.

Roy Orbison has also appeared as guest vocalist/instrumentalist on miscellaneous recordings by other artists. When signed to Sun, he sang backing harmonies on discs by Ken Cook, Sonny Burgess and others. Though it was likely that Roy himself could not have recalled all the records on which he appeared since then, among those on which his presence is most evident are:

'You've Got Love' by Johnny "Peanuts" Wilson (US Brunswick 9-55039);
'I'm In A Blue, Blue Mood' by Conway Twitty (US MGM K13011);
'I Belong To Him' by Jessi Colter (with Waylon Jennings – US Capitol 4472);
'Indian Summer' by Larry Gatlin and The Gatlin Brothers (on the LP *Smile* – Columbia FC 40068 – produced by Barry Gibb);
'Leah' by Bertie Higgins (on the LP *Pirates And Poets* – Columbia FZ 38587);
'Beyond The End' by Jimmy Buffett (on the LP *Last Mango In Paris* – MCA 5600);
'Zombie Zoo' by Tom Petty (on the LP *Full Moon Fever* – MCA 6253).

Many limited editions – sometimes of less than 100 copies – have been issued by the Roy Orbison International Fan Club, Schutterlarn 43, 5632 JF, Eindhoven, Holland. Most of these recordings feature Roy in concert, alternate takes, Coca-Cola commercials in which he was involved, and the rarer singles. *Roy Orbison Returns* – a mini-album – has German language versions of his songs while *The Connoisseur's Roy Orbison* in two volumes – mixes concert performances (including 'What'd I Say' with The Everly Brothers) with both sides of the Je-Wel disc, different versions of 'This Kind Of Love' and 'Almost Eighteen' and Orbison-composed instrumentals by Jerry Byrd. Among the recordings of complete concerts is *Big O Live At The SNCO* from a Dutch army camp in September 1972. This contains versions of the biggest Orbison hits – as do the majority of the few extant Roy Orbison bootlegs – which defy every known copyright law. Perhaps the best of these illicit recordings is a cassette of Roy's last British show. The fidelity is rather low at times but it captures the celebratory atmosphere of a memorable occasion.

As well as those mentioned in the text, there have been numerous cover versions of most of Roy Orbison's hits. Below is a list of some of the songs and the more notable artists concerned:

'Claudette':	The Four Pennies, The Compton Brothers, Kris Jensen, Jack Laiiner (French version) and Robert Johnson;
'Uptown':	Robert Gordon, Chase Webster, Ian Crawford and Johnny Seaton;
'Only The Lonely':	Sonny James, Kitty Wells, Arlene Harden, Glen Campbell, J Frank Wilson and his Cavaliers, The Flamingoes (Swedish version), Johnny Tillotson, Prelude and Roger Whittaker;
'Blue Angel':	Denny Martin, Ronnie Shaw and Bogdan Kominowski (who took over from PJ Proby in the title role of the London West End musical, *Elvis*, in 1979);
'I'm Hurtin'':	Arlene Howard;
'Running Scared':	The Fools, Peter Ringle, Peggy March, Bob Luman, Jay Black, The Four Pennies, The Indians, The Lettermen, Glen Campbell, Ted Herold (German version), Paul Rich, Del Shannon and Neil Brian;
'Cryin'':	Jay And The Americans, Lyn Anderson, Ronnie Milsap, T Ford and his Boneshakers, Glen Campbell, Floyd Cramer (instrumental), Freddie And The Dreamers, Waylon Jennings, The Lettermen, Gene Pitney, Del Shannon, BJ Thomas, Bobby Vinton, Don McLean (Spanish and Italian versions), Jeanne de Roy (German version), Little And Large and Suzi Stevens;
'The Crowd':	Arlene Harden, Frank Ifield and Waylon Jennings;
'Working For The Man':	Sherwin Linton;
'Leah':	The Canadian Beetles, The Delltones, Martin Denny (instrumental), The Federals, Tony And The Initials, Fred Jasper (in Dutch), Gert Timmerman (in Dutch), Ronnie Mason, Grant Tracy and Billy Stack;
'In Dreams':	Tom Jones, Spencer King, Alf King, Les Carlo, Vince Hill, Carl

Gibson, Wayne Newton, Tiny Yeng (in French), Marty Wilde, Sandalwood, Peter London and John Otway;

'Falling': Darryl Ford, Ry Pilgrim and Tim Reynolds;

'Blue Bayou': Glenn Barber, The Hillsiders, Hargus "Pig" Robbins, Towa Carson (in Swedish), Frank Ifield, Marielle Mathieu (in French), Dick Rivers (in French), Paela (in German), Linda Ronstadt (in Spanish, as 'Lago Azul'), Mike Roland (in German), Floyd Cramer (instrumental), Bert Weedon (instrumental), The Tielman Brothers, Barry Crocker, Jodi Vaughan, Billie Jo Spears, Nana Mouskouri, Frank Chacksfield and Slim Whitman;

'It's Over': Gene Pitney (in medley), Jerry Tawney, Arlene Harden, Jack Bedien and his Chessmen, Terry Brandon, Bubblerock, Karel Gott (in Czechoslovakian), Hal Prince, The Tramps (instrumental), Peter Kamp (in German as 'Wie Damals'), Dalida (in French as 'Je T'Aime'), Cocki Mazzetti (in Italian as 'La Fine Di Tutto) and Terry Urandon;

'Oh! Pretty Woman': The Newbeats, Tony Kaye, Arlene Harden (as 'Lovin' Man'), Andy Kim, Geno Washington And The Ram Jam Band, Jerry Allen (instrumental), Die Tommies (in German), Count Basie Orchestra (vocal by Leon thomas), Gerd Boitcher (in German), Al Green, Peter Holm (in Swedish), The Lifeguards (instrumental), The Mercey Brothers, The Nutty Squirrels, Real Pascal Et Les Rockatones, Ray Pilgrim and his Beatmen, Benny Quick (in German), Roy's Boys (instrumental), Laurent Rossi (in French), Del Shannon, Wayne Thomas, Sylvie Vartan (in French), The Ventures (instrumental), Dick Rivers, Jan Hammer (instrumental), Johnny Carroll, I Campioni (in Italian) as 'Se La Sola'), Out Of The West, Leroy Van Dyke, Blue Steel, Grace "Shirl" Strachan, Bruce Channel and John Spencer.

Perhaps the most intriguing version of 'Oh! Pretty Woman' was the "fish in the sea" (see text) rendition by Curtis Byrd and the Joe-Ray Singers – released well before Roy's hit. Less fascinating are the multitude of orchestral recordings of Roy Orbison hits on budget labels by the likes of The Sunset Strings, The Big Ben Hawaiian Band and The Nashville Brass.

Finally, there are the multitudinous compositions of Roy Orbison that were given away to other artists. Other than those mentioned in the text, the following list of titles (with performers concerned) contains those known – at the time of writing – to have been released on disc:

> 'Valley Of The Roses' (Jerry Byrd), 'Time And Again' (The Velvets), 'Suzie' (Sue Thompson), 'Spring Fever' (The Velvets), 'Sugar Love' (Don Gant), 'So Long I'm Gone' (Jerry Lee Lewis, Warren Smith, Jay Brown), 'See Ruby Fall' (Johnny Cash, Lester Flatt), 'Sad Eyes' (Don Gant), 'When The Blue Hour Comes' (Rodney Crowell – husband of Rosanne Cash), 'Wings Of Glory' (Bobby Bond), 'The Runaround' (Bobby Goldsboro), 'Rita' (Curtis And Del), 'The Puppet' (Gene Thomas), 'Peace Of Mind' (Gene Thomas), 'Once Again' (Dannie Dexter), 'Another Lonely Girl' (Mark Dinning), 'Baby's Gone' (Bobby Wright), 'Bad Boy' (Sue Thompson), 'Cast Iron Arm' (Shakin' Stevens, Johnny Devlin), 'Long Time No Love' (Ronny Smith), 'Bobby And The Boys' (Gene Thomas), 'Can't Forget' (Mark Dinning), 'No-One Really Cares', (Joe Melson, Kris Jensen), 'Memories Of Maria' (Jerry Byrd, Buddy Merrill), 'Lovestruck' (Terry McGill), 'Lavender Lace' (Nellie Rutherford), 'Daydream' (Don Gant), 'Fancy Dan' (Boots Randolph), 'Hey' (Don And Eddie), 'I've Had My Moment' (David Box, Cohn Cook). And, recorded by both Bobby Barker and Gene Thomas, 'The Last Song'.

INDEX